FIVE-BRANCH GOVERNMENT

FIVE-BRANCH GOVERNMENT

THE FULL MEASURE
OF CONSTITUTIONAL
CHECKS AND BALANCES
by Henry J. Merry

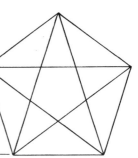

UNIVERSITY OF ILLINOIS PRESS : URBANA, CHICAGO, LONDON

© 1980 by the Board of Trustees of the University of Illinois
Manufactured in the United States of America

Library of Congress Cataloging in Publication Data
Merry, Henry J
  Five-branch government.
  Includes bibliographical references and index.
  1. Separation of powers—United States.   2. United
States—Politics and government.   I. Title.
JK305.M47   353.02   79–22499
ISBN 0–252–00797–2

*Dedicated to those Political Scientists
who have devoted their primary efforts to improving
the basic course in American National Government*

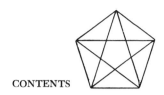

CONTENTS

FIVE-BRANCH GOVERNMENT

CHAPTER ONE

INTRODUCTION

A SIMPLE CONSTITUTIONAL MODEL with geometric imagery may be a useful approach in the study of American national government. It may help us grasp introductory generalizations, such as the basic reason for the institutional distribution of governmental functions. Americans often use a triangular design to stand for the idea that constitutional government consists of three separately functioning institutions, that is, a legislative Congress, an executive President and a judicial Supreme Court. This doctrine, usually called *separation of powers*, is idealized and even idolized.[1] At times we extend it beyond its introductory role and make it an ultimate standard.

The assumption that this tripartite scheme of allocation commands the whole activity of the governmental system provides a ready basis for positive or negative judgments, but it may need to be examined even as a take-off point. We may ask how appropriate it is as a representative design for the Constitution, the institutions, and the functions of the United States government. Even a symbolic pattern cannot be taken entirely for granted: it may have had a limited capacity from the start, and it may have become even more inadequate with the passing of time. A model needs to grow with basic developments so that it may continue to guide us to the major channels of essential interactions within the governmental system.[2]

Political scientists have a variety of reactions to the tripartite symbolism. In general, they pay respectful homage to the principle of three separate powers and make it a starting point in the explanations of American national government.[3] But, in varying ways and degrees, many analysts indicate that the tripartite model is an inadequate or even misleading representation of various aspects of the system. A number of political scientists even challenge expressly the common beliefs about the separate-power doctrine. For one thing, they criticize a tendency to idealize and even rigidify the simplest idea of the work of the 1787 Constitutional Convention. "It is curious that we still identify the framers with a doctrinaire view of separated powers" asserts one who explains that the Constitution both separates the presidency from the houses of Congress and provides for an intermixture of powers among them. Another, a specialist in the presidency, makes a similar statement. "The American reverence for the framers and their work," he says, has "kept alive a vision of politics" that becomes "more and more unrealistic with each passing year." The "traditional vision," he points out, is that the Congress and the other branches "for the most part go their separate ways," whereas "the important fact is their mutual dependency."[4]

These comments suggest that there are at least two rather contrasting patterns of constitutional distribution—a simple threefold allocation and a mixed, multiple arrangement. The first usually is based upon only a small portion of the Constitution, that is, the initial clauses of Articles I, II, and III. These similar provisions separately vest legislative, executive, and judicial powers in a Congress of two houses, a President, and a Supreme Court.

The common language and comparable positions of the three vesting clauses indicate an integrated concept of government with a one-to-one correspondence between a set of three separate functions and a set of three separate institutions. The three clauses as a related trio imply that the government consists of Congress making the laws, the President executing them, and the Supreme Court making final adjudications concerning them. That scheme is neat and simple and thus lends itself to the development of an appealing ideological model. Yet triangular symmetry provides a severely limited picture of governmental interrelationships.[5] The three vesting clauses are only the tip of the constitutional iceberg, and three institutions with separate functions are only the tip of the governmental iceberg. Accordingly, the three-power model may tell us little about the less visible mass of government. We may wonder whether the visible or the invisible portion is responsible for the action or inaction of the government.

The main body of the Constitution presents a complex pattern of authorizations and limitations in a variety of distributional arrangements. This more extensive and less symmetrical scheme of allocation is often called *checks and balances*, but political scientists increasingly term it *separated institutions sharing*

powers.[6] Its most striking feature in the political system of today
may be the three kinds of elected officials, that is, the representatives, the senators, and the President. Each differs from the
others in length of term and in their having been chosen by
different and often competing constituencies. They share a
number of the more important activities or functions, such as
legislation, communication, and supervision of administrative
processes, as well as representation and personification. Also
provided for in the Constitution are three types of executive
officials. The Constitution expressly authorizes a class of officers
to be appointed by the President with the consent of the Senate
and two types of inferior officers to be chosen by the President
alone or by the heads of departments.[7] The different types of
appointed executives may have distinct, counterbalancing
sources of political or professional power.

The relationship between elected officials and appointed officials may be, from the viewpoint of democratic and republican
accountability, the most important internal aspect of the national government. It is also an aspect of government that has
changed tremendously since the adoption of the Constitution.
In the 1790s executive employees were counted by the hundreds; now they are counted by the millions. In the year 1800,
the ratio of appointed personnel to elected officials was less than
thirty to one. Now it is more than five thousand to one.[8] Expertise has become much more complex—even incomprehensible.
The vast appointed officialdom may be a leviathan—or an ocean
of leviathans. The difficulties experienced by elected officials in
trying to control it suggest that we may need new applications
of the doctrines of separation of powers and checks and balances
for the executive branch itself.

The phrase *separation of powers* may be confusing or even
misleading, because the word *powers* can refer either to institutions or to functions, or to both. The initial vesting clauses
suggest simple, comparable patterns for institutions and functions, but the main body of the Constitution assumes a more
complex pattern for each. A basic question for this study is
whether the separation of institutions is an end in itself or
merely a necessary preliminary to the functional arrangements.
The answer may depend largely upon the extent to which the
proper functions of different institutions are explicitly or im-
plicitly interdependent and not merely independent.

Political science explanations of the national government often depart from the idea of a separate function for each of three types of institutions. Such analyses may go in either of two directions. Some indicate that all government officials engage in a similar function, such as making policies, converting inputs into outputs, or resolving conflicts. Other analyses point out a diversity of functions.[9] In addition to legislation, execution, and adjudication, there are appropriation, appointment, investigation, communication, and supervision of administration, as well as amendment of the Constitution. These various functions are distributed in a variety of ways—more mixed, joint, or shared than separate. This may be another reason to question the adequacy of the tripartite representation of the forces at work.

The three-separate-functions pattern indicates that Congress creates legislation and the President executes it. But the actual operations are often quite different from that process. Increasingly, Congress has delegated legislative authority to the executive or administrative units and has devoted much of its time to the investigation of administration and to the direction of particular areas of application. Many political scientists have pointed out the extent to which Congress and the executive/administrative forces have exchanged traditional roles. As one political scientist puts it, "The executive branch bears a larger burden of the legislative power, while Congress expands its administrative roles."[10]

At the same time, many of the more specialized officials of the executive branch engage in functions other than executive actions. One leading political scientist asserts that "administrative *functions* are not so much executive as they are *legislative* and *judicial*."[11] That, of course, tends to increase the responsiveness of specialized administrators to Congress and the courts and to decrease the influence of higher executive officials. It also challenges the constitutional model of three institutions with three separate functions and raises the possibility that the administrative force, with its mixed functions, may be a coordinate branch in a pattern of essential interactions.

This is related to another question that challenges the adequacy of a three-power pattern. The query Who Governs? has different answers. "Today the president *is* the government for millions of Americans" declares one book on the presidency;[12] and some journalists appraise administrations according to whether or not the President can govern.[13] On the other hand, some analysts suggest that it is the civil servants who govern. "In a very real sense the administrative bureaucracy *is* the government in any political system" asserts one political-science explanation of the national government.[14] Both views may be improper or inadequate. The basic facts are that a system governs and that it is a complex system. The three-power model tells us that Congress and the Supreme Court, as well as the President, are integral parts of the government; but it does not tell us about the discretionary functions of the less visible and much larger forces of specialized administration.

The three-power doctrine is troublesome, also, with respect to institutions. We have more structures than the Congress, the presidency, and the Supreme Court. Congress has established many other institutions, including committees, departments, agencies, commissions, and several types of courts. We try to preserve the three-power ideology by assuming that each of these sundry institutions is an integrated and controlled part of either a legislative, executive, or judicial branch, even though the Constitution does not use the word *branch.*

The formulation of the three-separate-powers doctrine in terms of legislative, executive, and judicial branches may lead to the belief that the branches are monolithic entities under the full control of Congress, the President, and the Supreme Court respectively. But that is far from the actual condition of things, particularly for the legislative and executive branches. One of the many political scientists who have called attention to the disunity within these branches comments: "It is highly misleading to speak of *the Congress* as if it were a collective unity. . . . Congressional power is divided among 16 major fiefdoms (standing committees) and 97 petty fiefdoms (standing subcommittees) in the Senate; 20 major fiefdoms and 124 petty fiefdoms in the House. . . . The executive branch is no more a monolith than the Congress. There are multiple power centers."[15] Even the official classification of executive-branch institutions is a virtual admission that symmetry is lacking. The *Government Manual* lists them under three general designations: the Executive Office of the President, the Executive Departments, and the Agencies.[16] These last are more than forty separate administrative units, often called *independent agencies.* The departments have little collective unity, and most of them are conglomerates in themselves either overtly or covertly. Political science efforts to characterize the divisions of the executive branch deal with classes of officials more than with institutions. The principal boundaries are more horizontal than vertical. There is a common differentiation of the presidency and the bureaucracy. More penetrating are the attempts to distinguish two general classes of appointed officials in the executive branch. The contrasting labels vary, and of them the following seem to be a fair sample:

> Political Executives and Professional Careerists
> Political Appointees and Merit System Appointees
> Political Executives and Career Executives
> Political Executives and Bureaucrats
> Noncareer Administrators and Career Administrators
> The Political Executive and the Professional Bureaucracy
> Political Personnel and Career Personnel
> Politically Appointed Bureaucrats and Top Career
>   Bureaucrats
> Political Executives and the Career Service[17]

The principal distinction seems to be between political and career officials. The terms *political* and *career* are not categorical opposites, and in this context they are more relative than absolute. Most political officials are appointees of the incumbent President, but professional as well as party-policy considerations probably enter into their selection. Career executives are likely to be chosen under the civil service or other merit system, but certain supergrade executives may be on noncareer or otherwise temporary assignment. Career officials are apt to be experienced in the politics of administration as well as in the professional functions of their respective offices or bureaus. Thus the labels *political* and *career* may each stand for several factors.

A division of appointed executives has underlying support in the constitutional provision on the appointment of different classes of officers. That distinguishes superior and inferior officers. One type is to be appointed by the President with the consent of the Senate and the other type by the President alone or by the heads of departments. These categories may presuppose differences in primary responsibilities, that is, accountability to the presidential-senatorial sphere of politics, to the presidential institution itself, or to the departmental managements.

Several political scientists sharpen the division of executive officials by asserting that the administrative bureaucracy, or career civil service, constitutes a "fourth branch of government" with the coordinate status of the three better-known branches.[18] At least two leading analysts of the presidency designate the two parts of the executive branch the *presidential government* and the *permanent government*.[19] These also are primarily divisions of officials rather than institutions or functions. The one includes at least the White House assistants and the top executives or advisers of the Executive Office agencies, while the other includes the career civil service. These are only general classes; they do not provide an exact division. There may be a considerable number of departmental officials who are neither definitely presidential nor permanent, but the recognition of two contrasting forces is another indication that the treatment of the executive branch as a single unit may be an unrealistic approach to the national government.

The separation between the presidential forces and the career officials of the executive branch, and perhaps some of the political officials as well, arises not merely from the sense of autonomy among the administrative bureaucracy but also from the diversity of presidential roles and the White House emphasis upon nongovernmental or external relationships. There is much more to the presidency than the execution of legislation enacted by Congress. This role is given to the President in the vesting clauses at the start of Articles I, II and III of the Constitution. But the execution of statutes is largely the function of lesser officials in the departments and agencies, and their executive actions are often in accord with regulations written by their respective units. In contrast, political scientists stress such presidential roles as chief diplomat, commander in chief, chief of state, chief legislator, and in a less official but more vital way chief party leader, chief citizen, and chief headline personality. These roles usually have a higher priority than that of chief administrator. For example, during May 1978 an adviser to President Carter gave to the press the following explanation for a campaignlike trip to the Midwest: "I reminded him the other day that he was elected to lead the country, not manage the bureaucracy."[20] This suggests that the three-power model gives a faulty image of both the presidency and the bureaucracy.

The position of the administrative bureaucracy may derive

less from opposition to the White House than to association with the Congress and its subunits. Many political scientists assert that the Constitution makes Congress responsible for the establishment and maintenance of operating departments, agencies, and offices. Congressional powers for these purposes include those of legislation, appropriation, communication, and investigation. The Constitution refers to departments but does not prescribe them specifically. Apparently the Constitutional Convention took for granted that Congress would establish departments, such as those existing under the Confederation for foreign relations, military affairs, and finances.[21] The broadest provision for this purpose authorizes Congress to "make all laws which shall be necessary and proper for carrying into execution" the powers of the government or "any department or officer thereof."[22] Congressional enactments provide funds, offices, and authority for executive operations. Congressional committees often guide and restrict administrative actions through investigations and other hearings. In these endeavors, Congress has developed specializations and fragmented structures largely comparable to those of the executive branch.

The interrelationships between legislative and executive subunits often make demands of and require support from specialized-interest pressure groups. Political scientists give much attention to the group process, even disagreeing upon its character and impact. Some stress its pluralism and others its elitism,[23] but from either viewpoint the specialized group phenomenon is a considerable challenge to the three-power design of government and to the electoral theory of control. One political-science explanation of American government gives this evaluation: "In the realities of the policymaking process, there is little in the way of a separation. The emergence of subsystems has served to bridge whatever gap was intended to exist between branches, as interest groups, executive agencies, and congressional subcommittees all operate in a particular policy area serving their specialized constituencies."[24] This suggests that the executive branch may be an agglomeration of subunits, many of which may be closer to the congressional subunits than to the President and the members of his cabinet. It indicates that in appraising the adequacy of the constitutional model of power distribution we need to consider the basic interactions between the major classes of executive officials and all three of the popular branches.

These observations of political scientists raise the possibility that there are checks and balances of substantial force within the executive branch itself, as well as between the major divisions of executive forces and the three primary branches. We may ask whether such interrelationships are within the constitutional principles of authority distribution.

The problem of reconciling the complex character of operational interactions with the constitutional pattern of balanced powers is not at all new for political scientists. J. Roland Pennock, writing in 1941, gave this description of the challenge:

> In short, what we are witnessing with the development of the administrative branch of government is not so much a violation of the fundamentals of the separation of powers as a supplementation of that principle by a diverse and complicated system of procedural arrangements. We still have the basic check of an independent legislature free to do what it will with the administrative branch and all its works. The judiciary also retains ample power. But this basic division of powers is far too crude a device to protect against arbitrary action in all the convolutions of the modern governmental machine. That function can be performed only by a continuous application of inventive genius which devises for each new development of administrative power the appropriate method of rendering it both accountable to the public and reasonable in its actions.[25]

There seems to be no effort here to limit the control of administrative forces to presidential authority. Rather, Pennock assumes that control is to be governmentwide. He even stresses the roles of the legislature and the judiciary. In fact, he recognizes both the scope of the political system and the specialized character of operations. He seeks a method of control for each new development and a method that includes both internal and external checks upon the administrative power.

The scope of the problem before us is evident in the comment of one leading analyst of Congress and the presidency. In discussing the question How many branches of government? he presents this picture:

> The point of these observations is to suggest that, in this day and age, the Constitution is a fallible and incomplete guide to national policy-making. Instead of three branches of government, each with its clearly defined sphere of competence and activity, there may be five branches of government in any particular issue area, or seven, or twenty, or only one. The number

of "branches" involved varies from time to time and from issue to issue. And the roles these branches play may vary greatly too: an Executive agency may "legislate" a regulation.[26]

This last point is another indication that the pattern of relationship is complex and also that it may differ considerably from subject to subject.

These developments raise three primary thoughts about theories of constitutional distribution. One is that the model of three types of institutions with correspondingly separate functions does not apply to many operations of the government. The second is that the doctrine of checks and balances may be fundamentally relevant to the whole realm of the government in its full scope and complexity. The third is that the principle of interrelationship may provide a means of bringing the vast, diverse activity of the executive/administrative units within the effective force of underlying constitutional doctrines. Accordingly, the next chapter will review the principles of constitutional distribution, with particular attention to the scope of separate functions, mixed power systems, and specialized government.

Then, we will proceed to examine the general character of the executive branch, with particular attention to the congressional basis of its institutions and functions, the diversity of the specialized functions, the political competition within the executive branch, departmental disunity, the levels of executive policymakers, and the checks and balances within the executive branch. Next, we will undertake a more concentrated effort to measure the major forces within the executive branch, to ascertain if they can and should be represented in the constitutional pattern of essential interactions.

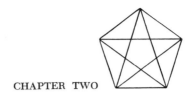

CHAPTER TWO

THE GENERAL CHARACTER OF CONSTITUTIONAL DISTRIBUTION

THE EXTENT TO WHICH a distinguishable class of appointed officials may qualify as a coordinate branch of the United States
government depends upon its separate contribution to the objectives of the Constitution in the distribution of power or
authority. (In this subject area, the terms *power* and *authority*
are often used interchangeably.) Those objectives are, in general, to prevent an undue concentration of power and to assure
the adequate checking and balancing of governing authority in
a comprehensive pattern of responsible assignment.[1]

The Constitution embodies three distinguishable but often
intermingled principles of structural arrangement or functional
distribution. The first features the parallel vesting of three types
of legal process in three separate institutions. This is often called
separation of powers; we will examine it under the title "The
Narrow Realm of Unshared Functions." The second, which involves the sharing of diverse rights and duties in a variety of
ways, is commonly designated *checks and balances;* we will dis-
cuss it under the heading "The Wide Realm of Shared Functions." The third principle, which concerns executive departments and agencies and different categories of appointed
officials, as well as congressional subunits and general- and
special-interest groups, we will consider under the heading "The
Constitutional Basis of Specialized Structures." This chapter
contains a separate review of each of the three types of constitutional distribution.

The Narrow Realm of Unshared Functions

The simplest and most idolized model of institutional-functional
arrangement is derived from the initial clauses of Articles I, II,
and III of the Constitution. Those comparable provisions vest
legislative, executive, and judicial powers respectively in a Congress, a President and a Supreme Court. These clauses give us
two sets of labels: one for institutions—that is, Congress, President, and Supreme Court; another for functions—that is, legisla-

tive, executive, and judicial processes. Together they suggest three possible objectives: separation of institutions, separation of functions, and parallel separation of institutions and functions. The last is the strictest pattern of distribution.

The similarity of the three vesting clauses indicates that they were integral parts of a common conception and that they should be interpreted in relation to each other. They may form a general pattern of limitation.[2] For instance, the vesting of executive power in a President may mean that the President does not have the power to legislate or to adjudicate.

Chief Justice John Marshall interpreted the three vesting clauses as an integrated unit with interrelated limitations. In an 1825 opinion he set forth the tripartite formula that "the legislature makes, the executive executes, and the judiciary construes the law."[3] This is a reduced or restricted concept of government, however. The President and the Supreme Court, for instance, engage in policy-making functions other than the execution and application of laws made by Congress. Yet the three-separate-functions model is not entirely inappropriate. It may be descriptive of some important functions of some legislative, executive, and judicial institutions.

The three-separate-functions model may still obtain in the criminal law process. That area is more strictly proceduralized than are most other fields. Criminal punishment must be based upon statutory definitions of the crime and punishment, and final determination must be within the jurisdiction of a court.[4] Penal laws must have markedly more specificity than is required in general of statutes. The Supreme Court upheld a conviction under a World War II price-control law that authorized an administrative agency to specify conditions which would bring the penalties into play; but the Court asserted that "the statute, not the regulation, creates the offense and imposes the punishment for its violation."[5]

Congress apparently has never authorized administrative officials to make a final determination of criminal liability. When there has been a grant of subpoena power to a regulatory agency, Congress has placed the final decision with the courts. This is probably a constitutional requirement. The Supreme Court indicated as much in an 1894 dictum.[6] If there has been no relevant decision since then, it is probably because Congress has not tried to place such final authority with executive or administrative officials.

The peculiar relevance of separate legislative, executive, and judicial functions to the criminal-law process may help to explain devotion to the concept of separation of powers during those centuries when government was more thoroughly coercive. Historically, the doctrine of exclusive processes appears to have had a close connection with the field of criminal law enforcement. Scholarly inquiries into the intellectual origins of the idea of separate functions indicate that the doctrine emerged in opposition to attempts made by the House of Commons to try individuals for criminal offenses during the English Civil War.[7] Three and even two centuries ago, theories of government generally placed more stress upon coercive rather than corrective processes.

The professors who have made the most scholarly investigation into the origins of the theory of separate legislative and executive functions distinguish that doctrine from such other patterns as mixed sovereignty, balanced government, and the limitation of powers.[8] The differentiation of legislative action on the one hand and executive and judicial action on the other entails legislative supremacy and the premise that general rules control particular orders.[9] Historically, legislative supremacy had political merit, because the largest of the joint legislative institutions was composed of elected representatives.

The one-to-one correspondence between three functions and three institutions as declared in the initial clauses of Articles I, II, and III of the Constitution is the principal feature of what M. J. C. Vile calls the *pure doctrine* of the separation of powers.[10] That consists of (1) the division of government into three branches, (2) a distinct function for each branch, and (3) a separation of persons in one branch from the others. This last might be implicit in the first, but it need not depend upon the vesting clauses. A strong tradition recognizes separate independence of judges, whereas the Constitution expressly provides that the members of Congress should not hold an office of the United States.[11] This last disqualification, too, has a long history. It originated in English attempts to prevent the king or his chief minister from giving members of the Commons sinecure positions. A 1701 statutory prohibition was not enforced, and the British government features parliamentary-cabinet integration rather than separation. There was a similar provision in the American Articles of Confederation,[12] so that the provision in the 1789 Constitution seems to be less a peculiarly separate-power element than a protection of legislative integrity. Yet it is an express basis for legislative-executive separation, so that we need not depend upon the initial vesting clauses.

The Supreme Court has made some efforts to preserve the theory that the Congress is the only legislative institution and is solely legislative, even while approving the dispersion of legislative and congressional activity. The 1825 opinion of Chief Justice Marshall, which set forth the tripartite-power formula, asserted that the Congress could not delegate what is "strictly and exclusively legislative" but that it could delegate other functions.[13] The Court has not defined what is strictly and exclusively legislative, at least not expressly; but, as noted before, the enactment of penal statutes could constitute that category. Much more evident is that the Court has approved almost every delegation of noncriminal law or rulemaking authority to a public agency. Now congressional legislative action is largely either a general grant to an executive or administrative unit, with only meager indication of standards or limitations, or the adoption of legislative measures proposed by such a unit.[14]

At the same time, Congress extended its investigative power. The Supreme Court in 1927 held that investigation "is an essential and appropriate auxiliary to the legislative function." Then in 1959 the Court said that Congress could investigate into areas "in which it may potentially legislate or appropriate."[15] Thus, the investigative power is as broad as the other two powers combined.

The Constitution does not define *executive power*, and the majority of the delegates at the 1787 Convention both preferred and assumed the supremacy of the legislative power.[16] James Wilson, while advocating a single chief executive, said: "The only powers he conceived strictly Executive were those of executing the laws, and appointing officers, not appertaining to and appointed by the Legislature."[17] The Convention used specific grant provisions to give the President various limited powers with respect to legislation, treaties, appointments, diplomatic relations, military command, and other matters. The formula of Chief Justice Marshall noted previously that the legislature makes the laws and the executive executes them seems to place executive power in a narrow, subordinate position. Not much of the contemporary presidency conforms to this pattern.

The middle- and lower-level administrators may fit into the formula better than does the President.

The developments of this century with respect to the presidency have made the office still less relevant to the pure doctrine of separate powers as expressed in the three vesting clauses. The increase in foreign-affairs problems has resulted in the President's frequently acting apart from and in advance of Congress, even though the Constitution gives Congress several powers with respect to external and military affairs. Further separation of the presidency from the regular and less visible forces of the government derives from the increased emphasis upon the public relations of an incumbent President and upon his episodic actions in selected situations. Such developments enhance the personal and political character of the office and subordinate relationships with Congress and the administrative units.

The independence of the judiciary from legislative and executive institutions has historical support that antedates the separation of the colonies from the British crown.[18] Moreover, judicial procedure is more strict and steadfast than are the processes of other institutions. The clause vesting judicial power in the courts seems particularly redundant, because courts and judicial power often are defined in terms of each other. Moreover, the Constitution contains specific provisions, such as those prescribing tenure for "good behavior" and protecting the rate of compensation, which assure autonomy of the judges more than does the general theory of separate functions.[19]

The tripartite formula of Chief Justice Marshall that the courts act upon laws made by the legislature and executed by the executive is particularly inappropriate to the Supreme Court. Much of that Court's activity is to determine the constitutional law that controls or limits even the legislative efforts of the houses of Congress. The formula may fit the inferior courts to a greater degree and may be even more applicable to the adjudicative functions of several administrative institutions.

Montesquieu and Madison warned against a situation in which, in Madison's words, "the whole power of one department is exercised by the same hands which possess the whole power of another department."[20] If there is any danger of that in the government today, it would be in the concentration of different types of power in a single executive branch. Accordingly, the existing separation into a number of counteracting forces may be serving the original purposes more than would a monolithic executive branch.

The Wide Realm of Shared Functions

The Constitution of the United States embodies a much more complex distribution of authority than the separate vesting of legislative, executive, and judicial powers in three corresponding institutions. The body of that document consists of at least seventy-five paragraphs (before the amendments) which specify procedures, limitations, and functions. The Constitution directs operating interdependence among the houses of Congress and the presidency on such important matters as the consideration of the state of the Union, the approval of statutes, the adoption of treaties, the control of expenditures, the appointment of officials, and the carrying of powers into execution. The common designation for this more inclusive and less systematic arrangement is *checks and balances,* but political scientists increasingly are using the term *shared powers* to designate the mixed constitutional pattern of explicit and implicit distribution of authority. Both concepts presuppose separate institutions, and the vital element of each principle is the interdependence of functions in one way or another.

Checks and balances, as a theory of constitutional allocation distinct from separation of powers, has breadth and flexibility, because it embodies a basic psychological formula of checking political power with political power. It may work against new types of concentration, including those involving the administrative bureaucracy, because it permits a sharing of basic functions and an expanded pattern of relationships among the diverse institutions. It also allows the interbranch development of corrective or positive policymaking in the various noncriminal law areas of government.

The Constitution shows the breadth of checks and balances by establishing three mixed systems of making law. In addition to the process of statute enactment by the two houses of Congress and the presidency, there is the method of treaty adoption. For this last, the President and the Senate have absolute negatives upon each other because only the President may initiate a treaty and no provision exists whereby he may override senatorial disapproval.

The third system of legislation concerns amendments to the Constitution. This entails proposal by two-thirds vote of each house and ratification by the legislatures (or special conventions) of three-fourths of the states. The Constitution prescribes no role for the President in the amending process, but he may be involved politically. The Supreme Court participates in the matter officially only as issues requiring adjudication are brought before it.

Thus, the four constitutionally prescribed institutions have varying types of participation in different areas of governmental activity. Even the number involved may change—constitutional distribution is a flexible and even self-changing matter.

The Supreme Court gave its approval to the doctrine of mixed powers or checks and balances in a 1925 case involving the judicial-like power of the President to pardon or reprieve. The Court pointed out that the Constitution was not designed to provide completely exclusive categories and that it contains several instances in which types of functions are more mixed than separate.[21]

If the two principles of separate powers and checks and balances are taken to be distinct, they can be counterprinciples[22] and serve both sides in a presidential-congressional dispute. Thus, if an issue arose whether the Congress may require the President to obtain prior approval by relevant committees before sending military units outside the country, the theory of separate powers would tend to support the claim of the White House that such a restriction is unconstitutional; whereas the principle of checks and balances would favor the position of Congress.

The more common practice is to consider the two doctrines as one or as closely related.[23] Frequently, the name of one stands for both. Separation of institutions is, of course, a necessary preliminary to mixed or balanced powers as well as to separate functions. The two doctrines may differ most basically in whether functions are to be exclusive or shared.

During recent decades the foremost development in the political-science explanation of constitutional distribution is probably the broad acceptance of the idea of "separated institutions *sharing* powers."[24] This formula, advanced by Richard E. Neustadt,[25] can serve to integrate the different theories of allocation and to provide legitimacy for the dispersion of legislative and executive functions among different classes of officials. Whether functions are or can be shared may depend upon the degree of generality. Only the President may exercise the veto of bills adopted by the two houses of Congress; and only Congress may override such a veto. But all three entities share in the general process of making legislation. Likewise, Congress and the administrative units have particular functions in the appropriation and expenditure of funds, but together they share in the supervision of the public monies.

This sharing is of two general types. In one type, two or more institutions perform the same kind of particular action on a mutually negative basis. A clear example of this is the constitutional requirement that the two houses of Congress vote separately on a proposed bill. The other type involves functions that are different in particular but interdependent in general. The prime example of this type is the trio of processes necessary for criminal punishment: the enactment of penal laws, the execution of them, and the making of judicial determinations based upon them. Another example is the establishment of offices by the Congress and the appointment of officials by the President or by a department head, such as the secretary of labor, as the Congress may stipulate. Judicial review may be of this type, because appellate consideration differs from the primary action.

There may be a type of sharing in the relations between the noncareer political officials and the career merit officials. Executives of the higher level may determine general policies, and the lower-level administrators may then formulate the rules by which such policies are carried out. But the actions of the latter are likely to involve substantial discretion in the interpretation of the general policies and in the manner of application. Thus, the lower executive officials may facilitate or restrict a program through the exercise of discretion. In a sense, they hold a negative upon the higher executives.

The highest form of shared function in the United States government may be representation. The Constitution does not refer expressly to the power of representation; but, from the viewpoint of republican and democratic legitimacy, that function is more fundamental than is legislation, execution, or adjudication. The constitutional pattern of representation corresponds to that for the enactment of statutes. The three institutions for each— the two houses of Congress and the presidency—vary in a number of ways, such as length of terms and size of constituencies, which variance makes for political and programmatic conflicts. This tripartite arrangement is similar to the classical model of mixed sovereignty and the counteraction of monocratic, aristocratic, and democratic forces. The interrelationships among President, Senate, and House may provide the most visible example of checks and balances and shared functions. Each is directly concerned with official representation and public communication, as well as with the adoption or revision of statutes.

There are shared functions of a more complex type in various areas of operation. They are apt to entail relationships of the major classes of appointed executives among themselves and with the elected institutions. Such interactions may make distinct, coordinate contributions to the system of checks and balances.

The doctrine of separated institutions and shared functions can have a negative or restrictive effect upon the total government, as well as upon particular branches.[26] That may have been part of the original purpose, but a number of observers suggest that the objective should be not inaction but action in concert.[27] This last may be more appropriate to activist, corrective government. The Supreme Court has articulated a principle of cooperative effort: "While the Constitution diffuses power the better to secure liberty, it also contemplates that practice will integrate the dispersed powers into a workable government. It enjoins upon its branches separateness but interdependence, autonomy but reciprocity."[28] This last suggests a common duty to cooperate and share responsibility.

The area for action in concert most relevant to this study seems to be that of guidance of the administrative policymakers by Congress and the presidency. The Constitution may vest executive power in a President, but it also authorizes Congress to make laws "necessary and proper for carrying into execution" not only the powers granted to Congress but also "all other powers vested . . . in the government . . . or in any department or officer thereof." This is the principal basis of the congressional power to establish executive departments and agencies.[29] The Constitution also authorizes Congress to provide for three classes of executive officers, that is, those to be appointed by the President with the consent of the Senate, those to be appointed by the President alone, and those to be appointed by the heads of departments.

The particular actions of Congress with respect to the administrative branch include the establishment of institutions and offices, the definition of their authority and standards, the allocation of administrative responsibilities, and the appropriation of operating costs, as well as other matters.[30] Congress is a constant guide or threat to the administrators; it may enact new legislation that can enlarge, decrease, or revise the administrative functions. Also, its annual review of appropriations gives several senators and representatives special opportunity to influence operating attitudes and activities. Likewise, committee investigations and the publication of findings may affect, in varying ways and degrees, the courses of policy-making in the executive departments and agencies.[31] The relationships of the elected institutions to the specialized administrators may be the most important aspects of the functional structure of the government and of the operation of the principle of checks and balances.

The Constitutional Basis of Specialized Structures

The third pattern of distributed functions concerns the multiplicity of specialized structures and the diversity of officials in the different branches of the government.[32]

The institutional relationships are much more complex than the separation of three branches or even the mixed allocation of functions among them. This set of distribution principles pertains not only to the executive departments and agencies and their subdivisions but also to the elements of the congressional and judicial systems to which they are related in practice. Moreover, legitimacy may involve the special publics or groups of the national society.[33]

The constitutional foundations include the inherent necessity of departmental operation as well as the express authorization of Congress to enact laws for "carrying into execution" the powers of the government. In this respect, the Constitution is virtually open-ended.

The inherent character of operating structures and specialized relationships is evident in the evolution of Anglo-American constitutional government. Specialized administrative and adjudicative structures preceded in substance the development of independent legislative assemblies. Twelfth-century England had a chancellor and an exchequer, each with a separate seal of its own, as well as three types of common law courts,[34] while the

Parliament was still an intermittent agency serving mostly to develop moral support for the king. The model Parliaments came a full century later, and then they were more like appellate courts than legislative assemblies.[35] Their legislative roles evolved in later centuries.

Historical surveys also show the inevitability of specialized administration. Virtually every government of any size or degree of advancement has embodied subject specialization. One scholarly study of "the profession of government" concludes that there have been five areas of administration—that is, foreign affairs, military, justice, finance, and internal affairs—in almost every government of historical note.[36] Today there are several departments concerned with internal affairs. That is true of most countries, including Germany, Great Britain, the United States, and to an even larger degree the USSR and China. Governments probably have more similarity in their types of administrative structures than in the kinds of higher political arrangements.[37]

In the United States the development of the national government shows both the historical priority and the inherent power of specialized administration in relation to general policy institutions. We had committees of correspondence before we had the continental congresses. We established a postmaster general and a commander in chief before we signed the Declaration of Independence and the Articles of Confederation. Moreover, we had executive departments before we had an executive President. In 1781 the Confederation Congress established departments of foreign affairs, war, and finance.[38] With a few adjustments these departments were continued under the Constitution of 1787. Likewise, there were appointed administrative officials who served under both the Confederation and the new Constitution as many career officials now serve under successive presidential regimes.[39] Later, the number of executive departments and agencies increased in spurts, as the nation expanded functionally as well as geographically. Four departments (State, Defense, Treasury, and Justice) concern general governmental functions, while other departments concern rather particular aspects of the domestic economy.[40] Also, there are a few specialized courts, as well as "independent regulatory commissions" and, most significant of all, the civil service and other merit systems. This last, we will see, accounts for a very evident division within the appointed officialdom.

Departmentalization, specialization, and fragmentation have been at work in Congress as well as in the administrative establishment. Committees and subcommittees match much of the administrative specialization. The major power in the houses of Congress seems to be in the senior members of the committees and subcommittees. There are now more than a hundred subcommittees in each house, and their relationship with corresponding administrative officials gives much strength to the middle and lower levels of executives in their contests with the White House. Whether the prime source of specialization or fragmentation is in Congress or in the administrative conglomeration is debatable. Most important is their close relationship with each other and with the general- and special-interest groups and other subpublics of the national society.[41]

Probably no aspect of the American sociogovernmental system is more analyzed and debated by political scientists today than are the extent and quality of the role of special interest organizations in representative democracy. The involvement of such groups has a constitutional basis in both the operation and legitimacy of specialized government. The First Amendment guarantees the rights of petition and expression, and the Supreme Court has found an implied right of association.

James Madison made the interplay of multiple factions or groups an element of the system of checks and balances. His statements at the Constitutional Convention and in *The Federalist* disclose his fear of radical action by the House of Representatives and his belief that the Senate and presidential veto provide insufficient restraint. He argued for the large American republic in lieu of the thirteen small ones on the ground that a multiplicity of factions would check a self-interested majority. In his time, factions may have had a bad name because they were associated with irrational thought; but today they have become elements of sociological democracy. De Tocqueville's study of democracy gave acceptability to the American tendency to form associations. Later, the specialization of industry and unionization made groups the foremost elements of economic and political interaction.

The political science discipline, beginning in the 1930s, gave increasing attention to the group process. By the 1950s there was growing recognition that the openness of input channels is a major test of legitimacy. Now virtually all American national government texts give interest groups a key role in unofficial representation and the practical control of specialized administration. The texts differ in depth of analysis, appraisal of impact, and classificatory terminology. Compositely, they differentiate among six general types: *social groups*, mainly religious and fraternal, which are value protective; *special interest groups*, mainly income protective, such as labor, business, and professional associations, which compete among themselves; *political interest or pressure groups*, mainly special interest groups, which endeavor to influence governmental decisions more or less directly; *public interest groups*, which tend to have broader concerns, such as consumer or environmental advocacy; *governmental pressure groups*, which are particularized bureaus, committees, and other entities with a concentrated self-protective mode of activity; and *potential interest groups*, which may arise among underprivileged persons when conditions of awareness and leadership are developed.

Political scientists differ, sometimes sharply, on whether the effect of the interest-group system is elitist and nondemocratic or pluralist and democratic.[42] In part the conflict derives from differing attitudes toward liberty and equality and in part from varying assumptions about the extent of participation. The consensus seems to be that about one-third of the adult males belong to no organized associations and that another one-third belong to groups that exert little or no pressure upon government.[43] It is also generally agreed that pressure groups differ in their inclination and capacity to influence public decisions. There is a consensus that internal organization is often elitist or unequal and that the system may aid the *haves* appreciably more than the *have nots*. During the past decade or more the group representation of minorities and the underprivileged has increased, as also has the representation of groups that exert pressure for such public interests as consumer and environmental protection.[44] These developments may make the group process somewhat more responsive to a few general interests, as well as to many special interests. The system is still more elitist than egalitarian. Moreover, congressional and administrative subunits tend to respond more to persons with group representation than to those without such support.

The legitimacy of specialized government has grown in importance during the past two decades because of the further micronization of major political institutions. The drives to democratize the representational system, including the electoral processes, the political parties, and the houses of Congress, have resulted in still more proliferation. These developments are examined by ten leading political scientists in a recently published collection of essays.[45] The concluding review by Anthony King focuses upon the increased difficulty of building legislative majorities. He points out that coalition building was what the Founding Fathers wanted and that this concept is "a fairly accurate description of the way in which American politics has in fact operated for the past two hundred years."

Coalition building, King says, assumes first "the prior existence of distinct political formations" and second "a degree of internal structure" within those formations. Metaphorically speaking, there must be previously existing building blocks or, more precisely, blocs. Yet, he asserts, "fewer and fewer cohesive blocs are to be found in the American polity." The integrating forces have dissipated; there is no such overriding public philosophy as, for example, the New Deal; power in Congress is diffused; party organization is weakened; most groups lack internal cohesion; and "the old 'iron triangles' (coalitions of a sort) have given way to much more amorphous issue networks."[46] American politics, King declares, have become highly atomized. "Building coalitions in the United States today is like trying to build coalitions out of sand."

King suggests that atomized politics "may share one characteristic with a human crowd—a tendency to move either very sluggishly or with extreme speed." He finds recent examples of these sharply contrasting patterns of group behavior in Congress's handling of the energy question on the one hand and its abolition of the mandatory retirement age on the other:

> In the case of energy, the issue was almost universally agreed to be of great importance. It has been on the policy agenda for several years. Yet in the early summer of 1978, more than fifteen months after President Carter had introduced his original energy package, no effective action had been taken. In the case of mandatory retirement age, the issue was not one that had been widely discussed. If it was on the policy agenda, hardly anyone had noticed the fact. It certainly did not rank with energy as a matter of major national importance. Yet in March 1978 both houses of Congress passed the measure abolishing

mandatory retirement—an action unprecedented in any major industrial society—by overwhelming majorities. In the first case, coalition building proved impossible; in the second case, unnecessary. A careful comparison between Congress's handling of these two issues would probably throw considerable light on the functioning of an atomized political system.[47]

Today presidential efforts to gain congressional approval of the legislative proposals are much more like the merchandising of packaged goods than the constructing of a majority coalition from blocs and factions. The Carter administration "sold" the Panama Canal Treaty, the civil service reform, the delivery of planes to the Far East, and other proposals with much emphasis upon the symbolism of the package label and with the use of widespread merchandising techniques among diverse types of audience.[48]

These developments mean that the constitutional pattern of specialized representation and specialized operations is more prevalent than the simpler models of power allocation. The separation of legislative, executive, and judicial functions still controls the criminal law processes, and the checks and balances among the constitutionally prescribed institutions invigorate political competition and the journalistic description of the national government; but, otherwise, the multiplicity of subunit power centers dominates the governmental process.[49]

The atomization of politics and government makes the executive branch more and more agglomerative. A top White House assistant remarked at the end of 1978 that the Carter administration took a year and a half to learn that the executive branch is a sieve.[50] Richard Nixon apparently never did accept the actuality of executive branch divisiveness.[51] Many persons seem unwilling to acknowledge that disturbing but basic fact. Yet, to comprehend the difficulties of presidential leadership and the problems of pubic control, we need to recognize that the governmental operations are not held together in three branches but are spread among three hundred or more mounds of sand and gravel.

That is where we need to begin in trying to comprehend the problems of effective administration and national responsiveness which arise within the executive branch. In other words, we need to see the plurality of departmental managements, of subunit self-centeredness, and of public-interest-group pressures against the reality of a few hundred subgovernments rather than against the mythology of a presidential-executive unity. The next chapter will analyze in some detail the character of the executive branch in relation to the basic problems that arise from the multiplicity of specialized power centers.

CHAPTER THREE

THE GENERAL CHARACTER OF THE EXECUTIVE BRANCH

THE CONGRESS, THE PRESIDENT, AND THE SUPREME COURT are the most visible elements of our constitutional government; but much of the legislative, executive, and adjudicative activity of the United States government is undertaken by appointed officials of the executive branch in the general manner of a coordinate force. In considering whether the major classes of executive officials merit separate recognition in a constitutional model of essential interactions, we need to examine the general relationships of the executive structures among themselves and with other institutions.

There are many difficulties in analyzing the executive branch; we noted a few of these in the preceding chapters.[1] The Constitution is sketchy on the matter and leaves several uncertainties. Its location of legislative power and executive power suggests that the former is prior, or even superior, to the latter. It does not define executive power, and its specification of presidential rights and duties suggests limitation as well as authorization. Moreover, the Constitution mentions executive departments but leaves their establishment to the discretion of Congress in the use of its general power to enact "necessary and proper" laws.

This chapter will examine several aspects of the executive branch: its congressional basis, its diversity of functions, its internal political competition, the disunity of the departmental structures, the principal levels of executive policymakers, and the checks and balances within the executive branch.

The Congressional Basis of the Executive Branch

"The Constitution gives and takes away. On the one hand, it vests executive power in the President; on the other hand, it assigns numerous administrative powers to Congress. As early as the Treasury Department Act of 1789, Congress created administrative offices with distinct responsibilities. Since then, except in emergency legislation, Congress has given statutory powers directly to agencies or agency heads instead of to the

President. Supreme Court decisions—in 1838 and 1935—upheld
this doctrine."[2] These statements, made by Stephen Hess, a senior fellow at the Brookings Institution, are preparatory to his
assertion that the primary role of the presidency is not to manage
but to make political choices. The statements indicate that Congress has legal power to place executive authority in agency or
department heads apart from the presidency.

The practical or effective power that Congress has over the
relationships between the President and agency heads seems to
depend most basically upon how specific Congress is willing and
able to be. The outstanding evidence of this may be an 1838
opinion of the Supreme Court, a case involving Postmaster General Kendall in the cabinet of Andrew Jackson. Kendall, at Jackson's instigation, refused to pay a certain sum to one Stokes, and
Congress passed a special act ordering him to make payment.
Kendall still refused, and Stokes asked the Court for a mandamus ordering payment. That writ applies only to a *ministerial
duty* in its strict legal meaning of a nondiscretionary obligation.[3]
The Supreme Court, in granting mandamus against the postmaster general (and in effect against the President), said that,
whereas political duties may be under the direction of the President, Congress here had ordered a ministerial duty.[4] A few
years later the Court held that courts should not order an executive official to perform an act when it is not ministerial but executive and political.[5] This time, Congress was specific.

The effect of congressional action is indicated also in other
cases. The Supreme Court has been most protective of the presidency when an incumbent is endeavoring to execute an Act of
Congress, in contrast with situations in which a President tries
to take action unsupported by legislation. In 1867 the State of
Mississippi petitioned the Supreme Court to enjoin President
Andrew Johnson from enforcing the Reconstruction Acts
adopted by Congress. The laws called for military governors
and, hence, involved presidential actions as commander in chief.
The Court refused the injunction. It distinguished the *Kendall*
case, asserting that the duty here imposed upon the President
was not ministerial but "purely executive and political." The
Court based its self-limitation upon the three-separate-functions
theory of government, in which there is first legislation, then
execution, and finally adjudication. The Court, in fact, spelled
out the basic pattern of distinguishable legal processes: "The

Congress is the legislative department of the government; the President is the executive department. Neither can be restrained in its action by the judicial department; though acts of both when performed, are, in proper cases, subject to its cognizance."[6] This last suggests that the essential role of the judiciary is to act retrospectively and not prospectively. The Supreme Court is reluctant to enjoin prospective execution, and in fact, it rarely does so.

The Supreme Court, even when reviewing enforcement actions retrospectively, has tended to favor the government in situations where the executive is proceeding under congressional authorization. It made such a decision in 1936. That decision concerned a joint resolution of Congress prohibiting the sale of arms to certain South American countries if the President should issue a proclamation that such a ban would aid the reestablishment of peace in the area. The President made such a proclamation, and a corporation charged with violating the joint resolution claimed that it was an undue delegation of authority. The Court upheld the authority of the national government in general and of the President in particular. This was an instance in which Congress and the President were acting in concert in the roles of legislator and executor. A contrary situation arose in 1952 when the Truman administration decided to seize strike-threatened steel mills because of a potential danger to the Korean War effort. The President, through the secretary of commerce, acted not on the basis of a congressional enactment but according to a procedure that Congress had not adopted and may have rejected by deliberate choice. The Court held the seizure invalid despite the connection with the conduct of the Korean War.[7]

The essence of these holdings is that a President is in a stronger legal position when his action is based upon express congressional authorization.[8] An Act of Congress is not indispensable, at least when the security of officials is involved,[9] but it definitely strengthens the presidential position. Thus, separation of institutions does not justify independent action; rather it provides the means by which there may be interdependent action.

The President is not, of course, the whole of the executive branch. The Supreme Court's 1867 statement that "the President is the executive department" involved an attempt from the outside to enjoin the execution of an Act of Congress and not a distinction between executive officials. In fact, a year later the Court denied such an injunction against the secretary of war. Here our analysis of the executive branch concerns internal relationships. They are complex and multifarious. "The first point to be made by a book on the Executive Branch of the United States government," James W. Davis, Jr., asserts, "is that the President and the Executive Branch are not synonymous." Davis describes its conglomerate character: "The Executive Branch is composed of numerous organizations—departments, agencies, administrations, bureaus, services, and commissions—and millions of employees."[10] Only one of those types of organizations, the department, is mentioned in the Constitution.

The Constitutional Convention of 1787 did not expressly prescribe or authorize executive departments. It probably assumed that Congress would establish in new legal form the then existing departments (foreign affairs, finance, and military) and agency (post office), and perhaps others as well. The Constitution expressly authorizes Congress to establish "post offices and post roads," "to raise and support armies," and "to provide and maintain a navy." The principal power of Congress to set up executive institutions is the general clause to enact laws "necessary and proper for carrying into execution" the powers of the government and of "any Department or officer thereof." The Constitution also authorizes Congress to determine which inferior officers there shall be and which shall be appointed by the President alone or by the heads of departments.

The only provision to call departments executive says that the President "may require the opinion, in writing, of the principal officer in each of the executive departments, upon any subject relating to the duties of their respective offices."[11] This is sometimes said to give the President administrative power, but it may suggest a general lack of such authority. If the Constitutional Convention assumed that the heads of the cabinet departments are the President's men, why did the Convention set forth, not a provision on general obligation, but a specific clause on the duty to furnish written opinions? The specification of a particular duty implies the absence of a general duty. The constitutional stipulation of an obligation to give an opinion to the President upon request suggests that the department heads are not simply the President's men and may have general responsibility to Congress.

At its first session in 1789, the Congress made selective use of

the phrase *executive department.* The authorization of the Department of State designated it to be an executive department.
Congress did the same with respect to the Department of War,
but not with respect to the Treasury.[12] Moreover, it expressly
required that certain top officials of the Treasury report directly
to the houses of Congress.[13]

The early Congresses seemed anxious to place responsibility
upon the President. They specifically made the presidential office responsible for many matters of apparently subordinate importance. For instance, Congress made George Washington accountable for the construction of lighthouses.[14] Subsequently,
Congress required the signature of the President on every transfer of public land. The Supreme Court gave a practical interpretation and held that the signature of the relevant department
head was adequate for that purpose.[15] Thus, the authority of the
President in relation to the department heads depends much
upon how Congress and the courts utilize their respective
powers of enactment and interpretation.

The extensive constitutional power of Congress over executive
institutions and operations is widely recognized by political
scientists. Peter Woll gives the following picture in his analysis
of public policy: "The 'organic power,' which is the power to
create and abolish agencies, is entirely contained in Congress.
There is no way in which this authority can be inferred from
Article II. When the Constitution is viewed in this light, the
bureaucracy is always an agent of Congress, unless the legislature chooses to set up different arrangements."[16] Woll adds:
"From the standpoint of the formal distribution of authority in
our government, it is a common mistake to assume that the
bureaucracy is 'the executive branch' and entirely accountable
to the White House." He tends to designate the bureaucracy as
the administrative branch, while pointing out that, as an extension of the organic power, Congress "also determines conditions
of appointment, removal, and the general organization of the
administrative branch." In addition, he asserts that "Article II
gives the president seemingly very few powers over the administrative branch."[17]

Louis W. Koenig expresses similar views on the authority of
Congress over the operating structures:

The mission and structure of the departments are determined
by act of Congress. Congress can give authority to subordinate

officials to act independently of their department heads, prescribe specific and detailed administrative procedures, petrify
the internal organization of an agency by statute, and require
Senate confirmation for bureau chief appointments. . . . All executive agencies require annual appropriations that Congress
provides as it chooses. The programs they administer Congress
authorizes and amends. Congress can investigate departmental work in close detail, and its habit is not merely to query
the leadership but to reach far down into the hierarchy.[18]

This last indicates that Congress may seek to guide third- and
fourth-level officials and not merely the President or department
heads. Hence the lines of influence may be more horizontal than
vertical.

Grant McConnell comments upon the contrast between the
authorizations of Congress in Article I of the Constitution and
those of the presidency in Article II:

> Whether taken as a mandate of power or as a description of
> the office, Article II and the few supplementary passages else-
> where in the Constitution are grossly inadequate. The list of
> functions and duties assigned the president is short and sketchy;
> at points, it is vague and trivial. . . . The greater clarity of Ar-
> ticle I on the powers of Congress suggests that the power of the
> president could come only from congressional enactment. And
> yet, if this were so, why should the few items of power given
> the president in Article II be stated at all? It is difficult to avoid
> the conclusion that either the framers were extraordinarily care-
> less with this part of their work, or they were unaware of the
> implications of what they were creating. The former is too harsh
> a judgment; the latter is more probable.[19]

There may be other reasons. The Convention of 1787 spent
much more time on the composition, selection, and authorization of Congress than on the presidency, because most delegates
assumed that the legislature not only should, but also would,
control the operation of the government. Even those who, like
James Madison and James Wilson, wanted a strong presidency
were mainly interested in the counteractive power of the President as a check upon the House of Representatives. Madison
and Wilson sought in vain to fortify the veto power of the President with a council of revision. That would have included members of the judiciary as well as the executive.[20]

Other political science specialists on the national government also remind us of the powers of Congress over the administrative operations:

The President is not made master in his own Executive house by the Constitution. The constitutional structure of separate institutions sharing powers gives Congress the authority to establish Executive departments and thereby to attempt to control them through the process of making appropriations and writing statutes. (Erwin C. Hargrove)

Congress, constitutionally, has at least as much to do with executive administration as does an incumbent of the White House. "The executive power" may be vested in his office, but four tangible, indispensable administrative powers rest with Congress: organization, authorization, financing, and investigation. Departments and agencies—the operating arms of the "executive branch"—are created by acts of Congress. They gain operational authority, programmatic jurisdiction, from laws passed by Congress. They gain funds to pay for personnel and programs from congressional appropriations. And their use of both authority and money is subject to "oversight," to inquiry in Congress. (Richard E. Neustadt)

Even more than its power to legislate, congressional powers to appropriate, to investigate, to mediate, to alleviate, and to repudiate give Congress its special role in the American governmental system. (Stephen K. Bailey)

Many congressmen and senators, working through committees and subcommittees, consider themselves bosses of administrative agencies. They take it upon themselves to oversee both administrative and substantive decisions made by agencies. The legal justification for this tendency is sometimes termed legislative oversight, and is based on the assumed right of the boss to check regularly on employee work. (William L. Morrow)

Congress . . . has become more inclined to participate in detailed administrative decisions. Since 1932 almost 300 provisions have been enacted to allow Congress or its committees to review, defer, approve, or veto executive actions before they take effect. Of these provisions, four-fifths have been enacted since 1960 and over one-half just since 1970. Several agencies in recent years have even been required to submit their budget proposals to Congress at the same time they send them for inclusion in the President's budget, defying the system of central control in executive branch budgeting that has prevailed since World War I. (Hugh Heclo)

The conflict between president and Congress over authority to superintend the departments has never been settled. . . . There seem to be two constitutionally established "chains of command," and the doctrine of coordinate powers makes it clear that neither Congress nor the president needs to subordinate its authority to the other branch. (Richard M. Pious)[21]

The Supreme Court gave its views on the relationship of Congress to an executive agency in a 1958 opinion. This concerned the Panama Canal Company, a government corporation. A steamship company sought to compel the Canal Company to prescribe new tolls in accordance with a ruling of the comptroller general. The Court denied the request, and it explained that the Canal Company may have been carrying out the intent of Congress. It pointed out that the government corporation "is not only the agent for the President but a creature of Congress"; and it noted that the Canal Company "is on close terms with its committees, reporting to the Congress, airing its problems before them, looking to Congress for guidance and direction."[22]

The pervasive authority of Congress with respect to the establishment, review, and maintenance of executive or administrative operations means that a basic pattern of constitutional distribution of power may need to include the essential interactions between the action units of Congress and those of the executive branch, as well as the relationships among the Congress, the President, and the Supreme Court. The relationship of the executive institutions to the President and the Congress is shown in Figure 1.

The Spread of Specialized Functions

"The function of public administration is quite similar to the functions of other political institutions: legislative bodies, chief executives, courts, and special interest groups." The two main points in the introductory sentence of Herbert Kaufman's explanation of the functions of public administrators concern diversity and discretion. Kaufman points out that "administration has never been a single limited set of activities, rather it has had a variety of functions so broad as to constitute the means by which most of the business of large governments has been conducted throughout history." He states also that "When administrators act in their legislative, executive, judicial, and interest group or

FIGURE 1
EXECUTIVE BRANCH OF THE UNITED STATES GOVERNMENT

Relationship of the Institutions to the President and the Congress

PRESIDENT

CONGRESS

EXECUTIVE OFFICE OF THE PRESIDENT

EXECUTIVE DEPARTMENTS

INDEPENDENT AGENCIES
(FORTY OR MORE)

White House
Office

Council of
Economic Advisers

National
Security Council

Office of Manage-
ment and Budget

Others

Inner Group

State
Defense
Treasury
Justice

Outer Group

Interior

Agriculture

Commerce

Labor

Health and Human
Services

Housing and
Urban Development

Transportation

Energy

Education

Management
Agencies

Banking
Boards

Regulatory
Commissions

Government
Corporations

Others

partisan capacities, they enjoy wide discretion for several reasons." Foremost among these reasons is that "the directives they receive from the other participants often express abstract principles in highly general terms."[23] In the preceding chapter, we noted that Congress often leaves to administrative officials much of the task of legislating types of regulation.

An implicit assumption throughout this explanation is that administrative operations are characterized most of all by their specialization. They cut across the traditional concept of three separate functions, because they involve, in particular fields, varying mixtures of legislation, execution, adjudication, and representation. Authority is distributed by area of specialization rather than by general type of function. Kaufman further explains that administrative agencies produce "large quantities of legislation" and that they "dispose of a great deal of business essentially judicial in character." The bulk of this last consists of "rulings on appeals from administrative actions," such as "complaints by private citizens and pleas by public officers and employers against acts of their superiors." He states that more such judicial-like business is "handled within administrative hierarchies than in the courts." His explanation of the way in which administrative officials act like "nongovernmental interest groups" is that they "draft and propose legislation to legislatures, testify at legislative hearings and inquires, rally support for bills they favor, and mobilize opposition against bills they oppose."[24]

In an analysis of the American bureaucracy, Peter Woll calls attention to such lobbying activities. He writes, "Administrative agencies function to a considerable extent as freewheeling interest groups, and in their use of propaganda activities they are no exception." Congress, he explains, may endeavor to limit some of such actions, but administrators in general are freer to lobby than are private groups or persons. He also asserts that "there has been a major delegation of legislative and judicial power to the administrative branch by Congress for political and regulatory reasons that do not fit the traditional constitutional pattern." He points out that there have been other changes in that pattern, such as the role of political parties and the popular election of Presidents. The activities of the bureaucracy are not unconstitutional, he says, so long as they are within "the broad purposes of constitutional government," that is, so long as they are subject to limitation.[25] We will see that the bureaucracy does function within a system of checks and balances.

Woll explains why the bureaucracy has developed its extensive coordinate status:

> It is difficult to grasp the concept that the bureaucracy is not subordinate to one or more of the three initial branches of American government. But the fact is the three primary branches have necessarily supported the creation of a semiautonomous bureaucracy as an instrument to enable our government to meet the challenges it has faced. Given the needs of modern government for economic regulation, specialization, continuity, and speed in the dispatch of business, to mention only a few, it is the bureaucracy that has stepped in to fill the gap created by the inability of the other branches to fulfill all of the requirements. The other branches, particularly the Presidency and the Supreme Court, have also greatly expended their ability and willingness to meet the challenges of the twentieth century, but they could not possibly solve by themselves the extraordinary problems that have confronted our government.[26]

A similar view is expressed by Robert Presthus: "As the scale and complexity of government increased, civil servants assumed a larger role in policy-making, in addition to their traditional—and still major—role of implementing policies designed by their elected masters."[27] This last may suggest some distinction between politics and administration, but most political scientists consider such a dichotomy untenable, at least in present-day government. Policymaking and even politics are defined with such breadth that they include administration as well as legislation. For instance, one explanation of American national government defines *politics* as "the process by which power is employed to affect whether and how government will act on any given matter."[28] This is broad enough to embrace many types of function. Another such analysis observes that there is little of the traditional separation in "the realities of the policymaking process."[29] There is a different type of separation: it appears less in the kinds of institutions or functions than in the diverse subject areas of the specialized subsystems.

The extent to which bureaucratic agencies of the executive branch engage in legislative and adjudicative types of activity is reflected in the passage of the Administrative Procedure Act of 1946. That statute tended to avoid the terms *legislative* and *judicial* by using *rule* and *order* instead. But the object was to impose a minimum set of procedural limitations upon actions that are essentially legislative and adjudicative in character. The Act required that agencies give notice and offer hearings before final issuance of rules or orders.[30] This judicialization of the operating process may be responsible in many instances for the delay and the legalistic mode of many bureaucratic actions. Robert C. Fried says in his study that this effort has encumbered the administrative process "with the anachronistic or archaic procedures dear to traditionalistic and conservative judges and leaders of the bar."[31] Most likely, lawyer groups urged its enactment, but deliberate procedures have long been a helpful means of safeguarding the rights of represented individuals.

Political Competition within the Executive Branch

The idea that civil servants as well as members of Congress, the President, cabinet members, and judges engage in discretionary making of policy is related to the political science proposition that government is a "conflict resolution process" that determines "who gets what, when, and how."[32] That general function embraces and tends to explain all particular functions. It is associated with the rejection of any categorical differentiation between *politics* and *administration,* such as the assertion by Paul H. Appleby that administration is "the eighth political process."[33]

The premise that politics and administration are interrelated involves broad conceptions of both and, in fact, makes *politics* a synonym for *making policy.* Such a view is presented by James W. Davis, Jr., in support of three propositions: (1) that the term *President* is not a synonym for *executive branch;* (2) that the executive branch is composed of numerous uncohesive organizations; and (3) that the various subunits of the executive branch may ignore the President, because they "do not need him and will continue long after he has gone."[34] The differences between the President and the civil servants may derive in part from the contrast between short and long tenure; but there are more fundamental forces, such as the differences in the constituencies of various officials. Davis points out the connection of these factors with the more inclusive conception of the governmental process:

The political system includes the Congress, the President, the Court, and the bureaucracy; it also includes organized interest groups, political parties, and individuals as voters and expressors of opinion.

It is obvious from this list of participants that one characteristic of the American political system is pluralism. This characteristic is critical, because it means that many participants may demand a voice in governmental decision-making. The pluralism of American politics means that any bureau chief may have to serve several masters. One cannot understand bureaucratic behavior unless one appreciates this fact of bureaucratic life.[35]

Later on, Davis gives further attention to the relative position of the presidency and the bureaucracy and the manner in which they enter into the political competition of the executive branch:

... despite the Constitution, tradition, the law, and folklore, the President is frequently not chief of the Executive Branch. He is more accurately viewed as chief persuader and chief bargainer.

If the President is viewed as only one of several players in the game of politics, it is easy to understand that he is not and cannot be the ruler of the Executive Branch. We realize that the President may have to rely on persuasion or patronage to get what he wants from Congressmen; that these are also required when it comes to ostensible subordinates in the Executive Branch contradicts our myths. Nevertheless there is no more accurate way to view the Executive Branch than as a political arena. The President may be more than "first among equals," but he is hardly the only man with power.[36]

The idea that the power of the presidency is less to command than to persuade and to bargain is a key point in the landmark study by Richard E. Neustadt.[37] That idea is related to Neustadt's notable theory of constitutional distribution discussed in the preceding chapter. It holds that the Constitution establishes, not separate institutions with separate functions, but rather separate institutions sharing powers. Davis's treatment of the executive branch as a political arena is itself recognition that that branch may be composed of separate institutions sharing powers. Viewed from another perspective, the Congress, the presidency, and the administrative bureaucracy are in substance separate institutions sharing the executive/administrative powers.

Other political scientists have argued in various ways that administration cannot be categorically separated from politics. For instance, Louis C. Gawthrop states that "The executive apparatus is structured to respond to the forces of bargaining, negotiation, and compromise—in short, to the powers of persuasion. It is not geared to respond to the forces of direct commands from top-level executive officials, and least of all to direct commands from the President."[38] The principal reason why administrative officials do not answer to the direct commands of their immediate executive superiors is that they have a number of masters, such as at least four subcommittees of the houses of Congress, the segments of the public they serve, their own bureaus, and their own professional standards.[39]

The counteraction between the bureaucracy and the presidency often is attributed to the differences in career and noncareer tenures, but more fundamental forces may also be at work. For one thing, there is a contrast in the constituencies they seek to serve in their various policy decisions. The difference between the substantive roots of the presidency and the bureaucracy is explained by Theodore J. Lowi in his general analysis of the national government:

> The president is directed by the Constitution and supposed by the public to be chief executive. Yet, the chief executive in the American system is a product of representative government, and the executive branch is a product of bureaucratization. The two belong to the same governmental galaxy, but to tie them together as one political process would suppress the special political features of the executive branch. In our system of government there are tensions inherent in the relationships between the chief executive and the executive branch.[40]

This statement is not at all unique in its general import. Many political scientists have pointed out the deep-running, persistent chasm between the presidency and the bureaucracy. Lowi's special contribution here is his identification of the different roots of the two forces. Presidents are basically elected officials, most of them coming to the White House because of success in that curious bundle of operations we call presidential nomination and election. Those who enter the office by the vice-presidential route also have political differentiations. A vice-presidential candidate often is chosen because of political identifications not possessed by the presidential candidate. Even the appointed

Vice-Presidents Gerald Ford and Nelson Rockefeller had distinct political associations and, hence, both limitations and assets of a political character.

The appointed officials of the executive branch generally have political or professional foundations that differ from those of the President. Lowi says that the executive branch is "a product of bureaucratization." That may pertain mostly to those appointed under civil service or another merit system. Their entry depends upon technical or professional specialization and may involve definite occupational points of view and certain functional standards.[41] With service in the government, they acquire attachments and loyalties to a particular bureau or agency and also considerable understanding of the clientele they serve most directly.

Lowi and Davis are typical of many political scientists in using the terms *chief executive* and *executive branch* even though neither appears in the Constitution. We noted before that the Constitution is particularly sketchy in dealing with executive institutions and functions.[42] The 1787 Convention refused to decide what, if any, cabinet there should be; and it did not even authorize in a direct and express manner the establishment of executive departments. Rather, it assumed they would be continued or established by Congress.

The majority of political scientists associate strength in the presidency with a capacity to initiate corrective legislation. Dorothy James, in her recent study, identifies two facets of power, that is "the positive ability to initiate" and the "negative ability to prevent," even while recognizing the scholarly association of strong Presidents with the initiation of policies.[43] This tends to reduce the importance of the role of chief administrator and to give priority to the legislative roles, particularly those of giving Congress information on the state of the Union and of recommending "necessary and expedient" measures. This specific constitutional emphasis upon policy initiation by the President seems to be a departure from the general implications of the related clauses vesting legislative power in Congress and executive power in a President.

Limitations of tenure upon the Presidents and, as a consequence, upon their appointees in the upper levels of the executive hierarchy tend to set them apart from the other forces in the government, that is, members of Congress, the judges, and the civil service administrators. The average tenure of the Presidents has been about six years, and since 1960 it has been four years. Departmental political executives have average tenure of less then four years, and surveys of such positions as assistant secretaries indicate an average of less than three years. In contrast, leaders of the houses of Congress and chairmen of most committees have had much longer periods of service. Moreover, they have a much greater opportunity to concentrate upon a particular area than do the Presidents. The tenure of most merit system administrators is even more striking: many have had twenty or more years of experience in their respective bureaus or agencies, and even those who are transferred to different units have general governmental experience considerably beyond that of their immediate superiors. As a consequence, Presidents view the bureaucracy as too slow and often turn to their White House staff.[44]

Other factors are also at work here. Officials near at hand in the White House Office generally have no political base or constituency and have unqualified loyalty to the incumbent President, whereas the departmental executives are apt to have political or professional attachments relevant to their department or agency. They have a loyalty to the President but also to their clientele, to the committees of Congress, and to others.

This touches upon another question. Are the differences in the constituencies and the attitudes among major classes of executive officials constitutionally functional or dysfunctional? In other words, do counteracting approaches to particular needs of public groups have a positive or negative effect upon the politico-governmental system? Some political science analyses may suggest that the conflict between the presidency and the bureaucracy is evidence of a malfunction in the governmental operation. But recently there seems to be increasing recognition that each can make a positive contribution and that they are coordinate and complementary parts of a mixed government. For instance, Lowi suggests more appreciation of the contribution of the civil servants. "Bureaucracy," he asserts, "is one of the great secrets of success in all of the 'developed countries' of the world." He concludes that there "may be no available solution to the problem of presidential power" but that there may be some progress "through a more thorough appreciation of the bureaucracy problem."[45] Then Philippa Strum states that it "is the greatest achievement of the American bureaucratic system that it continues to function no matter what happens on the electoral scene."[46]

The tendency of some political scientists to see the presidency and the bureaucracy as coordinate forces with distinguishable, positive contributions appears also in Thomas E. Cronin's *The State of the Presidency:*

> Bureau chiefs and career civil servants often do avoid initiative, taking risks, and responsibility, opting instead for routine and security. The bureaucracy most assuredly has its own way of doing things, often more conservative or more liberal than what the president wants. But the fact that bureaucratic interests and presidential interests often differ does not mean that the permanent employees of the federal executive branch constitute an active enemy force. Bureaucratic organizations act, rather, in reasonable, rational ways to enhance their influence, budget, and autonomy. And they generally believe that in doing so they act in the nation's interest.
>
> Thus, the bureaucracy often defines the national interest quite differently from the way it is defined in the White House. But a close examination of these two definitions often reveals that both are valid and representative views of what is desirable about which reasonable people can legitimately differ. The task for a president, then, is to understand the strategies and tactics of federal bureaus and appreciate the underlying motivations. Properly diagnosed, the bureaucratic instinct for competition, survival, and autonomy can be creatively harnessed by the White House both to educate itself and to develop cooperative alliances.[47]

The observation that the bureaucracy may be either more conservative or more liberal than a particular President may be attributable to a desire on the part of civil servants to be considered neutral, whereas the presidency is marked by alternating partisanism. The deviation from center is more in the particular Presidents than in the bureaucracy. Civil servants, in their private political leanings, may be more Democratic than Republican because that is true of the country in general. Different agencies, such as those in commerce and labor may attract persons with contrasting views on economic liberality; but, by and large, career civil servants, in their official decisions, tend to be appreciably less partisan than the White House.

William E. Mullen is another political scientist who seems to view the presidency and the bureaucracy as positive, coordinate forces. He observes that:

> Presidents and administrations come and go, but the careerists linger on. They are the ones who are most familiar with the legislative mandate of their departments and who have the oldest and closest ties to the clients served by the departments. In many cases they believe that their experience and professionalism puts them in a better position than the president to determine which policies best further agriculture, the defense of the United States, business or urban housing. (They of course may be right).[48]

The idea that both the Presidents and the bureaucrats may be right in different ways is further evidence of the counteractive and interdependent character of the elements of the executive branch.

Departmental Disunity

The ideological belief that the executive branch is a unified pyramid with the President at the top in full command often assumes that the cabinet, composed mainly of heads of the executive departments, brings the whole array of structures into a single operating force. Such a belief overlooks a number of factors. One is that the cabinet is more a representative body than an administrative institution. Members are more often selected for identity with a professional or political constituency than for managerial experience or capacity. The full cabinet extends across a socio-political spectrum. Another factor is that each department head serves several masters—the President, congressional committees, departmental personnel, the relevant subpublics, and so on. A third factor is that the center of administrative operation is less in the department than in the subdepartmental units. We will examine the views of political scientists on each of these matters.

David C. Saffell makes these pertinent observations in his general explanation of the American national government:

> The cabinet is weak in part because of its lack of constitutional status. Its influence is weakened further by the limitations placed upon the president in selecting cabinet secretaries. Unlike the members of the executive office, who are chosen primarily on the basis of knowledge and good personal relations

with the president, cabinet membership represents an attempt by an incoming president to take into account the need for harmony within his party, geographical balance, the wishes of interest groups, and the availability of first choices to accept positions. At the time of the selection process, the president may have had only the most casual personal contact with some cabinet nominees.[49]

This last was true in the case of Presidents Eisenhower, Kennedy, Nixon, and Carter, as well as others.

Saffell's differentiation between members of the executive office and the cabinet is evidence of a basic division within the presidential appointees. The special assistants and advisers on the White House staff and in other executive office units are chosen for their commitment to the presidential constituency, and most of them do not have a preestablished political base of their own. Many of the White House aides do not need senatorial approval. In contrast, department heads require consent of the Senate; and, with the exception of some heads of the Departments of State, Defense, Treasury, and Justice, they have politico-economic attachments. In fact, that is often a principal reason for their appointment. As a consequence, each tends to represent a socio-political constituency that differs from the others and also from the most crucial constituencies of the incumbent President. For instance, the heads of the Departments of Labor, Agriculture, and the Interior, and probably others in the Carter cabinet, had to make hard choices between the presidential policy and their own political bases.[50]

These factors are also dealt with by Dorothy B. James. A President, she writes, "must appoint individuals to his Cabinet for reasons quite different from their personal loyalty to him. Especially in the initial Cabinet appointments, he must consider factors of balance in terms of geography, religion, and ethic background." She also points out a requirement of appropriateness: "For example, New Yorkers are unlikely to be selected secretary of agriculture, whereas Kansans have little hope of being secretary of labor." She also explains the causes for differences between the political interests of a President and his department heads:

> . . . each department has its own attentive "constituency" of organized interest groups affected by its actions and of congressional committees established to consider the policy areas with

which it deals. Since the relevant interest groups and congressional committees are powerful allies or antagonists for any executive department, the department secretary's loyalty must necessarily be divided. He must often represent *their* interests to the President rather than the President's interests to them. Thus Cabinet members can be useful to the President because they represent other interests, but for that very reason they cannot be depended upon as a source of bureaucratic control.[51]

Hence, the identification of cabinet members with different constituencies serves both to broaden the political basis of the presidential regime and to increase the difficulties of achieving unity within the executive conglomeration.

Commenting on this phenomenon, Theodore J. Lowi explains that those who have political support sufficient to be attractive to the President in the choice of cabinet members also have their own goals in life. There is every reason to expect, he points out, that they will continue to pursue their own goals even while in the cabinet, and once in a while these goals are likely to be in opposition to those of the President. Lowi also observes that all top political appointees are special pleaders and that there may be difficulty in knowing when they are operating on their own behalf and when they are disinterestedly working for the President. Moreover, he asserts, "the political following a cabinet member brings is not necessarily translatable into effective control over the department the appointee is supposed to administer."[52] In other words, the cabinet is not likely to bring unity to the executive branch, and the individual members may not assure the unity of even their respective structures.

Lowi calls attention to the idea that Presidents often feel their department heads are their natural enemies. This designation, which goes back at least fifty years, gives some indication of the duration of the presidential-cabinet difficulty. Charles G. Dawes, the first director of the Bureau of the Budget after its establishment in 1921 and later Calvin Coolidge's Vice-President, remarked at a hearing in the 1920s that cabinet members are natural enemies of the Presidents, because they instinctively seek larger budgets for their respective units. Political analysts have kept the designation alive.[53]

Aaron Wildavsky gives a pointed explanation of the mixed loyalties of many cabinet members in his 1976 analysis of the past and future presidency:

Secretaries of the great departments must serve more than one master. They are necessarily beholden to Congress for appropriations and for substantive legislation. They are expected to speak for the major interests entrusted to their care, as well as for the President. They need cooperation from the bureaucracy that surrounds them, and they have to make accommodations to get that support. A Secretary of Agriculture who is vastly unpopular with farmers, a Secretary of Interior who is hated by conservationists, and all Secretaries whose employees undermine their efforts, cannot be of much use to the Chief Executive. Nevertheless, Presidents (and especially their personal staffs) appear to behave as if there were something wrong when Cabinet members do what comes naturally to people in their positions.[54]

This last is another indication of the general division of presidential appointees between those in or near the White House and those beyond the Executive Office complex. That substantive boundary may need to be considered in any pattern of the distribution of power in the national government. Wildavsky's comment is also another sign that political scientists tend to regard conflict of attitude among administrators as inevitable and even empirically fitting.

The operating gap between the presidential contingent at the White House and the top departmental officials is apt to cause the latter to develop ties with lower levels of policymakers within their respective departments, including many career administrators of the subunits. This development was described in 1977 by Hugh Heclo, a senior fellow of the Brookings Institution:

Weaknesses among political executives lead inevitably to White House complaints about their "going native" in the bureaucracy. The image is apt. To a large extent the particular agencies and bureaus *are* the native villages of executive politics. Even the most presidentially minded political executive will discover that his own agency provides the only relatively secure reference point amid all the other uncertainties of Washington. In their own agencies, appointees usually have at least some knowledge of each other and a common identity with particular programs. Outside the agency it is more like life in the big city among large numbers of anonymous people who have unknown lineages. Any common kinship in the political party or a shared political vocation is improbable, and in the background are always the suspicions of the President's "true" family of supporters in the White House.[55]

The tendency of presidentially appointed political executives in the departments to find security among the continuing subunits lessens their opportunities to be a unifying force in the executive branch. "Political executives have no common culture for dealing with the problems of governing," Heclo asserts, adding that "it is seldom that they are around long enough or trust one another enough to acquire one."[56] Surveys show that the tenure of such officials as the assistant secretaries of the departments averages less than three years and often is more like two years.[57]

Other political scientists have pointed out that departmental managements need to cultivate the lower level administrators if they are to achieve any appreciable degree of unified control:

> A cabinet secretary must also spend considerable time and energy promoting the interests of the permanent civil servants within his or her own department. Many of these people have devoted years of service to developing expertise in carrying out their agency's mission. . . . They are the ones who are most familiar with the legislative mandate of their departments and who have the oldest and closest ties to the clients served by the departments. (William E. Mullen)

> Just as the President faces great difficulty in controlling policy-making by his departments, the department secretary is faced with an array of bureaus not uncommonly in a state of incipient or actual mutiny. (Louis W. Koenig)

> . . . the real power in each bureaucracy lies with the middle-level management: those civil servants who make the day-to-day decisions and keep the bureaucracy functioning in spite of the vagaries of electoral politics. (Philippa Strum)

> In short, the President has limited control of his Cabinet and sub-Cabinet members; they in turn have limited control over the operations of their own subordinates. (Louis C. Gawthrop)

> In Washington, congressional committee and subcommittee chairmen normally prefer to talk to civil servants, whom they have known and done business with for many years, rather than with secretaries and assistant secretaries, who came to town only last month and probably will be gone before the cherry blossoms next appear. (Rowland Egger)

> It is actually possible that in terms of effective power most of the noncareer officials are inferior to the careerists. . . . Nor

should we delude ourselves into believing that the executive transients at the Cabinet and sub-Cabinet levels are automatically and necessarily the loyal instruments of Presidential direction and control over the executive departments and agencies. (Stephen K. Bailey)

. . . Cabinet members are not wholly the President's men. Most of their time is spent, not with the President, but rather in their departments, where they are subject to constant internal and external pressures from clientele groups represented by the department. Frequently the objective of these pressures is to move Cabinet members in directions that are not compatible with the President's goals. (Robert E. DiClerico)[58]

General political science explanations of American national government often strike a similar note. One such volume asserts that a new cabinet secretary in Washington often discovers that a title does not assure actual authority over his or her department. It explains that the bureaucracy has its own sources of power that enable it to resist political authority and points to the difference in tenure: "Cabinet secretaries come and go; the civil service remains."[59] Thus, the most knowledgeable and most enduring forces are the subunit officials. "The career administrator provides invaluable continuity compared to the frequent and steady turnover among top-level policy executives," Louis C. Gawthrop declares.[60]

The third major cause of departmental disunity is this semiautonomous character of the constituent subunits. Several political scientists recognize their central operating position. Hugh Heclo observes that the administrative machinery represents a number of fragmented power centers, and Louis W. Koenig asserts that the single most powerful figure in the great pyramid is the bureau chief. Harold Seidman is even more pointed. He states: "It is the agency heads, not the President, who have the men, money, materiel, and legal powers." Grant McConnell says that "it is questionable whether the presidency has kept up with the centrifugal tendency of the government" and that many parts of the government have a "large degree of autonomy" and "their own political sources of support." Often, they "can act independently of presidential wishes."[61]

The departmental subunit is typically an operating center with vital relationships extending out in a number of directions. Richard E. Neustadt describes this phenomenon: All agency administrators are responsible to the President; but "they *also*

are responsible to Congress, to their clients, to their staffs, and
to themselves. In short, they have five masters. Only after all of
those do they owe any loyalty to each other."[62] In other words,
a sense of executive branch unity is low in their scale of values
as long as it may conflict with the welfare of their own respective units.

James MacGregor Burns explains that a bureau is usually both
independent and dependent with respect to President, Congress,
clientele group, and public and that the agency chief, as best he
can, "works out his own 'mix' of organizational alliances and in-
dependences." The idea that the subunit occupies a coordinate
position is implicit also in the comment of Dorothy B. James
that the bureaucracy "cannot be controlled by the President,
Congress, or any of the extra-constitutional actors involved" and
that, therefore, "alliances have to be worked out."[63] This is also
evidence of the political competition within the executive
branch and the mutual interdependence of the major classes of
executive officials. And it leads to the possibilities of horizontal
arrangements among these policymakers.

The Levels of Executive Policymakers

Stephen K. Bailey, in 1956, called the executive branch "a many-
splintered thing,"[64] and we may wonder whether it can have a
general structural pattern. The official classification of executive
units into the Executive Office of the President, Executive Departments, and Agencies (often designated *independent agencies*) is a virtual admission that no comprehensive symmetry
exists. There may be a common belief that at least a single department has the tight unity of a pyramidal hierarchy, but the
preceding section showed that there is apt to be much operational disunity *within* the particular departments as well as
among them.

The complexity and even confusion of the executive branch
has not deterred political scientists from endeavoring to divide
the various executive policymakers into two general categories,
even though the differentiating concepts or terms may vary.
Each set or pair of terms may be an oversimplification, but that
is almost inevitable in any attempt to develop an identifying
model for the essential interactions of a governmental system.
Fred A. Kramer presents a dichotomy with a long historical

record: "There seems to be a natural separation between 'merit,' on the one hand, and the 'spoils' of politics on the other. The merit system, where appointments and promotions are based on more or less objective measures, is usually contrasted with the spoils system, where personnel decisions are made primarily on political criteria."[65] The spoils system often is associated with the presidential politics of Andrew Jackson. He may have been more outspoken about rewarding his supporters than any other President, but his percentage of replacements in 1829 probably was not much larger than those of Thomas Jefferson when the presidential party changed in 1801.[66] The probabilities are that there have been both merit and spoils appointments in all governments of substantial size or complexity during the whole course of history. At the height of the Athenian "democracy," lot was used to select administrative personnel, a practice that seemed to favor some families or districts over others. Yet there was deliberately a more careful selection of military leaders. In the history of our own nation, there were probably both merit and spoils appointees in the administration of the departments under the Articles of Confederation and under the new Constitution beginning in 1789.[67]

That differentiation acquired new terms and somewhat more exact meaning with the beginning of civil service legislation in 1883. "The Civil Service Act created a dichotomy within the executive branch between career and noncareer administrators," in the words of Louis C. Gawthrop.[68] Political scientists seem to have less objection to the career/noncareer set of terms than to other sets, such as politics and administration or political executives and professional bureaucrats. The discipline tends to reject the use of *political* as a term of limitation, probably on the ground that the whole field of governmental operation involves the political process of adjusting or accommodating conflicts between persons or groups.[69]

The analytical identifications and designations of two major classes of executive policymakers tend to differentiate in one way or another the basic distinction between the permanent character of the specialized bureaucracy and the come-and-go aspect of the White House and most presidential executive appointees. Rowland Egger articulates the contrast in his study of the President. He asserts that a measure of conflict "is instinct in the relations between a permanent bureaucracy and a tem-

porary political executive."[70] Arthur M. Schlesinger, Jr., one-
time adviser to President John F. Kennedy and a leading historian of the contemporary American presidency, made a similar
distinction. In 1969 he stated that we have, in effect, four
branches of government, because the executive branch has come
to be divided between "a presidential government" and a "permanent government."[71]

Some political scientists also use these terms. Erwin C. Hargrove defines them: "The Presidential government is that thin
layer of Presidential appointees in the White House and Presidential agencies and at the top of each department. . . . The permanent government is composed of those civil servants whose
jobs are secure regardless of changes of Administration."[72] This
dichotomy, like the others, has the merit of simplicity, but there
may be executive officials who are, at least much of the time,
neither presidential nor permanent. The boundary between the
classes of administrative policymakers is much more a zone than
a line, and that also suggests the possibility of various levels of
executive officials.

These differentiations endeavor to divide officials rather than
institutions or functions. As a consequence, the boundaries are
more horizontal than vertical. They cut across most of the institutional categories of the executive branch, including the Executive Office of the President. There are not apt to be career policymakers in the White House Office, but there are many in the
Office of Management and Budget. The staffs of the National
Security Council and even the Council of Economic Advisers include some continuing officials along with carry-over problems.
Informally, there is a horizontal division within the cabinet.
Often heads of the Departments of State, Defense, Treasury,
and Justice, as individual advisers, may be closer to the Oval
Office than are the other department heads.[73] In one sense, the
inner four have a higher status than the outer group. In another
sense, both cabinet groups have a higher elevation than is en-
joyed by most top officials of the independent agencies, with a
frequent exception for the chairman of the Federal Reserve
Board and one or two others.[74]

An understanding of the essential interactions among the various types of officials in the executive branch entails a basic
appreciation of the idea of horizontal boundaries and a considerable recognition of the diverse levels of policymakers. Accord-

ingly, we will illustrate such a classification of executive-branch officials by suggesting a pattern of six general levels:

1. *The presidential level.* The assistants and advisers in the White House Office, the key officials of the other principal agencies of the Executive Office of the President, and those cabinet members who are particularly close to the President.

2. *The secretarial level.* The other members of the cabinet and the general undersecretaries or deputy secretaries of the several departments.

3. *The assistant-secretarial level.* The specialized undersecretaries or deputy secretaries, the military secretaries, the substantive assistant secretaries, and the general counsels of the various departments.

4. *The administrator/director/commissioner level.* Those appointees of the presidential regime who are in charge of the principal bureaus, agencies, and services, as well as the administrative-assistant secretaries of the departments.

5. *The civil service supergrade level.* Those officials appointed under the civil service or other merit system in Grades 16, 17, and 18 or their equivalent. These may include excepted, temporary, noncareer, and career assignments.

6. *The regular civil service level.* Those executive policymakers in Grade 15 or below and comparable positions in other merit systems.

This classification concerns, primarily, the officials within the executive departments, but with a number of adjustments it can be extended to most of the independent agencies. The structure and nomenclature of the agencies differ widely. Moreover, the members of boards and commissions often have functions and responsibilities that differ from those of the single executives.

Checks and Balances within the Executive Branch

Political scientists, from time to time and in varying ways, associate the interactions of executive officials with the basic principles of constitutional distribution. In 1953 Bertram Gross stated that "there are more checks and balances within the executive branch itself than the Founding Fathers ever dreamed of when they wrote the Constitution."[75] In 1963 Peter Woll described the American bureaucracy as "a powerful and viable branch of government, not properly subject to complete control by Congress, the President, or the judiciary," and he asserted that it "functions within a checks-and-balances system in much the same way as the original three branches of government."[76] He did not say expressly that it was the same system that obtains with respect to the three better-known institutions, but he did indicate that the limits are set by congressional and judicial action. In 1967 Grant McConnell observed that a whole series of obstacles to presidential influence has been built into the federal bureaucracy. He identified as one of the most important obstacles "inertia . . . a tendency to go on doing what has always been done," and he stressed the need for political leadership. The administrative part of the presidential task, he said, is as political as anything a President does.[77]

The more substantive forces of a checks-and-balances system derive from political competition, such as that among the President and the two houses of Congress. Among three classes of executive officials, we may have a pattern of interaction somewhat analogous to that among the three elected institutions. We noted earlier in this chapter the conclusion of James W. Davis, Jr., that "there is no more accurate way to view the Executive Branch than as a political arena."[78] That tends to place the departments, agencies, and even their subunits in the position of coordinate forces. Dorothy B. James, also, points out that attempts to supervise the administrative units may involve alliances among various forces of the government, including the Congress and the President.[79] Likewise, Harold Seidman paints a similar picture:

> An alliance—which is what the executive branch really is—is by definition a confederation of sovereigns joined together in pursuit of some common goal. Some members may be more powerful than others, but they are nonetheless mutually interdependent. Individual purposes and goals are subordinated only to the extent necessary to hold the alliance intact. Each member will find it necessary at times to act contrary to the interests of the alliance when compelled to do so to promote his own vital interests. Unless a President is able to convince his departmental allies that they need him as much as he needs them, inevitably they will gravitate to another power base.[80]

Seidman, a one-time management specialist with the Bureau of the Budget, explains further that the executive branch is composed of multiple power centers and that that is the essential character of a confederation or alliance. Other political scientists have emphasized the existence of diverse pressure or veto points.[81] The essence of checks and balances is, of course, the existence of mutual negatives which make for limitation and a broader base of action in concert and cooperation.[82] The presence of emergencies may stimulate agreement. Strong political parties also may facilitate agreement among some forces, but the weakening of major parties and the strengthening of constituency politics make the multiplicity of power centers increasingly evident and more and more dominant.[83]

One of the most comprehensive sketches of the possibilities of the administrative bureaucracy in bringing new dimensions and force to the checks-and-balances system is a 1974 analysis by Stanley Bach:

> The mutual control or balance model asserts that presidential power can be limited by the countervailing powers of the Congress, the courts, and even the federal bureaucracy (as well as by less formal political groups). To evaluate this model, we must ask if, in fact, the balance of powers among these institutions is even enough to control abuses by any one of them. Traditionally, the focus of attention has been on presidential-congressional conflict, most recently over such questions as executive privilege and the control of information, impoundments and the control of money, and war powers and the control of American military forces. At the same time, there has also been a growing recognition that a President's relations with his own administration involve more than giving orders and assuming obedience to his commands. The bureaucracy can do almost as much as the Congress to limit presidential power. But civil servants are not elected and, therefore, not directly accountable to the public. In the future, we may have less to fear from the White House or the Congress than from the huge and anonymous public bureaucracy, exercising its discretionary powers to thwart the will of elected and accountable representatives. To the extent that any of these institutions become effectively independent of the others, to that extent the prospects for mutual control are weakened.[84]

This places the bureaucracy in a system of coordinate powers that challenge each other in both negative and positive ways. Bach warns against bureaucratic dominance, but other political scientists suggest that there may be inadequate checks upon the presidency. Stephen Hess, for example, points out that White House staffs grow less and less willing to express a protest. Conflict continues, but as the less loyal depart, the more loyal gain ascendancy. "What may then happen is that the President is left without the necessary internal checks and balances, which are nearly as important as the checks and balances built into the Constitution."[85]

That brings us to the most explicit recognition of the separate identity of the administrative bureaucracy as a coordinate force in the constitutional pattern of distributed authority. Several political scientists have asserted that there is in recognizable degree a fourth branch of government that is presumably comparable to the congressional, presidential, and judicial branches. Following are some of the declarations to this effect:

> The bureaucracy must be maintained as a semi-autonomous fourth branch of government to check any potential excesses on the part of the president or Congress. (Peter Woll)

> The theory of our constitution needs to recognize and understand the working and the potential of our great fourth branch of government, taking a rightful place beside President, Congress, and Courts. (Norton Long)

> . . . a strong case can be made out that we actually have "four-way" government instead of the classic tripartite; Congress, the presidency, the bureaucracy, and the judiciary are the four. (Ernest S. Griffith)

> The executive today consists not only of a chief executive but of numerous departments and agency heads. It also consists of thousands of civil servants (what some have called the "fourth branch of government") who, in fact, do most of the executing of the laws. (Dale Vinyard)

> While bureaucracy (or administration) is in many ways executive in nature—and thus commonly considered to be an offshoot of the presidency—both in the terms of the diversity of its responsibilities and its tenuous relationship to the presidential office, it must be viewed as a fourth branch of government. (Charles E. Jacob)

> . . . such are this bureaucracy's formidable size and independent disposition that it can loom as an almost autonomous fourth branch of the government. (Emmet John Hughes)

This agency independence has led to the accusation that the bureaucracy constitutes, in effect, a powerful fourth branch of government. (William L. Morrow)[86]

In a few instances, scholarly analysts have said that the presidential contingent is a "fourth branch";[87] but, usually when used in relation to government officials, the term is applied to the administrative forces in the departments and agencies. For example, the 1979 study of executive processes by Kenneth J. Meier is entitled *Politics and the Bureaucracy: Policymaking in the Fourth Branch of Government*.[88]

Those political scientists who undertake to explain the general character of the American national government for the basic university course on the subject tend to point out a lack of controlled unity within the executive branch. Examples from a number of them who expressly apply the term *fourth branch* to the more permanent officials follow:

At every level of American government—indeed, in most governments of the world—the strings of power are pulled by enterprises variously called the "administration," the "fourth branch of government," and the "bureaucracy." (Blanche D. Blank)

The Constitution established only three branches of government, but the demands of a modern industrialized society have combined with a variety of political forces to establish a "fourth branch" of government—the bureaucracy. (David A. Caputo)

Taken together, federal government agencies spend vast sums of money, employ very large staffs, and make great numbers of decisions, some of enormous significance to the lives and fortunes of millions of people. There is power here—enough to suggest that the federal bureaucracy has become what amounts to a fourth branch of government. (Leonard Freedman)

No treatment of the operations and functions of the federal government's established institutions would be complete without devoting considerable attention to the "fourth branch." . . . The bureaucracy is very much an important political force independent of the president. (Thomas G. Ingersoll and Robert E. O'Connor)

The bureaucracy has become a "fourth branch of government" not only because it was able to respond to the needs of public policy but also out of the inability of the other branches of government to meet these needs. (Harvey M. Karlen)

Ironically, the specter of a powerful and relatively autonomous Fourth Branch of government in the form of a bureaucracy is the result of the Founders' fear of unrestrained power. (Fred R. Mabbutt and Gerald J. Ghelfi)

This national bureaucracy of ours, with its three million civilian employees, has been called the fourth branch of government. Some people think it has grown into the most powerful branch of all, with perhaps the most profound effect upon the daily lives of Americans. (Dennis J. Palumbo)

The reason the separation of powers into three branches fosters the formation of a relatively independent fourth branch—the bureaucracy—is that bureaucracies learn to play one branch against another. In this way they enhance their independence. (Kenneth Prewitt and Sidney Verba)

Bureaucracies have become a fourth branch of government. . . . The bureaucracy is not accountable to the public at large. It is in a position to regulate itself as an autonomous institution. (Sam C. Sarkesian and Krish Nanda)

The federal bureaucracy is sufficiently large and independent of presidential control to constitute a fourth branch of government. (Raymond E. Wolfinger, Martin Shapiro, and Fred I. Greenstein)

. . . the bureaucracy is not clearly responsible to any one of the three branches. In effect the bureaucracy has become a "fourth branch" of government often acting in a semi-independent fashion. (Peter Woll and Robert Binstock)[89]

The unsystematic recognition by many political scientists of the substantial division of executive branch officials and the assertions of several analysts that there is in effect a fourth coordinate branch composed of middle and lower levels of policymakers seem to justify a more penetrating effort to mark out the boundary between the major classes of executive/administrative officials. In such an endeavor, this book will utilize the idea that there are within the executive branch both a presidential government and a permanent government. However, in place of the term *permanent* we will use the more relative term *continuing*. The next two chapters will examine the dimensions of the continuing government and the presidential government for the purpose of determining their boundaries in relation to each other.

CHAPTER FOUR

THE DIMENSIONS OF THE CONTINUING GOVERNMENT

THE REVIEW, in the preceding chapter, of the general character of the executive branch of the United States government came to the conclusion that the most fundamental division within that vast and complex array of structures is a more or less horizontal one between two general types of policy-making officials. Political scientists use different sets of terms to identify the two forces, none of which is entirely satisfactory. These include *political* and *career executives* and *presidential* and *permanent governments*.[1] We consider the latter pair to be more helpful than the former for the purposes of this study, but we are changing *permanent government* to the more relative designation of *continuing government*.

This chapter undertakes to measure the extent of the continuing policymakers of the national government. We will be particularly interested in ascertaining the upper limits of the continuing government and its boundary with the presidentially selected executives. For this we will use four approaches. The first will examine the method of appointment as a basis of division; the second will evaluate conditions of tenure as a basis for relevant differentiation; the third will consider the effect of specialized knowledge and information about the operation of the governmental units; and the fourth will inquire into the comparatively long-range relationships between career administrators and specialized subunits of the houses of Congress.

Method of Appointment as a Basis of Classification

The Constitution expressly differentiates general types of executive officials in prescribing the methods of appointment. The relevant portion of the Constitution provides:

> The President . . . shall nominate, and by and with the advice and consent of the Senate, shall appoint ambassadors, other public ministers and consuls, judges of the Supreme Court and all other officers of the United States whose appointments are

not herein otherwise provided for, and which shall be established by law: but the Congress may by law vest the appointment of such inferior officers, as they think proper, in the President alone, in the courts of law, or in the heads of departments.[2]

The constitutional use of the designation *inferior officers* for the last clause implies a general distinction between superior and inferior positions. The Supreme Court justices and the higher foreign service officers are expressly in the superior group, and by necessity the heads of departments are also in that category. Otherwise, Congress may decide which offices shall exist and may determine whether or not the appointment of particular officers requires senatorial approval. The inferior officers are of three types, according to the identity of the officials making the appointments. One of the three types pertains to the judiciary and the other two pertain to the executive branch. Thus, the Constitution expressly recognizes three kinds of executive appointees: (1) officers appointed by the President with the consent of the Senate, (2) officers appointed by the President alone, and (3) officers appointed by the heads of the departments.

In 1789 the first Congress established in new legal form three departments, designated State, War, and Treasury. It authorized the President to appoint the "principal officer" or head, with consent of the Senate, and to remove a department head without approval of the Senate.[3] Congress authorized the department head rather than the President to appoint the second in line. For the first two departments, that officer was called the chief clerk, whereas the Treasury title was assistant to the secretary.[4] If a distinction can be made between politics and administration, the political sector for most of the time prior to 1829 consisted only of the department heads. Subsequently, more of the other important officers were chosen on the basis of political considerations. But there was in substance a career service in practice if not in legal definition.[5]

There has been, of course, a considerable expansion in the number and variety of appointed executive officials. For the purpose of determining the dimensions of the continuing government, the establishment and enlargement of the civil service and other merit systems beginning in 1883 are primary matters.[6] These systems result in a large portion of the executive force having not only career status in a legal sense but also an occupational and operational advantage over noncareer officials, including those immediately superior in the formal hierarchy.

Congress has established one clear line between two types of appointed officials by providing for two salary schedules, one definitely above the other. The first is designated the *Federal Executive Schedule* and the second the *General Schedule of the Civil Service*. These are not the only pay schedules, but they are the most important of such schedules for this study. The Executive Schedule concerns the highest levels of civilian positions in the executive branch. A new President moves promptly to place his appointees in these offices. The General Schedule concerns the next highest government-wide category of officials. In general, the highest salary under the second schedule cannot exceed the lowest salary under the first.[7] The boundary between the two may correspond roughly to that between political and career executives. However, the boundary is much more a zone than a line. Not all of the officials in the higher grades of the civil service General Schedule are in career protected positions; some of the executive assignments may be noncareer or otherwise temporary.[8]

The Federal Executive Schedule pertains to about seven hundred officials, most of whom are appointed by the President with the consent of the Senate and the large majority of whom are theoretically removable or replaceable for policy or political reasons.

The positions in the Executive Schedule are in five levels. Level I usually consists of the heads of the cabinet departments. Recently the President's Special Representative for Trade Negotians has been included. Level II includes from twenty to twenty-five positions. The list has grown recently. The more usual positions are the three military secretaries, the deputy secretaries for some departments, and the following bureau or agency heads:

Chairman, Council of Economic Advisers
Director, Office of Management and Budget
Director of the Office of Science and Technology
Director of Central Intelligence
Administrator, Agency for International Development
Administrator, Federal Aviation Administration
Administrator of Veterans Affairs

Administrator of the National Aeronautics
and Space Administration
Chairman, Board of Governors of the Federal
Reserve System
Director of the United States Arms Control
and Disarmament Agency
Director of the International Communication Agency
Director of the National Science Foundation

The first four positions are included in the Executive Office of
the President, the next two are in departments, and the others
are heads of independent agencies. This indicates the importance of nondepartmental institutions.

The other levels are much larger than I and II. Level III includes the undersecretaries of several departments; the chairmen of about fifteen management, banking, and regulatory
commissions; about twenty administrators of departmental and
nondepartmental agencies; and the members of the Board of
Governors of the Federal Reserve System. This last board appears to be the highest paid of any commission or board. Level
IV includes most of the substantive assistant secretaries, while
administrative assistant-secretaries are on Level V. The lower
two levels include many members of commissions, as well as
numerous administrators and deputy administrators.

There seems to be little public awareness of the separate character of the political executives in the upper levels of the departments and agencies. They are not bureaucrats in the scientific
meaning of the term, but there is a common tendency to include
them.

The General Schedule does not specify positions as the Executive Schedule does but rather establishes salary grades with in-
grade steps. It sets the levels of pay for the large majority of
technical and professional employees in the nonmilitary portion
of the executive branch. There are other salary schedules, such
as that for the foreign service. More than a million employees
are under the postal and wage systems, and the military services
have their own pay systems.[9] A rising force in the control and
compensation of governmental employees is unionization. In
1976 there was union recognition for 83 percent of the trades
and labor employees and 51 percent of the General Schedule
personnel.[10] But in an analysis of the division of appointed exec-

utives between career and noncareer or between merit and political administrators, it is the General Schedule that stands in contrast with the high-level Executive Schedule.

The General Schedule has eighteen salary grades, which we will place in three categories with rough, unofficial labels. First are the supergrade executives in GS 16, 17, and 18; then the regular-grade executives in GS 13, 14, and 15; and finally the regular-grade nonexecutives in GS 12 and below. This is using the term *executive* in a broad sense, which includes advisers and professional experts with policy-making contributions. The broad use of the term is common in governmental, newspaper, and political science literature. The regular-grade nonexecutives come close to being a career, nonpolitical force. They are in definite contrast with the noncareer political executives in the five levels of the Executive Schedule. "Between these two extremes of the executive establishment lies a patchwork of intermingled political and career appointments that become more tentative and variegated in the higher levels." That is the commentary of Hugh Heclo on the officials in grades GS 13 through 18 of the General Schedule of the Civil Service.[11]

The difference between the political officials appointed under the Federal Executive Schedule and the career personnel selected under the civil service or other merit system[12] is not complete or absolute. A number of factors modify the distinguishing aspects of the two types of appointment.

The competitive examinations for even the middle- or lower-grade positions of the civil service necessarily embody some human elements. Then the authorized practice of allowing the appointing officer to select from among the three highest on the list of approved applicants[13] permits some leeway for personal or political inclinations. Moreover, merit appointees have private attributes and preferences which may affect their manner of applying rules to specific instances or otherwise exercising discretion, even though these influences are latent rather than patent.

A more overt factor affecting the political/merit differentiation concerns the excepted schedules of positions. Congress has excepted from the general civil service examination procedures three groups of positions designated Schedules A, B, and C.[14] Schedule A relates to positions "for which it is not practicable to examine." About 100,000 employees, mostly attorneys, come

under this exception. Congress has, in effect, banned the examin-
ing of an attorney who is a member of the bar of a state.[15]
Lawyers probably have the least difficulty of any major group
entering government service and also of leaving and returning
to private occupation. Schedule B concerns positions "for which
it is not practicable to hold competitive examination." There are
fewer than 2,000 positions in this group; examples are crypto-
graphic technicians and bank examiners.

Schedule C, unlike Schedules A and B, pertains to positions
"of a confidential or policy-determining character" at GS 15 or
below. This is a direct political invasion of the merit system,
because it allows a new presidential administration to appoint
some 1,200 persons on a political preference basis. The aim is
as much to gain confidentiality among assistants for high-level
executives as to reward partisan election workers. This category
was introduced at the start of the Eisenhower tenure, because
the outgoing administration had placed the positions of confidential aides under civil service limitations to prevent replacement of the Democratic incumbents. The hierarchy of the new
Republican leadership needed such aides of its own persuasion
and choosing.[16]

There is even more intermingling of political and career systems among the supergrade positions in GS 16, 17, and 18. These
are considered to be executive positions, and the authorized
regulations of the civil service and other systems permit at least
1,200 of such positions to be noncareer executive assignments
for three-year periods or temporary assignments for shorter
periods.[17]

At all grades, as many as 2,500 political or partisan appointments may be replaced whenever there is a new presidential
administration. Combined with the 550 presidential appointments in the Executive Schedule, a new administration means
a come-and-go force of some 3,000 officials and employees.

Another practice that disturbs the political/merit contrast is
the appointment of career officials to political positions because
qualified candidates are not otherwise available.[18] This may affect one-third or even one-half of the lower-level political executive positions.[19]

Civil service executives are not entirely careerists. A leading
book on public administration categorizes three-fifths as full
careerists, one-fifth as in-and-outers, and one-fifth as high-level

entrants who joined at the senior level (GS 13 or above) and remained.[20] Turnover in the total service is at least 20 percent per annum. During the fiscal year ended in 1976, there were 640,887 separations, against 618,751 accessions. The separations included 187,684 terminations, 21,718 discharges, and 56,214 reductions-in-force, as well as "quits," transfers, deaths, and retirements.[21] The average length of service is about fourteen years, but the high turnover among newer employees in the lower grades means that those in the higher grades may have much more than fourteen years of service.

There are few tabulations of the numbers of political and career executives. The report of the second Herbert Hoover commission on the executive branch, issued in 1955, estimated the numbers in the two groups to be 755 and 4,000.[22] About half of the first category were heads, deputy heads, or assistant heads of departments or agencies; and most of the others were political aides and assistants to the political executives. The second category includes the administrative assistant-secretaries of the departments and a few hundred heads of bureaus or staff offices. But three-fourths of them were either assistant bureau or division chiefs, or regional office directors.

No comparable tabulation seems to have appeared until that included in Hugh Heclo's 1977 book *A Government of Strangers*.[23] In general, Heclo uses the designations *political executives* and *bureaucrats*,[24] but the heading of the relevant statistical table speaks of noncareer and career positions and then further explains each category. The one category consists of "political, or excepted, noncareer positions," and the other of "competitive civil service career positions." The data for 1975-76 are shown in the table on page 68.[25] These statistics may have a number of limitations. For one thing, the numbers for at least the higher grades of the General Schedule may concern only appointees under the civil service proper and not the other merit systems. There may be as many as 5,000 executive officials in the supergrade levels of the other systems, including about 2,000 in the Foreign Service.[26] Heclo's figures for the Public Law 313 supergrades in the defense agencies[27] indicate 430 noncareer and 808 career positions. Likewise, he points out that classification of the noncareer positions is not a simple matter, and he observes that "from 9 percent to 25 percent of the executive supergrade positions can be considered as political appointments."[28] One of the

SCHEDULE	NONCAREER	CAREER
Executive		
Level I	12	
Level II	71	
Level III	115	
Level IV	353	4
Level V	194	19
General		
Grade 18	246	221
Grade 17	386	771
Grade 16	646	3,213
Grade 15	310	28,940
Grade 14	150	50,930
Grade 13	140	108,100
Grade 12 and below	720	2,100,000

difficulties is that some of the excepted positions are permitted only certain types of political activity. Because of such factors, we need to recognize that the boundary between the continuing type and the changing type of administrator is rather fuzzy. Heclo concludes that "for almost 7,000 people near the top of the government, the formal demarcation between bureaucrat and political appointees is far from obvious."[29] For many such officials the uncertainty may relate to the particular assignment at the time rather than their long-term status. They may have career status in a regular-grade category, such as Grade 15, and be on assignment in a Grade 16 or 17 position. In such a situation, they may be more responsive to the political appointees in higher levels than if they held a career position at the higher grade.

The uncertainty of the political/career boundary is the result of nearly thirty years of proposals, pressures, and programs to lessen the disadvantage of the presidential appointees in trying to manage the career administrators and other continuing officials. President Carter's civil service reform included further steps in this direction.[30] Hence, the boundary is not only a broad zone that is not well marked, but also is subject to pressures from above and to rather frequent adjustments designed to lessen the advantages of career administrators.

Conditions of Tenure

There may be a general correlation between the policy-making attitudes of an executive official and the extent of protection from political replacement. An administrator effectively subject to policy removal is likely to be more responsive to presidential wishes than an official with the security of position commonly associated with judges. The extent to which Presidents may replace or remove executive officials for political or policy reasons is a complex matter from both a practical and a legal point of view.

The Constitution says nothing about removal except for impeachment and trial, and that rests with the houses of Congress rather than with the appointing official. The issue of presidential removal of a department head arose at the first Congress in 1789. The immediate question was whether removal should involve consent by the Senate when that body's consent was needed for appointment. The 1787 Convention had not clarified the reasons for senatorial approval. At that time, legislative appointment was common, and the Convention first gave to the Senate powers that we now consider to be executive, such as the negotiation of treaties and the appointment of judges and ambassadors. Also, some delegates suggested that the Senate might serve as an executive council.[31]

At the first Congress, James Madison argued repeatedly for exclusive authority in the President to remove department heads. He asserted that, if consent of the Senate were needed, the President could not be held responsible for the administration. Madison here, as in his arguments for executive veto of legislation, favored restrictive power in the presidency. He also probably did not wish the Senate to be an executive council or cabinet. He had been defeated in his bid to become Senator from Virginia, but his desire for a strong "corrective" presidency goes back to the Convention.[32]

The 1789 legislation giving the President sole authority to remove officials for policy reasons was treated as "organic law" by the Supreme Court in a 1926 disapproval of a post–Civil War statute that required Senate approval.[33] The case concerned a postmaster, but the opinion of Chief Justice Taft indicates that he may have been thinking also about the situation of a department head, even the secretary of state. In 1915 lectures the former President said that, whereas *political* tenure may be necessary for the departmental secretary and undersecretary, the assistant secretaries and bureau chiefs should have *permanent* tenure so as to avoid throwing "the administration of the department into the complete control of minor subordinates."[34]

Congress has authority to impose conditions upon the removal of certain types of officials. Its statutes provide protection for the tenure of civil service appointees. It also has limited the presidential removal of quasi-judicial officers, such as members of the Federal Trade Commission and other regulatory agencies. The President may not remove such officials for policy reasons but only for legal cause, such as criminal misconduct or culpable neglect. The Supreme Court has upheld such limitations[35] and has imposed them upon the removal of quasi-judicial officers even when the limitation is not expressed in the statute which established the office.[36] Some restriction upon dismissal may be implied in a fixed term for an official, particularly a member of an independent commission or a corporate board of directors.[37]

The several restrictions upon a President's power to remove officials for policy reasons raise the fundamental question of whether he properly can be held responsible for the decisions and actions of personnel he cannot replace should they not conform to his policies. The practical limitations upon a President may be more significant than the legal ones. As the official head of the party seeking to hold together its various elements the President may hesitate to dismiss an official for differences in policies. This seems particularly true of cabinet members. Franklin Roosevelt tended to counteract rather than remove department heads who displayed independence in their views. President Nixon ousted his first secretary of the interior, Walter J. Hickel; but he went along with other none-too-loyal cabinet members until he had won re-election.[38] After he encountered the Watergate affair, his ouster of the special prosecutor provoked resignations among the heads of the Department of Justice. President Ford encountered strong criticism when he replaced a secretary of defense.[39] In mid-1979, when President Carter was at the low point in public approval ratings, he changed cabinet members to improve his public image in preparation for 1980 nomination and election battles. The changes, of course, accentuated the discontinuity of top-level management. The full historical record indicates that a cabinet may not be a very effective means of bringing unity to the executive/administrative system.[40]

The effect of conditions of tenure upon executive-branch unity involves, among other things, differences in the average length of service among the levels of both the executive branch and the congressional branch. We will consider the impact of these differences.

The average tenure of Presidents is about six years, of department heads less than four years, and of assistant secretaries less than thirty months.[41] Among politically appointed administrators, J. Edgar Hoover and Lewis B. Hershey had exceptional tenure; the usual period is more like three years.[42] In contrast, the general average of civil servants is in excess of a dozen years, with much of that time spent in the same bureau. The large majority of the civil service officials who are immediate subordinates of the come-and-go political executives are likely to have twenty years of experience or more in a particular bureau or agency, including a substantial period in the most recent position. Many have become acquainted with Capitol Hill specialists. Members of Congress in the controlling echelons of the committee structure necessarily have much longer periods of specialized governmental activity than partisan appointees in the departmental managements.

The short term of political executives is accentuated by the high degree of "lateral entry." Three or four years in one position may be normal in a business organization with much upward mobility, but the officials move up in the same hierarchy with related experience in the levels of management. In governmental departments the upper-level political executives are likely to come in from the outside, often with little experience in the particular field. Moreover, at a change in the presidency, with some exceptions for succession by a Vice-President, there is usually a rather complete change in the top three or four levels of executive officials. In contrast, changes at the career-executive levels and in the congressional committees are staggered so that there is considerable continuity in those policy-making structures.

The longer experience of merit-system officials in the affairs of their particular units and in the operating practices of the government, including relationships between congressional and executive forces, gives them substantial advantage in dealing with superiors among the political executives. Robert C. Fried describes this phenomenon:

Many department heads are taken from private life with little experience either in Washington or in the affairs of the department they are supposed to direct. Their turnover and that of other top political executives is quite high. But most of those who head the bureaus within the department are specialists, career executives with long experience both in Washington and in their specialty. Bureau heads work closely with congressional committee chairmen and with organized interest group leaders, and form with them the permanent cadre of political and administrative control. Congressional committee chairmen, because they are chosen by seniority, share with bureau heads long experience both in Washington and in the policy details with which their committee deals. Interest group leaders usually have the same expertise, experience, and permanence. Departmental political executives are at a disadvantage in dealing with alliances of bureau heads, committee chairmen, and interest group leaders, because, unlike the members of those alliances, many of them are transient, inexpert, and inexperienced.[43]

Thus the differences in tenure between the two major classes of officials are signs, if not causes, of contrasting qualities that tend to allow the more continuing officials to be a distinct force.

The comparatively short tenure of Presidents is accentuated by their political party connections. Since at least 1828, each elected President has been the candidate of one of the two major parties existing at the time. The essence of the presidency is its alternating partisanship. During the past thirty years, the presidential party has changed every eight years. This discontinuity is accentuated by the almost complete change of top executive officials that accompanies the coming and going of an elected President. Not only the assistants and advisers of the White House staff but also the higher two or three levels of executives within the departments change with the advent of a new presidential-party regime.

The differences between noncareer and career tenure have a number of consequences, and they accentuate the underlying conflicts that arise from contrasts in types of constituencies. Noncareer executives tend to be impatient, whereas career officials become attached to predictable procedures. The press and the public seem to demand that Presidents provide dramatic action on an almost day-to-day basis. Presidents seldom find help from bureaucrats in meeting such demands. Stephen Hess describes one aspect of this phenomenon:

> Operating in a much shorter time frame than that of the rest of the executive branch, Presidents have viewed the bureaucracy as too slow to respond to their leadership, too unimaginative in proposing policy change, too unwilling to accept political direction, too closely allied with special interests. They turn, often in desperation, to those closest at hand, their personal assistants. Yet the White House staff is not a sufficient fulcrum to move the weight of the federal establishment. It can never be large enough to do the job.
>
> The President's solution—salvation-by-staff—is self-defeating. An enlarged White House staff overprotects Presidents in a political environment where their greatest need is the need to know. Sycophancy can replace independent judgment. By extending the chain of command, Presidents have built additional delay and distortion into the system. Tensions between White House staff and Cabinet officers become inevitable. In the game of "who saw the President last," the department heads are badly positioned. Their exclusion from the inner circle creates a vicious cycle—the loss of power generating the further loss of power. Morale declines in the departments. Thus the careerists who ultimately must implement presidential policy no longer have as much of a stake in its success. They need only wait long enough and there will be another President.
>
> But Presidents cannot wait. Indeed the pressure of time often pushes them to try to overwhelm or end-run the bureaucracy and Congress.[44]

This account suggests that gaps occur among the President's own appointees, between those near at hand in the White House and the Executive Office and those away from this center of action in the hierarchies of the departments and agencies. These last may react by moving closer to the more permanent officials in their respective institutions or by beginning to plan new political or professional connections.

Specialized Knowledge and Information

A third general factor that characterizes permanent or continuing officials of the executive branch and helps to measure their scope is their possession of specialized knowledge and information and the capacity to use those assets in making administrative policy. All levels of departmental executives need to be both professional and political specialists. They benefit from both occupational expertise and a comprehension of the congressional subunits and the socioeconomic constituencies affected by their respective agencies or bureaus.

Specialization is the key to the semiautonomous policymaking of continuing administrative officials. Knowledge and information of their profession, their area of concentration, their bureau or office, the relevant congressional subcommittees, and the affected constituencies, set them apart from the presidential forces in and near the White House and also from the political executives who are their immediate superiors. Lack of similar knowledge and information by the presidential appointees in the higher levels limits their managerial capacity and causes them to depend heavily upon lower-level officials. Louis C. Gawthrop explains this aspect of the noncareer/career division of officials:

> Every incoming President must expect to inherit a vast army of career civil servants without whom the day-to-day operation of the federal government's administrative apparatus would grind to a halt. The career administrator provides invaluable continuity compared to the frequent and steady turnover among top-level policy executives. He provides the essential elements of stability and predictability. . . . Thus the dichotomy between career and noncareer officials has become an immutable and an *essential* feature of our fragmented executive structure.[45]

Gawthrop finds that this condition involves the interrelationship of politics and administration. "Given the nature of our pluralist political system there is virtually no such thing as a purely apolitical administrative decision." Almost any administrative decision "will almost inevitably run counter to the political objectives of some particular group in our society," he explains. The administrator "creates political sound waves every time he makes an administrative decision."[46] The politics involved is not as likely to be major party politics as the specialized politics of competitive groups or constituencies. The accumulated knowledge and information of the career administrator pertain not merely to the occupation or profession or to legal aspects of the area of concern, but equally to the specialized politics of the demands and supports of relevant constituencies and groups. We will see that this is one reason why specialized administrators develop long-term relationships with the specialized sub-committees of the houses of Congress and with the constitu-ency-minded members of the Senate or House.

One political science explanation of the national government presents this picture of the interrelationship of presidential appointees and merit system personnel:

> The political executives help make the policies of the Chief Executive and with him assume responsibility for the government. They come and go with the party in power. The career administrators, on the other hand, provide a reservoir of knowl-edge and managerial competence based on long-time experi-ence. Their main concern is with organization, methods, pro-cedures, techniques; they are the professional experts who know *how* to do *what* the political executive decides should be done. . . . Professional bureaucrats play a significant and sometimes crucial role at every stage in the policy process. When the principal officers of a government agency go before congres-sional committees to obtain legislative authorizations and ap-propriations, they are usually accompanied by their career officers to back up their presentation, to interpret the supporting documents, and to answer the difficult and technical questions. When a new policy is authorized, bureaucrats work out the personnel and fiscal requirements and the operating procedures. In addition to developing the rules and regulations for the implementation of policy, bureaucrats interpret and apply the rules in specific cases. They are expected to do all of this with professional competence and always to remain in the back-ground.[47]

This last may tell why there is not a full public awareness of the policy contributions of the career bureaucrats. Often they prefer to remain in the background, because they may be able to con-trol more if the public believes that the presidential appointees in the higher offices rather than the civil servants in the lower levels are making the policy decisions. The attitudes of the con-tinuing administrators may differ, either to the left or right, from views of the presidential appointees in the White House–Execu-tive Office contingent and even from the attitudes of the politi-cal executives in the departments. This may result from career officials adopting a neutral or middle position that is distinct from the alternating partisanism of the Oval Office.[48]

Hugh Heclo, in his study of executive politics at the national government, makes several comments concerning the depen-

dence of political executives upon the specialized knowledge
and information of career bureaucrats.

> . . . without higher civil service support, almost nothing
> sought by the political executives is likely to take effect. . . .
> The services of top bureaucrats begin with helping to orient
> new political executives to a particular agency. . . .
> A political executive always steps into a moving current of
> activity. . . . Civil servants are in a good position to describe
> the background of what has previously been set in motion—the
> inherited controversies and bargains that outsiders will prob-
> ably hold the new appointee responsible for. . . .
> Any substantive actions a political executive may wish to
> take are embedded in extraordinarily complex rules about ad-
> ministrative processes. . . . A monopoly of knowledge about
> those technicalities constitutes both the source of many bureau-
> crats' power and also the positive services they can supply. De-
> pending on how much help bureaucrats give, administrative
> processes and red tape will become a way of facilitating the
> political executives' aims or just another means of ensnarl-
> ment. . . .
> Experienced bureaucrats are in unique position to provide
> intelligence of all kinds for imputing the intentions and atti-
> tudes of these government and nongovernment power centers.
> . . . In a highly unpredictable environment, the civil servants'
> own networks help them anticipate what will be considered in
> a favorable light elsewhere and what signs suggest that a seri-
> ous explosion is in the making. . . .
> Policy, even presidential policy, rarely seems to involve a
> group of political executives walking in, thumping the table,
> and giving the administration's marching orders into an indefi-
> nite future. More often there is a continuing dialogue in which
> bureaucrats are important participants helping extract the mu-
> tual understandings that eventually become known as policies.[49]

The fundamental reasons for the strategic position of the career
officials may be the limitations upon Presidents and their political appointees. A President may have authority to direct or
order a bureau administrator to take a particular action, but a
President is not likely to issue a specific command until after the
White House has acquired a specialized knowledge of the area,
and the presidential staff can become involved to that extent in

only a few particular situations. The political executives in the higher levels of departmental management face a comparable dilemma. Robert E. DiClerico explains the difficulty: "A Cabinet appointee and his assistant secretaries frequently have very little expertise in the substantive concerns of the department. Furthermore, they are not likely to remain in their positions long enough to develop the expertise nor, for that matter, long enough to grasp thoroughly the internal operations of their department."[50]

In general, political offices are, of course, above career positions, even though the level of the boundary may vary from department to department or from agency to agency. However, the pattern of appointments may not coincide fully with the scheme of positions. Most Presidents encounter difficulty in finding outsiders with the appropriate political or professional qualifications for a number of the third- and fourth-level departmental offices. In such cases, there may be three possibilities which disturb the political/merit differentiation. The first is the appointment of career executives who were recruited originally under merit regulations and have permanent status in nonpolitical positions. The assignment may be temporary or for a short term, after which the career official reverts to the previously held civil service grade. A second possibility is that the higher position may remain vacant. As a consequence, "much important work filters down by default to the career civil service executives."[51] Thus the person in the lower, merit level does the work of the higher, political office at the salary of the lower grade. A third possibility is the appointment of a person who is neither strictly political nor career. A survey of the Nixon administration by Kenneth J. Meier found that 38 percent of the bureau chiefs were "politicians filling appointed positions," that 30 percent were civil servants, many of whom were assigned to political positions, and that the remainder were professionals. These last, in Meier's description, were persons with scientific or technical careers outside the government.[52]

These exceptional situations accentuate a number of operating problems in the executive branch, and while they indicate a somewhat indefinite boundary between political and career officials, they do not destroy the substance of that division of forces.

The importance of specialized information is evident also in this political-science description of presidential-administrative relationships:

> When we think of a top executive like the President of the United States and the bureaucratic agencies under him, we imagine that the President issues orders and the agencies obey. Most Presidents have found that this is not the case. . . . The President depends on his subordinates for two important things: information and compliance.
>
> The federal agencies are the only ones close enough to their own field to know what programs are working and what programs are not. Consider foreign policy. The State Department, the CIA, and the military have people on the spot. The President has to rely on them for information. The same is true in domestic affairs. The bureaucrats in the Agriculture Department have the facts and figures on grain production; the officials in the Nuclear Regulatory Commission have the details on nuclear power plant safety. . . .
>
> The size of the government and the fact that the lower levels control a good deal of information make it impossible for the President (or the Executive Office) to know what is going on in all parts of the government and to make sure their directives are complied with. Many Presidents have complained that they had no real control over parts of the government: Kennedy complained that he could not count on the State Department to carry out his foreign policy directives. No matter what he wanted, they acted in their established ways. And most Presidents have made similar complaints about one or another branch of the government.[53]

The hesitancy of career officials to carry out fully the policies of a President may not be mere obstinacy. They need to look beyond the current President's regime to the years when the opposing party may be in power. State department officials, in particular, have suffered in the past from association with a prior administration. Rowland Egger, explaining the presidential-administrative differences in his study of the presidency, remarks that "an established bureaucracy runs heavy risks in becoming too openly identified with novel program proposals emanating from the White House."[54]

Two recent political science surveys show that the differences between career and noncareer executives are relative in character. One study compares a political group of departmental assistant secretaries, Schedule C–exempt appointees and noncareer supergrades, and a bureaucratic group of career supergrades who were top officials of administrative subunits. Interviews taken during the Nixon period disclose that among 53 political appointees, 35 said they were Republican, 6 Independent, and 12 Democrat; whereas among 53 career supergrades, 9 said they were Republican, 19 Independent, and 25 Democrat. The same survey found that career officials were somewhat more in favor of government provision for social services than were the political appointees.[55]

The second survey, concerning 257 federal political and career executives, found that the two groups are similar psychologically, that is, that both are "cooperative sorts of people" who tend to accept "legitimate authority" and have "a high sense of purpose about their public service."[56] This may mean that neither group was antiestablishment, with room left for significant differences. The analyst, Lewis C. Mainzer, also presented this distinction: "Top political appointees, such as cabinet members and aides whom they bring along, are not bureaucrats of the Federal Government. Equally clearly, however, they are leaders of the bureaucracy. One must distinguish such short-term, politically appointed chieftains of the bureaucracy from regular career bureaucrats, yet recognize their importance in the bureaucracy."[57]

The relationship of noncareer and career officials seems comparable to the long-debated separation or connection of politics and administration.[58] The reality appears to be that an executive official is a mixture of politician and administrator and, even more important, that the mix varies with the level. We may construct a simple model to illustrate the variations by assuming six levels of policy-making executives. The top level may be something like five-sixths political and one-sixth administrative, while the bottom level is one-sixth political and five-sixths administrative. We cannot divide executive officials into rigid categories of politicians and administrators, but there is a discernible and meaningful difference between the top level with a five-to-one ratio of politics to administration and the bottom level with a one-to-five ratio. Similarly, there are at different levels varying mixtures of leadership and followership. The differentiations of political and career officials are not categorical, but they are substantial. Moreover, they derive not so much from contrasting methods of appointment or length of tenure as from meaningful variations in specialized knowledge and information.

Continuity of Specialized Relationships

The most pervasive cause of the continuing existence of an administrative force with a nonpresidential attitude is quite probably the relationship of specialized executive officials with specialized subunits of the houses of Congress. The presidential appointees in the upper levels of the departmental management have in general the same alternating partisanism and come-and-go tenure of the presidential force at the White House. Most of them serve for only two or three years,[59] and much of the time they do not have sufficient knowledge of what to do and how to do it. They may not be able to provide sound guidance for their subordinates.[60] Even more, the political executives in the departments are not likely to have a strong connection with either the power center at the White House or the other sources of political strength. Their subordinates are apt to look elsewhere for support that is both more potent and more enduring.

Executive officials who are career-minded are likely to find support that is relevant to their specialties, as well as comparatively strong, among the congressional subcommittees and the informal blocs of senators and representatives. These last are usually responsive to the political force of constituencies within their districts and among related special-interest groups.[61] That can, in several ways, provide long-range benefit to the administrator who deals with the particular area. Congressional committees have a continuing duo-party pattern. Their leaders have definitely longer tenure than the average President and the top departmental executives. Although the committee chairmen may change as time goes on, the committee memberships are more or less continuous. Replacement is gradual and future chairmen are often anticipated, so that a congressional committee is comparatively constant; whereas the top executive hierarchy of a department undergoes an almost complete revision whenever a newly elected president takes office, and other changes occur at more frequent intervals.

At the same time, the continuity in the career administrative personnel and their less partisan attitudes make them attractive to the senators and representatives, because they are less likely to have contrary political views and more apt to have the kind of specialized information and know-how needed by congressional committees.

These forces result in the on-going existence of hundreds of unofficial, informal triangles composed of a few members of Congress, interest group spokesmen, and an administrative chief in a specialized area of common interest. The extent to which these pragmatic arrangements control the policymaking and policy implementation in the executive branch is a somewhat debatable matter, but most political science analysts of the national government indicate they have considerable impact. In fact, the threefold relationship has become a conceptual model that may outrank the more official and idealized models of distributed or shared power. There seems to be a special appeal to any triumvirate, so that the bureaucratic-lobbyist-politician trio may be a simplification and an exaggeration; but we are designedly interested in the essential interactions, and our choices are limited largely to simple patterns. Political scientists seem to find this one particularly attractive. Of the five reasons for the opposition between the presidency and the bureaucracy identified by Rowland Egger, the final one is that "a triangle is one of the most rigid and durable structures known to man, and when bureaucrats, congressmen and lobbyists are able to keep a reasonable peace in the process of satisfying their different but closely related interests, not even the President of the United States is likely to shake the foundations of their fond relationships."[62] Another specialist in the presidency, Dorothy James, remarks that the most successful way for a bureau to deal with the "struggle for supervision" is to form a "cozy little triangle" with "organized interest groups and the chairmen of the relevant subcommittees."[63] Similarly, McGeorge Bundy, in lectures on the national government, refers to "the network of triangular alliances which unite all sorts of interest groups with their agents in the Congress and their agents in the Executive Branch."[64] (The term *agents* may be apt only in a general, not a legal, sense.) Philippa Strum asserts that "the major check on presidential power may well be not the Congress in its legislative capacity, but the Congress in its executive capacity allied with the bureaucracy and special interest groups."[65] This seems particularly relevant to the matter of essential interactions that make the national government more than an arrangement of

Congress, the presidency, and the courts. In fact, the underlying principles of authority distribution may be a contributing cause. William L. Morrow gives this interpretation:

> Atomized constitutional power encourages the formation of subsystems or triple alliances. Such alliances consist of coalitions between administrative agencies, legislative committee and subcommittee leaders, and private interests, each of which has a mutual interest in particular programs. Since the governmental structure does not afford them easy access to any single authority with plenary power, they form such alliances to work concertedly for programs that mutually benefit. This is one way of attaining de facto fusion of interests or pressures that the de jure assignment of power by constitutions does not permit.[66]

Such arrangements may not be constitutionally prescribed, but they are constitutionally protected. The constitutional requirement of congressional appropriations, as well as the legislative and investigative power, make congressional-administrative relationships necessary. Moreover, the least official and most criticized aspect of the arrangement—that is, the interest-group participation—is protected by the First Amendment right to petition the government.

How to deal with factions or special-interest groups was a problem even in 1787. James Madison argued for a national government on the ground that it would result in more restrictive counter-action than would a confederation of states. Political scientists of today also find that groups are natural to the economic society:

> For every organized economic interest there is an agency at some level of government. For every agency there is a constituency net work interdependent with it. (Eugene Lewis)

> Group competition and conflict is a natural way to control the "effects" of faction. As groups challenge each other, they serve as an informal supplement to the constitutional system of checks and balances. . . . In many respects, interest group representation is superior to party and electoral representation, because the bond holding interest group members together is stronger. (Charles W. Dunn)[67]

This last touches upon what may be the most fundamental and difficult problem arising from the separations within the executive branch, that is, how a concerned public may keep special administrators responsive to the general interest when the presidency is not available as a channel of control or communication. We face here an expanding problem because of the decline of major-party power and the increased role of group or constituency politics. This is recognized by Fred A. Kramer:

> This triangular relationship . . . describes much political bureaucratic behavior in American public administration and places the agency in a key political role. As C. Wright Mills has argued: "The executive bureaucracy becomes not only the center of power but also the area within which and in terms of which all conflicts of power are resolved or denied. Administration replaces electoral politics."[68]

Other political scientists also point out that these developments work against unity and central control in the executive branch:

> The administrative machinery in Washington represents a number of fragmented power centers, . . . the cracks of fragmentation are not random but run along a number of well-established functional specialties and program interests that link particular government bureaus, congressional committees, and interest groups. People in the White House are aware of these subgovernments but have no obvious control over them. (Hugh Heclo)

> Another constraint on Presidential authority within the Executive is the fact that many of the departments and agencies have developed symbiotic client relationships with organized interest groups, for example, the Department of Agriculture and farmers, or the Office of Education and school bureaucracies. These often become three-way alliance relationships between the department or agency, the interest group, and the relevant congressional committee or subcommittee, both legislative and appropriations. A web of horizontal relationships thus develops that can undercut Presidential vertical authority over his own Executive establishment. (Erwin C. Hargrove)[69]

This last means that in governmental operations specialized policymaking involving horizontal relationships of corresponding subunits of Congress, the executive, and the public is more dominant than generalized policymaking, whether led by Congress, the President, or the department head.

The effect of these special-interest relationships upon departmental management was expressed at a 1971 hearing by John

Gardner, a former secretary of HEW: "Questions of public policy nominally lodged with the Secretary are often decided far beyond the Secretary's reach by a trinity consisting of representatives of an outside body, middle level bureaucrats, and selected members of Congress, particularly those concerned with appropriations."[70] Gardner founded a public-interest association called *Common Cause* with the aim of reducing the special-interest character of Congress. Thomas E. Cronin's book on the presidency also recognizes the force of particularized policy-making: "Special-interest groups often effectively capture administrative as well as legislative officials and succeed in fragmenting the organization to their own ends."[71]

The special-interest alliances are not simply antipresidential. They are more fundamental; they are the key to effective operations at any level of making policy, even the presidential level. The White House, most analysts agree, is the number one special-interest pressure group in Washington. Presidents need alliances with members of Congress and with subpublics to achieve their legislative objectives. Two political science analysts have described the presidential participation in the process:

> In the image of wrestling, . . . Portions of interlocking power exist in many corners of the government. It is not a rare phenomenon to have one team of "wrestlers" made up of a congressman, a well-placed bureau chief, and a powerful outside interest group. These may be pitted in the ring against another team made up of the President, his budget director, and an opposing interest group; or a senator, another bureau chief, and a league of municipalities. If on a lonely Saturday morning a congressman feels overwhelmed by the power of the President and the federal bureaucracy, there are a score of executive branch officials who at the very moment are pondering the power of Congress or some key section thereof. Presidents may set budgets, but how many parts of those budgets have been prepared at the agency level with someone's eye on past or possible future congressional reactions? (Stephen K. Bailey)

> The interest group and congressional committee alternatives open to the ambitious or ambivalent administrator need not be considered mutually exclusive alternatives. In effect, a four-cornered interaction pattern results between the individual administrator, the interest group, the congressional committees, and the policy executive to whom the administrator is nominally accountable, for example, the President, departmental secre-

tary, or assistant secretary. The result, stated in simplistic terms, is that public policy decisions represent the consensus that emerges from a dominant coalition formed from these four elements. In actual practice, the interacting network becomes much more complicated; seldom is just one interest group involved in any policy or administrative conflict, and every administrative unit is accountable to at least four congressional committees—the authorization and appropriation committees of both the House and the Senate. In the final analysis, top-level executive officials (including the President) must frequently compete for the support and approval of influential and completely autonomous private interest groups and congressional committees in order to achieve their public policy objectives. (Lewis C. Gawthrop)[72]

Thus, the special-interest process involving congressional, executive, and group alliances is another example of the operational division between the presidential few and the subunit many. The White House participates in the few matters it selects for direct attention, while the large number of administrative subunits participate in the alliances for the innumerable cases of regular and more invisible policy determinations.

Many general political science explanations of American national government also recognize the mixed character of the administrative/political process. Some texts expressly refer to the threefold interaction of legislators, administrators, and lobbyists.[73] Others add to the three forces such competing elements as the chief executive, public opinion, and the courts;[74] while still others point out that the rivalry between the presidency and Congress allows the administrators much leeway in choosing their sources of support.[75]

There has been much criticism of the specialized subgovernments, because they make for disunity, and because the members of a triadic entity may be called politician, bureaucrat, and lobbyist. These units have much lasting power, however, because the socioeconomic public is highly fragmented, and because the three members may be conceived to share equally in respectability as legislator, administrator, and representative. The concept of "iron triangle" may be an oversimplification, which both scholars and journalists may use to suggest more structural identity than actually exists. Modification in the explanation of multiple specialization may be in order.

Hugh Heclo argued recently that the subsystems of the executive establishment are "issue networks" more basically than iron triangles.[76] The true experts are those who are "issue skilled." Heclo pointed to the growing percentage of supergrade civil servants and contended that lower-level political executives and upper-level career officials deal more and more with specialized policy conflicts in contrast with operating management. Heclo's new view may be the result mostly of more penetrating analysis. It emphasizes the struggles of formulation more than those of implementation. Issue networks involve goal debates and policy conflicts, whereas the iron-triangle concept relates more to making decisions and taking action. Heclo says there are more participants in the issue networks. Yet it would seem that there are at least as many specializations. An iron triangle may be involved in several issue networks. The fragments are numerous and even more amorphous and no less difficult for the President and cabinet members to control.

The Upper Limits of the Continuing Government

This chapter is a part of the general effort to assist the political science explanation of the American national government by portraying graphically the ways in which administrative officials have a substantive identity that is distinguishable from the presidential system, as well as the congressional and judicial systems. The starting points in this endeavor are the flexibility of the constitutional principles of distribution and the unsystematic recognition by many political scientists of a persistent division within the policy-making personnel of the executive branch. Analysts use a variety of terms in this dichotomization. The pairs of contrasting designations include career and noncareer officials, permanent and presidential governments, and civil service administrators and political executives. In this book we are using the terms *continuing government* and *presidential government*.

The examination, in this chapter, of the dimensions of the continuing government has been directed at the upper limits, with particular attention to the horizontal boundaries which may separate it from the higher echelon of executive officials. We have employed four general ways of trying to identify the boundary markers.

The first approach was by the method of appointment. We

looked at the distinctions, half expressed in the Constitution, between superior and inferior offices. The first involves senatorial approval of nominees by the President, and the second includes appointments by the President alone and by the department heads. That provision may furnish constitutional legitimacy for a division within the political executives appointed by the presidential party forces, but our concern now is the boundary between those officials and the continuing administrators. We found a more relevant differentiation in the statutory salary pattern and particularly in the contrast between the Federal Executive Schedule and the General Schedule of the Civil Service. Most of the officials of the first are appointed by the President or his department heads and hence change with the coming of a new presidential party or even a new President. But we found that there are thousands of positions in the grades of the General Schedule which are excepted from the merit system appointment procedures. Moreover, at least two thousand of these may fall within the "spoils system" of the winning presidential party.

The second approach was by tenure. There is a sharp contrast between those who serve legally at the pleasure of the President and the civil servants who have protected tenure for a lifetime career, but again there are a few thousand officials for whom tenure is a rather indefinite matter. Moreover, tenure may be the formal result of, rather than the actual cause of, more fundamental factors.

Specialized knowledge and information are the core of the third approach. Experience and capability in the work of particular bureaus and in the practical know-how of governmental methods may be the real distinguishing quality of the continuing body of executives. The multiplicity of specialized iron triangles and issue networks also tends to increase the autonomy of career officials in relation to political executives appointed by the presidential party.

The fourth approach seems equally basic. It concerns the close relationship between career administrators and corresponding specialists in Congress and in accepted group organizations. The continuity of each of the three forces of concentration tends to support that of the others and to form a common bond distinct from the come-and-go contingents at the White House and in the departmental managements.

The fourfold analysis leads to the conclusion that there is no

simple way of designating the dimensions of the continuing government. Official terms, such as civil service or merit system,
may include thousands of excepted positions, which in substance
are in the changing realm. Unofficial terms, such as *bureaucracy*,
are still less distinctive; that term often is used to mean any type
of appointed official. Moreover, there may be a number of executives who are not consistently presidential or continuing. For
instance, some executives are President's men at the start but
before long "go native" and become associated with career
officialdom.

The principal conclusion we may draw is that there is a substantial difference between the main body of the continuing
government and the presidential forces, but that the boundary
between them is much more a zone than a line. In addition, the
zone itself is neither regular nor consistent in its dimensions. The
continuing government may not extend much above the civil
service or merit systems, but each higher grade within these
systems is a mixture of political and career positions; and, in
fact, some middle-level professionals may be neither strictly
political nor career. In the top regular grade (GS 15), the portion of noncareer positions may be less than one percent; but in
the top supergrade (GS 18), there seems to be an even division
of political and career positions. Yet the absence of an exact official boundary does not detract from the substantive fact that at
least 80 percent of the more than 75,000 executive policymakers
are definitely in the continuing government rather than in the
presidential or political come-and-go realm.

CHAPTER FIVE

THE DIMENSIONS OF THE PRESIDENTIAL GOVERNMENT

DEVELOPMENTS DURING RECENT DECADES have increased the problems of explaining the boundaries of the presidential forces in the United States government. For much of this century and particularly since the late 1930s the activities of Presidents have been moving in two rather contrary directions. In the words of a leading commentator, the President has become "less a man who presided over the processes of government in Washington" and, at the same time, "progressively more a one-man generator and executor of national policy."[1]

As presidential regimes have come and gone, there has been in general less White House interest in trying to achieve a broad and enduring consensus among members of Congress, party leaders, public groups, and specialized administrators. In contrast, Presidents have given increased attention to public-relations events and symbolic actions, such as corrective proposals on those particular subjects that stir public anxieties and dramatic appearances that enhance their political images. Jimmy Carter was only accentuating the trend—impelled by media-led demands of the voters—when he stressed his communicative image and appealed to our romantic esteem of a peasant king. He had higher ratings in the 1977 polls for his style or manner and for specific self-denials, such as walking rather than riding down Pennsylvania Avenue or wearing a sweater on national television, than for his handling of substantive issues, foreign or domestic.[2]

Presidents frequently reassert familiar ideals and beliefs on which almost everyone agrees, but beneath those transcendent reaffirmations of our pride in historical uniqueness and national superiority there is little sustained effort to coordinate the basic policy conflicts among members of Congress, other political leaders, and government officials. Reconciliation and compromise usually come after a specific proposal encounters roadblocks; consensus is gained more in the retrospective and particular than in the prospective and general. President Carter's approach to the energy controversies was to send Congress a comprehensive bill containing a number of debatable specifics that he and his White House energy adviser had developed almost in secret. Virtually no preparation was undertaken to establish a foundation consensus among legislative and executive leaders or among the different states or segments of the American public. Then he placed much publicized emphasis upon a crusade momentum with a metapolitical slogan—the moral equivalent of war—and upon the quick adoption of the particular package, which he asserted would forestall the impending crisis.[3] But this last gets us into the second general trend.

Presidential performance in governmental matters is dominated largely by White House concentration upon selected issues, with mass media potential, often taken from a department or agency for quick action. Richard E. Neustadt puts it all in a nutshell: "Trying to stop fires is what Presidents do first. It takes most of their time."[4]

The two trends tend to feed upon each other. As Presidents are less successful in unifying diverse forces, they naturally turn to those issues on which they can act alone, with drama and without deference to legislators and administrators. There may be common causes for these developments, and this chapter will endeavor to identify and explain them under four general headings: (1) the elevation of the presidency, (2) the externalization of the White House, (3) the mixed institutionalization of the presidency, and (4) the White House government. Then we will undertake to mark out the lower limits of the presidential government.

The Elevation of the Presidency

"The tendency of all people is to elevate a single person to the position of ruler."[5] That was written nearly a hundred years ago in an analysis of the American presidency, and it may identify the principal reason for the White House separation from regular administrative functions. It may explain why both the public and the Presidents pay most attention to the monarchlike functions of the presidency and why the press and people esteem the drama and symbolism of singular activism. It may also tell us why most Americans are impatient with the slow pace of congressional deliberations and bureaucratic operations and why they prefer Presidents who have an active, corrective disposition over those who are passive or protective and defer action until a solid foundation can be established.

Analysts of the American governmental system have asserted repeatedly that the presidency includes a high degree of symbolic leadership. Henry C. Lockwood in 1884 attributed this to the American sentiment of hero worship.[6] Henry James Ford in 1898 observed that, as the presidential office has been constituted since Andrew Jackson's time, "American democracy has revived the oldest political institution of the race, the elective kingship."[7] Two decades ago Clinton Rossiter wrote that the President is "the symbol of our sovereignty, continuity, and grandeur" and that an incumbent "symbolizes the people" as well as "runs the government."[8] Alfred de Grazia, in 1965, declared that "the President is part man and part myth" and that most persons often attribute to every President qualities that "are either quite fictitious or large exaggerations of the real man."[9] At much the same time, Louis W. Koenig explained that, aside from the real one, there is an "imagined Presidency," which he described as "a euphoric impression of its past, present, and future."[10] Any post-Watergate demystification has not changed the picture. James D. Barber still declares: "The President is a symbolic leader, the one figure who draws together the people's hopes and fears for the political future."[11] Richard M. Pious, writing in 1979, elevates that symbolism: "Politics is the secular religion of America, its martyred presidents are the saints, and the incumbent is the high priest."[12]

A belief that the President furnishes unity of decision to the diverse forces of the government may be more in the mind of the perceiver than in the record of facts. The presidency is the only constitutional institution composed of a single person, and it can be a focal point for those who are perplexed by the apparent disarray of official relationships. There is relevance in the remarks made a century ago by English historian Walter Bagehot on the unique intelligibility of the monarchy: "The mass of mankind understand it, and they hardly anywhere in the world understand any other. It is often said that men are ruled by their imagination; but," he explained, "it would be truer to say that they are governed by the weakness of their imaginations." He argued that the "nature of a constitution, the action of an assembly, the play of parties, . . . are complex facts, difficult to know, and easy to mistake." In contrast, "the action of a single will, the fiat of a single mind, are easy ideas; anybody can make them out, and no one can ever forget them."[13]

This seems equally relevant to presidential appearances and actions. George Reedy, a press advisor to President Lyndon B. Johnson, while describing the person in the White House as an American monarch, makes this observation: "The most practical method of unifying people is to give them a symbol with which they can identify. If the symbol is human, its efficacy is enhanced enormously."[14] James D. Barber, in his examination of presidential personality, also points out the distinctive appeal of the American chief executive. "The President helps make sense of politics. Congress is a tangle of committees, the bureaucracy is a maze of agencies. The President is one man trying to do a job—a picture much more understandable to the mass of people who find themselves in the same boat."[15]

The symbolism of the presidency reflects not only its monarchlike aspects but also a hidden fondness of many Americans for some kind of royalty. Several political science analysts of the presidency have asserted this. John F. Murphy says that numerous "Americans secretly look for a king."[16] Louis W. Koenig states that the "appearance of Presidential power is enhanced by the color and pageantry of the office, the adaptation to American needs of the monarchical principle."[17] Louis E. Kallenbach notes that the presidential office is "a modified version of the English monarchy."[18] Grant McConnell finds the idea of elective kingship to be relevant to the modern presidency whereas Rowland Egger explains that the presidency has "a substantial part of the royal prerogative with respect to diplomatic and military affairs."[19] James D. Barber asserts that "the President is the only available object for such national-religious-monarchical sentiments as Americans possess."[20]

Paradoxically, the monarchical or monocratic attributes of the presidency often are regarded as democratic.[21] The American people have come to view the presidency to be, as Clinton Rossiter said, "their peculiar instrument" and "their peculiar treasure." He argued that we must ignore the traditional notion "that executive power is inherently undemocratic" and that we must recognize that the presidency "has been more responsive to the needs and dreams of giant democracy than any other office or institution in the whole mosaic of American life."[22]

The idea that a strong executive is necessary for a "giant democracy" is itself an indication that the presidency merges monarchical and democratic qualities. At the 1787 Constitutional Convention, one of the arguments against a national government for the thirteen states was the repeated contention of political analysts like Montesquieu that democracy and republicanism are for small and medium societies, whereas monarchy and despotism are necessary for large and immense societies.[23] Americans generally have made democracy seem appropriate for a large nation by assuming that a strong executive power is a guarantee of what they consider to be democratic ideals. President Carter sought to discard some of the monarchical or imperial aspects of the presidency but at the same time may have fostered a deeper and more complex mythology of moral superiority and peasant royalty.

The monocratic version (or vision) of the presidency enhances the belief that the office assures executive unity for the vast and diverse operations of the national government.[24] Woodrow Wilson, during his pre-presidential academic years, may have been the first political scientist to stress this symbolic power of a President. "Let him once win the admiration and confidence of the country," he declared in 1908, "and no other single force can withstand him, no combination of forces will easily overpower him."[25] Clinton Rossiter, writing in the 1950s, was more emphatic. "The President is easily the most influential leader of opinion in this country principally because he is, among all his other jobs, our Chief of State," he stated, explaining that the President's role as "the leader of the rituals of American democracy" enlarges his persuasive power in his other roles. The overriding strength of the presidency, he insisted, derives from the fact that the several elements of democratic leadership are focused in a single office filled by a single man.[26]

Similar themes appeared in writings of the 1960s,[27] including those which attributed presidential elevation to certain powers. Robert S. Hirschfield remarked that the "real foundations of Presidential powers" are those forces which "elevate the executive to a focal position in the government, allowing him to interpret his authority broadly and to exercise it boldly." Hirschfield explained that the presidential authority comes not merely from constitutional and statutory sources but also from the extraconstitutional forces of democracy and necessity. He concluded that the President as the "symbol of national unity has become an instrument of tremendous power, making him the center of our governmental system, and creating the basis for his leadership both at home and abroad."[28] President John F. Kennedy, in comparable observations made after two years in the White House, asserted that the office "is the center of the play of pressure, interest, and idea in the nation" and that it is "the vortex into which all the elements of national decision are irresistibly drawn."[29]

The unifying force of the presidency may be more symbolic than real, more myth than fact. The most striking evidence of this comes in his relations with the executive/administrative offices, where he is supposed to be not merely coordinate, as he is in relation to the Congress and the courts, but superior in legal as well as in ideological force. We have seen that almost every political scientist who examines, to any appreciable degree, the interactions of the presidency and the specialized departments and agencies challenges the idea that the operating units form a solid organizational pyramid under the full control of the chief executive. One favorite example is FDR's anecdote about the Navy Department: that while President he first learned from a newspaper headline that the Navy was embarking upon a two billion dollar shipbuilding program.[30] Another is President Harry S. Truman's remark about the difficulty Dwight Eisenhower would have if he were to bring his military sense of command into the White House. A broader comment on the symbolism of the presidency is that of William E. Mullen, who says that those who focus attention solely on the person in the White House "see only the drama and not the substance."[31]

The response of bureaucrats to the symbolic leadership of the presidency may be symbolic followership; that is, they may go through the rituals of subordination. Their compliance may be more style than substance.

The External Roles of the Presidency

The popular elevation of the presidential office and its monarchical symbolism are supported and extended by the externalization of the White House. This is another factor in the two general trends of the presidency in recent decades: the one toward less effort to achieve governmentwide political consensus and the other toward more media drama in selected crises. All of these related developments are, of course, aspects of the substantial separation of the presidential government from most departmental executives as well as from the continuing civil service personnel in the administrative subunits. Such events also bear upon our efforts to identify and measure the dimensions of the presidential government for the purposes of ascertaining the general pattern of essential interactions within the government of the United States.

The externalization of the White House involves definite emphasis upon world and national relationships in contrast with governmental relationships, particularly those with the administrative units. In simple, formal terms, priority goes to actions as chief of state, chief citizen, commander in chief, chief diplomat, and chief legislator above those of chief administrator. More specifically, it focuses upon the roles of sovereign representative in foreign relations and the roles of national representative in domestic affairs. These last include expressing the moral and even spiritual voice of the country, sharing the public anxieties, being a national rather than factional leader, addressing joint sessions of Congress, and representing the public in the government. Among the specific actions are: televised signing of noteworthy legislation, remembrance of historical events, press conferences, and reception of domestic dignitaries.

Such actions may seem to be ritualistic chores that take up a President's time and might better be performed by some other official, such as the Vice-President. Yet such work may be politically and personally necessary for a President. An event of this type usually has wide press and television coverage; it gives much exposure and is largely noncontroversial. It associates the President with the greatness and goodness of the national image; it is one of the reasons why an incumbent generally has considerable advantage over any other candidate. The very nonpolitical character of the action makes it a top political action.

It may also be helpful to a President in a more personal way. It can be a considerable relief from dilemmas and insolvable problems. There are few imponderables in the ritual of national personification. It is all a proper thing to do. George Reedy asserts that it lightens the burdens of the presidency, because the nonritualistic duties involve "the crushing responsibility of political decisions," where life and death may hang in the balance for many people. "A president is haunted every waking hour of his life by the fear that he has taken the wrong turn, selected the wrong course, issued the wrong orders," Reedy asserts. And only the president is authoritative; he can turn to no one for authoritative counsel. The workload of formalities "is a blessed relief which comes all too rarely," Reedy maintains.[32]

Any candidate for national office, even for that of representative in Congress, may attempt to set himself above regional and political interests by presuming to act for all the people, but an incumbent President has a decided advantage in maintaining that he is a national representative. Since about 1840, Presidents have claimed to be the representative of the whole nation, based upon the ground that their electoral constituency includes all the states, whereas senators and representatives are elected only by states or districts.[33] Yet a presidency may be more a personification than a representation. The role of national representative can be as ceremonial and symbolic as are the roles of chief of state and chief citizen. Actually, the votes for a winning candidate may be less than a third of the potential electorate, and that segment is not likely to be characteristic of the citizenry in general.

Many persons make a morally satisfying symbol of a President by assuming that upon entering the White House he is transformed into a representative of all the people. But a President usually retains much of the policy viewpoint upon which he was elected. If he did not continue his partisan position, there would seem to be little point to campaign platforms. The Democratic nominees of recent decades have been spokesmen of the urban minorities more than of the full society. James MacGregor Burns, writing in 1965, said that "the man in the White House has become the President of the Cities; he has become the Chief Executive of the Metropolis" and "has provided the main motive power for shaping legislation needed by the cities."[34] At about the same time, Louis W. Koenig wrote on the ways that President John F. Kennedy had "pitched his policies, such as civil rights, education, housing and the like to urban racial, national, and economic groups," so that he "could confidently cultivate state and local party leaders who determine the selection of and the support given to congressional candidates."[35] Burns and Koenig were writing of Democratic Presidents; Republican Presidents speak more for other factions. Jimmy Carter at times seems not to favor urban concentrations, but when confronted he expresses firm intentions to revitalize the cities.

The trends of the past four or five decades have made Presidents welfare liberals in comparison with the corresponding party forces in the Congress. Presidents Eisenhower, Nixon, and Ford were less conservative than were Republicans in general. Democratic candidates and incumbents, of course, were more clearly on the liberal side. They often asserted, in the words of Woodrow Wilson, that a President "is at liberty, both in law and conscience, to be as big a man as he can."[36] The majority of political scientists responded favorably until about 1967, when they began to have misgivings about Lyndon B. Johnson; but they disliked even more Richard Nixon's antipoverty efforts.

Now leading analysts of the presidency seem unwilling to leave the character of the office to the particular persons in the Oval Office. In effect, they say a President is not at liberty to be as small a man as he can; rather, he must continue with the course of progress. Dorothy James asserts that the path of the presidency has become so institutionalized that programs which once seemed novel and personal are now the normal expectation.[37] Richard Neustadt contends that now all Presidents must be strong and activist; Watergate has not altered his view.[38] Philippa Strum, writing in 1972, before Watergate, said Richard Nixon was not a strong President, because he was so isolated that he believed he embodied the ideals and aspirations of the people when he definitely did not. She is typical of many political scientists who assume that the principal object of government is to bring "disadvantaged groups into the mainstream of American political and economic life."[39] Although that may be the view of only the left half of the political spectrum, many journalists and academics emphasize it.

The relevant consequence of the presidential emphasis upon public relations, upon liberal or corrective proposals, and upon personification of national ideals is that Presidents need give less attention to administrative supervision of the regular and routine operations of the executive branch departments and agencies. Presidents may participate in selected problems, such as critical diplomatic encounters and strikes which threaten national welfare; but this is often a phase of the externalization development, because such matters have passed from the invisible government to the headline arena. They are withdrawn, in effect, from the regular department, bureau, or agency and thus are further evidence of the separation between the White House operations and the main force of departmental management and subunit administration.[40]

The foremost examples of externalization are, of course, those concerning foreign relations. There are three general reasons for this: (1) such issues are more likely to seem critical than most domestic problems; (2) a President usually has more opportunity to act alone without interference from Congress or the bureaucracy; and (3) there is a higher expectation of success in those matters which do involve Congress.

Although the priority of foreign relations is a common theme, a recent analysis by John H. Kessel has brought out some new angles. His survey found that during the years 1945–69 several Presidents gave priority to six policy areas. Their identity, with the type of politics involved, and their relative importance are

POLICY AREA	TYPE OF POLITICS	IMPORTANCE
International involvement	Symbolic	Major-imperative
Economic management	Regulatory	Major-imperative
Social benefits	Allocative	Major
Civil liberties	Symbolic and regulatory	Minor
Natural resources	Regulatory	Minor
Agriculture	Allocative	Minor

shown in the table above.[41] This list of priorities still seems relevant a decade later. There may be more attention to natural resources today, but this is an imperative area only as it becomes a part of economic management. Moreover, social benefits and civil liberties are apt to keep their priority status.

The most interesting aspect of Kessel's presentation concerns the type of politics. Presidents may prefer issues they can deal with symbolically, because there is less dependence upon

other institutions and less political opposition. Regulatory politics are likely to make one or another major group unhappy.
On the other hand, allocative politics is beneficial to certain
groups and not to others, but apparently there is short-range
benefit. Kessel maintains that "distribution of social benefits is
primarily the first-term phenomenon." It is most important in
the fourth year, when a President is preparing for re-election;
but interest "is apt to drop sharply" during the second term.[42]
    Most striking is Kessel's statement that "the politics of inter-
national involvement are primarily symbolic," despite the economic and military resources of the United States. He treats
this area as solely symbolic, and it is the only such area. The
area of civil liberties is regulatory as well as symbolic. Kessel
seems to be using *symbolic* in a broad sense. Foreign relations,
as long as they do not involve economic or social issues, are less
controversial politically, because in their pure state they relate
to national security and ideals. The media crusades of the Carter
regime against the 1980 USSR action in Afghanistan seem to
support Kessel's assertions that "the majority of our interven-
tions must be symbolic" because "against the range of our international commitments, American resources are finite indeed."[43]
    Presidents traditionally have dominated foreign affairs more
than domestic matters. Louis W. Koenig says that "the President enjoys broad power to engage in executive-centered policy-
making" when he acts as chief diplomat or commander in chief.
The classic example, he explains, is President Kennedy's policy-
making in the Cuban missile crisis of 1962. Kennedy had an
ad hoc advisory group of a dozen members, including former
heads of State and Defense but no member of Congress other
than the Vice-President, who was a statutory member of the
National Security Council. Kennedy informed a group of twenty
congressional leaders of the adopted policy shortly before it
was made public, but not even Senator Fulbright, then chairman of the Senate Foreign Relations Committee, was permitted any definite input. The Senator's objection to the use of
blockade was to no avail.[44]
    Political scientists tend to disagree on the extent to which
the presidential roles in foreign and domestic affairs can be dif-
ferentiated. The issue has grown more complex since 1967.
Aaron Wildavsky, writing in 1966, asserted that there are two
presidencies and that in foreign affairs a President "can almost

always get support for policies that he believes will protect the nation." He referred to President Truman's actions on the United Nations, the Truman Doctrine for aid to Greece, the Marshall Plan, and similar matters. But the difference is relative. Wildavsky reports that presidential success in Congress is 70 percent on foreign affairs and 40 percent on domestic issues.[45] Still, the difference is substantial. President Carter's approval rating shot up when Iran and Afghanistan dominated presidential public relations. Dorothy James continues to entitle her discussions of the presidency in domestic and foreign affairs as "Prometheus Bound" and "Prometheus Unbound."[46]

The congressional reaction to Vietnam and the adoption of the War Powers Act of 1973 suggests that Congress will be more restrictive, but the change of attitude has yet to face real tests. Congress is reluctant to accept much responsibility on its own in this area.[47]

The Mixed Institutionalization of the Presidency

"Modern executive leadership is an organizational process." Lester G. Seligman makes this assertion in analyzing the political aspects of leadership. He explains further: "In such an organizational context, 'leadership' may be attributed to an individual but it is in reality a collective product of organizational activity." Political scientists call this development "the institutionalization of the presidency."[48] The official elements have congressional authorization, directly or indirectly, and collectively they constitute the Executive Office of the President. The total personnel runs into thousands; those with policy-making discretion number between fifty and a hundred; perhaps more. They increase the consistency as well as the scope of presidential activity. Many political scientists would agree with this observation of Randall B. Ripley: "The development of an institutionalized presidency has provided increasingly large elements of stability and continuity in the performance of presidential tasks."[49] But we need to examine the specific areas.

The initial recognition by Congress of the presidential need for central institutions to support executive control was probably the Budget and Accounting Act of 1921.[50] That Act established a Bureau of the Budget to aid the President and a General Accounting Office to aid Congress in overseeing administrative operations. The Bureau of the Budget was placed under the Treasury, but it reported directly to the President.

In 1939 Congress, in response to a political-science report on the need of the presidency for administrative assistance, set in motion the steps for a general institutionalization of the presidency. Congress granted to the President reorganization authority, which permitted him to establish the Executive Office of the President.[51] At first it consisted of two bodies: the Bureau of the Budget was transferred from the Treasury, and a White House Office of assistants and advisers was commenced. In 1946 the Council of Economic Advisers was added, and in 1947 the National Security Council. There has been a varying number of other offices, councils, and agencies.

The term *Executive Office of the President* may suggest that there is a monolithic entity, but a more accurate explanation may be that the name is only a title to cover a group of individuals and agencies which more or less separately assist the President in meeting his more important and immediate responsibilities.[52]

The elements of the Executive Office differ in a number of ways. Some have been continuous, others come and go. Likewise, the persons filling the various positions have differing tenure: some are career specialists, some serve for several years, and most key officials change with the President. Loyalties to a particular President have a similar range: some are distant, others fluctuate, and a number are especially close.

The Executive Office of the President has, at one time or another, included from six to sixteen different offices, agencies, and councils.[53] There seem to be three general types. The first, the White House Office, is a unique governmental institution. It is closer to the President than any other body, including the cabinet. Its members are specialists in relationships with the press, the public, the interest groups, the Congress, the states, and so on. Each newly elected President replaces the principal officials with persons who were involved in his election or are otherwise committed to the maintenance of his political prestige. Their appointment does not require senatorial approval, and generally they are immune from congressional investigations. In sum, the White House staff is the institutionalization of the politically personal side of the President.

The second type of component agency combines, at least at

the top level, presidential loyalty and governmental responsibility. They deal with highly important specific areas. The largest is the Office of Management and Budget (until 1970 the
Bureau of the Budget). The director and deputy director are
subject to senatorial approval. The staff includes many career
administrators and specialists. The smallest of the continuous
agencies is the Council of Economic Advisers (CEA). Its three
members are subject to approval by the Senate. Usually they
are academic or professional economists with social viewpoints
similar to the incumbent President. They change with a newly
elected President and so does much of the small staff. A political-science analysis of the Executive Office concludes: As an
organization, the CEA more nearly resembles "a task force or
research institute than a governmental bureaucratic agency."[54]
The most crucial Executive Office unit may be the National
Security Council. Its statutory members are the President, the
Vice-President, and the Secretaries of State and Defense. Other
officials may attend as the President decides. It has a sizeable
staff of specialists, some of whom have career tenure in this or
another government office.[55] The head of the staff usually com-
petes with the Secretary of State as a foreign affairs adviser to
the President. One function of the Council is to oversee the
Central Intelligence Agency. Its major contribution may be to
lessen conflict between the State and Defense departments.

The third type of agency within the Executive Office is less
permanent and more specialized. This type has included the
come-and-go offices for equal opportunity, science and technology, and drug abuse. In total, since 1939 there probably have
been three dozen different units, including those for energy
resources, environmental protection, foreign intelligence, and
others. The maximum at any time has been about a dozen;[56]
Presidents change the units to meet new conditions and anxieties. Presidents wish to show that they are giving special
attention to persistent headline issues. President Carter has had
several such agencies transferred outside the Executive Office
as part of a general effort to reorganize the executive structure
and functions.[57]

The consequences of the institutionalization of the presidency
have been mixed. The Presidents have received much more effective support in their roles as a political personality than in
their roles as chief administrator of the government. The rela-

tionships with the public and with the leaders of Congress are mainly the realm of the White House staff. The other agencies of the Executive Office are more concerned with governmental policy and relationships. The Office of Management and Budget and the National Security Council, in their respective fields, have aided Presidents in appreciable degree. But there has been little help to the problem of total administrative control.[58] The whole realm of domestic affairs seems out of reach. No President has been able to establish an effective Domestic Council,[59] and President Carter preferred a staff assistant to a council.[60]

Two offices do make some efforts to effectuate presidential control of the executive operations, even though their personnel and performance differ appreciably with each new regime. One of these offices is that of Management and Budget; the other is the White House staff. We will here look briefly at the role of the former and in the next section will consider the contributions of the White House staff.

The establishment of the Bureau of the Budget to assist the President in the preparation of the annual budget and of the General Accounting Office to assist Congress in reviewing the way in which moneys are expended did basic violence to the general theory that the Congress is the legislative institution and the presidency the executive agency. Legislation, supposedly, is prospective rather than retrospective, while execution is particular and subsequent to legislation. The new budget and accounting arrangements gave to the President a larger prospective role and increased the capacity of Congress to act retrospectively. This is another indication that the traditional model, which stands for a legislative Congress and an executive presidency and does not recognize the administrative force, is substantially inadequate and even misleading.

Prior to 1921 each department submitted a separate budget to Congress; after 1921 and the establishment of the Bureau of the Budget, the Presidents, for more than a half century, increasingly prepared the total budget. As a consequence, Congress was more and more in the role of disposing of what Presidents had proposed. Congress undertook to reverse that trend with the Budget Act of 1974, and the establishment of a central Budget office within the houses of Congress.[61] There is also a joint Budget committee, in addition to the appropriations committees and subcommittees in each House. The joint Budget committee has responsibility for the total appropriation, and hence Congress now has more opportunity and obligation with respect to the total amount of the budget than it did formerly. The consequences seem to be beneficial in several ways, but the full impact is not yet clear.

Louis Fisher, probably the foremost legal analyst of the budget process, describes the complex interactive character of presidential-congressional relationships in his comprehensive study of presidential spending power. He challenges the view of Woodrow Wilson that Congress is to appropriate and the executive branch to administer:

> Public policy is not so easily apportioned into watertight compartments. Policy-making is a dynamic, ongoing phenomenon, beginning with the inception of an idea and carrying through to its enactment and implementation. Although we think of legislation and administration as consecutive steps, they continually interact and fold back into a larger process. If Congress is to play the role of major policy-setter, it must avoid situations where budget execution becomes a controlling factor, locking Congress into commitments and decisions ahead of time.[62]

This is more indication that government is not always a matter of separated, successive functions and that in many important areas, including the appropriation and expenditure of funds, there is virtually a constant interplay between elected and appointed officials, between generalists and specialists, and between congressional and administrative officials.

The institutionalization of the presidency reached a peak, temporarily at least, with the Nixon administration. President Nixon expanded the White House staff, enlarged the management sector of the Budget office, tried to build a domestic-council apparatus that could dominate the seven outer departments,[63] proposed that the seven departments be reorganized into four[64]—the heads of which would form a supercabinet within the White House—and at the start of the second term assigned to trusted Executive Office aides second-level departmental positions in what one analyst called a plot to establish an administrative presidency.[65] Watergate cut short his efforts, but the record shows the frustrations of a President who tried to turn the myth of unified control into reality.

The consensus among political scientists who have examined

the institutionalization of the presidency seems to be that it has helped the quality of the external functions far more than the governmental or administrative relationships.[66] The holding of press conferences, preparation of messages to Congress, arrangement of meetings, and—most of all—the public relations of the presidential personality now seem more consistent; but there has been little benefit to the supervision of departments and agencies. The contrast between the two types of institutionalization appear to parallel the difference between, on the one hand, White House staff leaders such as Hamilton Jordan, Jody Powell, and Stuart Eizenstat and, on the other hand, the Senate-confirmed heads of Executive Office agencies, departments, and independent agencies. Newspaper reports at mid-term (the start of 1979) indicate that the ten persons who conferred most with President Carter included only two in the second category, that is, the secretaries of state and defense.[67]

That thought prompts a further question. Is the Executive Office itself tending to divide horizontally, in much the same way as the entire executive branch, into a presidential sector, a permanent or continuing sector, and an intermediate sector of less identifiable and somewhat forgotten political appointees?

The White House Office may be all that is unique to a particular President. Its forces may have brought a new meaning to the term *personalized presidency*. Political analysts have noted that the concept of an institutionalized presidency is a challenge to the concept of a personalized presidency implicit in the 1908 observation of Woodrow Wilson that the "President is at liberty, both in law and conscience, to be as big a man as he can" and that his "capacity will set the limit."[68] Now the institutionalization may set a limit through its continuing structures, functions, and relationships. Some political scientists assert that there is now a relative permanence in ideological expectations as well.[69] But, at the same time, there are increased demands that the President personify in his own dramatic way our ideals of both the past and future.[70] We may have a new concept and dimension of a personalized presidency apart from the concept of a governmental presidency. For this the White House staff of personal assistants and advisers, changing mostly with each President, provides the means by which the person in the Oval Office may meet the public and political demands for a transcendent personality.[71] Thus, it may be the capacities, positive and negative, of the White House staff that above all determine how big and how limited a President can be.

White House Government

The two trends of the presidency, toward more episodic actions and less programmatic leadership, place double emphasis upon the ad hoc decision-making processes of the White House. In this a President needs quick, politically astute answers to varied questions. He is aided mostly by the principal assistants and advisers on the White House staff, with added help from top officials of the Executive Office of the President and a few members of the cabinet. This inner circle, for which *kitchen cabinet* is a traditional label, consists of a President's most trusted lieutenants. Nearly all of them change with each President, and their common characteristics are their single-minded attachment to the incumbent President and an innate tendency to feel superior to all other Washington forces. Methods of operation, as well as the priority of issues, may differ from time to time; but each President lives in a context of endless demands and supports.

Presidents come and go; but the problems, the public, the press, most of the civil service, and much of the Congress remain the same. The character of the difficulties and the means of trying to meet them are sufficiently uniform from one President to the next that we can with substantial validity make general classifications of the activity of the White House decision-contingent. There seem to be three principal types of effort: (1) to maintain the presidential personality at a high level of public prestige, (2) to exert guiding pressures upon various units of the government on behalf of the presidential policies of the moment, and (3) to provide crisis-subduing answers to the specific situations that threaten the standing of the presidential regime. We will consider these in order.

The primary responsibility of the White House staff is the public image of the President. Many Americans identify the United States government with the behavioral personality of the incumbent President. This is an easy way of appraising the character and progress of events; a simple means of feeling satisfied or dissatisfied with the operation of the political system. The various public demands for sovereign articulation of inner fears and hopes provide an opportunity for the public relations specialists at the White House. If they hit the right questions and answers, they can keep the President's communicative personality in a healthy and attractive state of acceptable visibility. They are aided by the mass media. Newspaper reporters, journalistic analysts, and radio commentators all focus upon the outward activity or passivity of the person in the Oval Office. There may be signs of antagonism between the White House and the press corps, but they are much dependent upon each other. Day in and day out, the President is the best news story in Washington, the country, or the world; and presidential prestige could not stand much neglect by the press corps.

The public-relations presidency is more than headline deep. It is a psychological phenomenon. Increasingly, Americans seem to consider the presidency to be a set of relationships with the mind and imagination of millions of individuals, much more so than a set of relations with legislators and administrators.[72] This is, of course, profoundly related to the separation of the President from the continuing force of executive officials.

The second general type of activity by the White House staff concerns support for the priority items among the President's legislative proposals. On these matters, the White House may be the number one pressure group in the country. The activities include the work of congressional liaison specialists and direct consultations with senators and representatives. But it also may encompass concentrated activity by political and public-relations experts upon other members of the party, upon favorable interest groups, upon leaders of public opinion throughout the nation, and upon the voters in general. The Carter White House developed such tactics into a standard operating procedure, moving from the energy program, through the Panama Canal Treaty to civil service reform, SALT II, and so on.

The direct pressures upon congressional and party leaders include personal persuasion by the President. The early stages in such crusades may be aimed at the relevant administrators in the executive branch. These may include noncareer officials appointed by the President as well as career civil service bureaucrats. Even here the personal participation of the President is likely to entail persuasion more than command. It rarely proceeds through the full cabinet, except perhaps on a formal or superficial note. It may involve small groups of cabinet members, such as members of the National Security Council, but most frequently this involvement is on an individual basis. Such methods indicate that the President is less chief administrator than chief adviser or chief critic; or, in military analogy, he is less a commanding general than a chief of staff, even in relation to presidential appointees in the departments and agencies.

We saw in the preceding chapter on the general character of the executive branch that these officials have to serve a number of masters in addition to the President. Most executive officials, of course, will abide by executive orders issued by the President; but what can be reduced to unambiguous writing is, in most matters, severely limited. In new and somewhat controversial and venturesome matters, which usually are the subject of presidential crusades, a President may not wish to be too specific on details because of the probability of subsequent revisions, compromises, and unexpected consequences. In these endeavors, the activity of White House aides, assistants, and advisers is much less with the determination of essential contents than with selling the package. Many are veterans of the presidential election campaign, and their talents are primarily in public relations. President Carter seems fond of comprehensive proposals, such as the energy bill, airplane sales in the Middle East, civil service reform, and so on. The inclusion of five or six specific matters in one legislative recommendation may prove a hindrance as well as a benefit in congressional procedure, but it does give the proposal a broad basis upon which to develop public acceptance.

The third type of activity for the White House contingent concerns specific situations in which the President reacts to crises of headline proportion, either actually or potentially. Here a President is responding to the pressure of daily events. Richard E. Neustadt, describing such presidential activity, explains that it is a "cardinal fact" of government that "presidents don't act on policies, programs, or personnel in the abstract; they act in the concrete as they meet deadlines set by due dates —or the urgency—of documents awaiting signatures, vacant posts seeking answers, audiences waiting for a speech, intelligence reports requiring a response."[73] Elsewhere Neustadt points out that Presidents spend most of their time "putting out fires." The need to respond to the pressure of events is one aspect of what Dorothy James calls the routinization of the Presidency.[74] But, even in larger matters, the White House contingent seems to be drawn into a succession of disconnected crises that are frequently forced upon the presidency through media-led demands. The necessity for immediate answers, which often serve more to subdue anxiety than to solve a problem, tends to isolate critical issues and make the presidential performance more episodic than programmatic.

The most fundamental factor in comprehending presidential performance here as elsewhere is that a President, even as institutionalized with a large supporting staff of loyal specialists and generalists, can deal effectively with only a small number of selected issues, leaving most matters to be handled by the multiplicity of less visible administrators in the executive subunits. Several political scientists who have written about the presidency and the administration have pointed out this limitation upon the President:

> Only the biggest problems can ultimately reach the President. The others have to be dealt with elsewhere. (Hugh Heclo)

> Professional bureaucrats dominate those vast segments of the policy process that do not become major issues. (Eugene Lewis)

> Because of the size of the executive establishment, the president . . . must deal with those matters he considers most important or urgent or troublesome, leaving much of the bureaucracy free to operate at the discretion of its administrators. (Dale Vinyard)

> There is, after all, a limit to the crusades a President can hope to handle successfully. (Dorothy B. James)

> A President should carefully pick and choose the issues which merit his personal participation in the give and take of policy formulation. (Harold Seidman)

> The President's political survival depends upon a nationwide electoral process in which his personality and a few key issues determine the outcome. (Peter Woll)[75]

The quantitative limitations upon a President have been especially evident in the Carter regime. The President was determined to relieve public anxieties in a large number of disturbing situations, but he has been able to achieve his aim in only a handful of instances, and these have been second- or third-level rather than top-level issues. Even when a President confines himself to critical issues, there may be more of them than he can cope with. In March 1978 a veteran Washington correspondent felt the need to analyse the question "How many challenges can a president handle?"[76]

The full scope of the limitation may not be apparent to persons with only a vague or special interest in the government, because the issues Presidents select for their own participation are apt to be headline crises or will become so as soon as the choice is made known. The strong tendency of much of the public and even of the media is to view the government in relation to presidential behavior, and that concerns only the tip of the policy-making iceberg. William E. Mullen may be a bit blunt in saying that when people's attention is focused solely on the man in the White House they see only the drama and not the substance;[77] but there is again the basic need of distinguishing between the presidential few and the subunit many.

President Harry S. Truman was probably our foremost episodic decision-maker, because he did not give much consideration to long-range programs even in connection with his legislative proposals. Erwin C. Hargrove, in his study of personality and political style in presidential leadership, gives us this analysis of the Truman method:

> He had no sense of strategy but made decisions as they came to him without considering their relationship to other decisions. Thus, he often let the initiatives of other men time his decisions and his political strategy suffered because of it.
>
> His manner of leading public opinion was much like his decision-making. He had no sense of grand strategy but took each case as it came. He seldom prepared the public in advance for policy departures. Of course, he had to face more crises than F.D.R., who excelled at such preparation, but Truman's episodic approach to leadership was also responsible.[78]

Truman's famous motto "The buck stops here" may explain, more than justify, his quick, unrelated decisions. It may suggest a high sense of responsibility, but it may also excuse an I-am-the-government attitude. President Carter adopted that motto and, like Truman, tried to place the blame on Congress when legislative proposals met without success.

When Americans became disillusioned with Lyndon Johnson

and Richard Nixon, they made a folk hero of Harry Truman. His approval rating twenty years after he left the White House was much higher than it had been when he was president. Jimmy Carter used the new Truman for a model; but there are also underlying similarities with the actual Truman, particularly his lack of overriding strategy and an episodic approach to leadership pointed out by Hargrove in 1974. James Fallows, Carter's former speech writer, stated in May 1979 that "Carter believes fifty things, but not one thing," and that he "fails to project a vision larger than the problem he is tackling at the moment."[79] Those comments were considered critical of, and even damaging to, Carter's public image; but they seem to reflect traits comparable to those of the real Truman. Moreover, we probably should expect almost every President to proceed in such manner.

President Carter is like previous Presidents, also, in having to allow White House staff members to enter intermittently into the realm of government operations. Despite campaign opposition to such actions, Presidents seem forced to permit them in practice. It could be that political assistants may wish to aid a supporter or a favorite cause; but, more than likely, the pressure is a headline crisis and the White House assistants are better at and quicker in providing a headline answer than are departmental officials.

Whatever the cause, White House staffmen have involved themselves and their respective Presidents in operational and policy decisions that primarily and ordinarily are made in the bureaus of the departments and agencies. Dwight Eisenhower's "assistant president" became so involved in regulatory processes that he felt impelled to resign.[80] President John F. Kennedy, according to Patrick Anderson, dispatched staff members "to be spies in the hostile land of the permanent government."[81] President Johnson's one-time press adviser George Reedy asserts that there is "on the part of the White House assistants a tendency to bring to the White House problems which should not properly be there, frequently to the disadvantage of the President." Reedy cites the number of times President Johnson himself tried to settle labor disputes.[82] Reedy's criticism may have had an effect on subsequent Presidents. After 1964 the White House did not again enter such matters until 1978, when President Carter was drawn into the coal strike. His hesitance to enter the dispute, which brought criticism from some circles, may have been a reaction to Reedy's criticism.

These developments are related to the broader issue of whether a President should rely more upon his cabinet and less upon his White House staff. Both the Nixon and Carter forces indicated at the start that they favored cabinet government, but both changed emphasis and accepted White House dominance. Nixon regretted having made a preinaugural remark that he would leave responsibility to the department heads.[83] Thomas E. Cronin reports one of Carter's men as saying that probably Carter's biggest mistake in 1977 was in giving so much power to the cabinet members.[84]

The experience of each President in having to rely upon his White House staff or Executive Office specialists to deal with particular operations of a critical or select character is more evidence that the institutionalization of the governmental presidency by the Executive Office establishment has not brought the hoped-for strength to the presidential-departmental system of command. The institutionalization of the public-personality President has been more successful. In fact, that side of the presidency tends to take over the few governmental decisions which are forced upon them by demands of the press and the public. Here again is the basic division between the presidential few and the subunit many; and the separation of forces within the executive branch may be caused more by the presidential need for quick action in selected instances than by the bureaucratic inertia in regular operations. Presidents Ford and Carter endeavored to reduce the size of the White House staff, but neither had much success. President Carter, after fifteen months in the Oval Office, apparently felt that he might need more high-level assistants in the White House.[85]

One of the best explanations of the effect of these developments on the character of the presidency comes from Judge Samuel I. Rosenman, Franklin Roosevelt's special counsel and favorite speechwriter. Judge Rosenman in 1973 criticized the "great recent growth of the White House staff around the President." One objection, he said, is that, the larger the staff, "the more clumsy and inefficient it becomes"; and that there is an inevitable tendency to take on more and more functional duties and to become an operational rather than an advisory body. That development, he explained, is doubly bad, because "it duplicates and conflicts with the action and responsibility of the departments" and "seriously impairs the chance of responsible relations with Congress, since it increases the number of staff officials empowered to act behind the shield of executive privilege."[86] Thomas E. Cronin has similar criticism: "The more the White House usurps responsibilities from their proper home in the departments, the more the White House undermines the goal of competent departmental managements."[87] However, the White House intervenes in only a few critical matters. Most operating policy decisions are made by the specialized executives in the departments and agencies.[88]

The action pattern of Presidents tends to be episodic and even spasmodic. This is due to a number of continuing factors. For one thing, a President can act dramatically on only a few issues. The choice is affected by circumstances beyond presidential control, such as the security and economic situation, and the state of the day's headlines. The maintenance of the presidential image and the approval rating requires dramatic action —or reaction—to the day's crises. Decisions must result in quick, lively action. They may make a President more like a solo player than an orchestra leader, but that is what the press and public demand. The pressure is such that a President must be guided by individual likes and dislikes. James Fallows says the "central idea of the Carter Administration is Jimmy Carter himself, his own mixture of traits."[89] This seems much like what Richard E. Neustadt wrote in 1960 about FDR: "Roosevelt, almost alone among our Presidents, had no conception of the office to live up to; he was it. His image of the office was himself-in-office."[90] Perhaps we should expect this of every President.

The Lower Limits of the Presidential Government

This chapter has reviewed the forces that tend to give the presidential contingent of executive officials a distinctive character apart from the other personnel of the executive branch. We have considered the strong tendency of the American people to elevate the presidency to the position of an elective monarch. We have noted also the external roles of the presidency in both foreign and domestic areas of government. Then we analyzed the institutionalization of the presidency and its benefits with respect to the public-relations presidency and its lack of success with respect to the governmental presidency. Finally, we examined the selective character of White House government and noted the demands of the press and public for a President who reacts quickly and sharply to headline crises and who can subdue public anxieties with headline drama.

These analyses tend to show that "the dimensions of the presidential government" correspond neither with a simple pattern of institutional arrangement nor with a legal definition of executive officials. Rather, presidential officials are those who can help a President in the demanding task of "putting out fires" in a quick and even heroic manner. By and large the presidential branch includes only those top officials in the Executive Office who are engaged directly in developing and implementing policy decisions for the Oval Office. It may exclude the middle- and lower-level policymakers in the Office of Management and Budget and the National Security Council who are professional specialists and who may have as much career status as comparable officials within the departments and agencies. It excludes also those Executive Office special agencies that relate to science, drugs, minority rights, and so on, which lose favor with a new President or a change of climate but still remain officially and perhaps dormantly within the Executive Office.

The presidential establishment usually includes a few members of the cabinet and, possibly, of the subcabinet. The cabinet collectively is rarely within the presidential government except in a formal and symbolic manner, such as drawing public attention to a presidential decision or program. The members of the "inner cabinet," usually the secretaries of state, defense, treasury, and justice, may enter into presidential policymaking, but even then they do so on an individual basis and on selected occasions. The most official and most regular participation by cabinet members is probably by the heads of the Departments of State and Defense, who are statutory members of the National Security Council. Otherwise, involvement is likely to be another episodic matter. Sometimes a general undersecretary may have special proximity to the presidential political establishment; but specialized undersecretaries, assistant secretaries, and bureau administrators usually spend much more time in relation to their subordinates and members of Congress than in relation to White House activity.

The uncertainties of the exact boundary do not preclude substantive differences between the selected policymakers in the Executive Office of the President and most of the political executives in the departments and independent agencies. A few of the administrators of independent agencies may be within the presidential orbit on some occasions; but many of them, as well as members of boards and commissions, are most known for their comparative autonomy.

Thus, presumptively, the presidential government generally includes little more than the upper levels of the Executive Office of the President, including key White House assistants and advisers and a few members of the cabinet. Its scope varies from time to time, but that indefiniteness does not detract from the more substantive fact that at least two levels of political executives, the assistant secretaries and the top agency and bureau administrators, are usually outside the essential force of the presidential government.

The principal determinant of the presidential realm is the relationship of officials to the Oval Office. Those within its scope are largely concerned with the public image of the President rather than with his governmental administrative power. This may reflect political realities. Presidential standing in office, the probabilities of re-election, and even position in history depend upon public relationships much more than upon governmental associations. Voters seem to prefer that a President be an inspiring public personality rather than a manager or supervisor of administrative operations. The nominating processes focus upon ability to meet the demands of diverse groups for symbolic rhetoric and behavior that is satisfying to their interests and ideals. Those processes test the ability of a candidate to deal with the press and meet critical media events much more than the ability to supervise governmental activities. The whole election mechanism stresses the capacity of the candidate to send back to the people the kind of messages they prefer to receive, rather than the ability to exercise effective control over the specialized executives who make most of the administrative policy decisions.

CHAPTER SIX

THE CHARACTER OF THE EMERGING FIFTH BRANCH

THE DELINEATION of the continuing and presidential governments in the preceding chapters left us with a considerable undistributed middle of specialized administrators and other policymakers in noncareer and temporary positions. They range from exempt appointees of the civil service to heads of some cabinet departments. But they are mostly in the intermediate levels, notably the assistant secretaries of the departments; the directors of bureaus, agencies, and offices; the members of controlling boards or commissions; and supergrade professionals in semipolitical assignments. These officials may not be fully aware of their emerging identity. The conditions of their original appointments and their individual goals differ widely; but circumstances cause them to be operationally separate much of the time from the power bases of both the merit systems of the civil service and the superior partisanship of the White House. They fill a critical no-man's-land between the upper limits of the continuing government and the lower limits of the presidential government. Their emerging identity as a fifth branch[1] involves not only the distinction between career-service officials and noncareer political executives but also a division of the latter. There is noticeably less recognition of the second boundary, but several political scientists indicate that there is such a differentiation among presidential appointees.

This chapter will review the extent to which political scientists recognize the identity and emergence of an intermediate group of specialized but changing administrators and will then examine five aspects of this fifth branch: (1) the general types of officials involved, (2) their potential for specialized activism, (3) the prospects for more neutral policymaking, (4) the matter of bipartisan guidance, and (5) the potentials of public control.

Recognition of Identity and Emergence

The sharpest instance of political science recognition of a division of presidential appointees for the executive branch concerns members of the President's cabinet. This is the idea that much of the time there is in effect an inner group and an outer group of department heads. Harold Seidman, writing in 1970 after serving as a management specialist in the Bureau of the Budget, made a distinction between the secretarial and the institutional roles of the department heads who compose most of the President's cabinet. The one role concerns relationships with the White House, the other relationships with constituent units and administrative officials of the respective departments. Certain members of the cabinet seem to be selected more to serve the presidential constituency than the departmental constituencies. Seidman asserts:

> Institutional loyalty is not as crucial when the Secretarial role is discrete and separable from that of department head. The Secretaries of State, Treasury, and at times, Defense, tend to function more as staff advisers to the President than as administrators of complex institutions. Their effectiveness and influence are only coincidentally related to their access to institutional resources. . . .
>
> For the Secretaries of Agriculture, Commerce, Health, Education, and Welfare, Housing and Urban Development, Interior, Labor and Transportation, as well as the heads of the major independent agencies, the Secretarial or agency head and institutional roles cannot be divorced. Without the loyalty, or at least neutrality, of their principal bureau chiefs, these officials can be little more than highly ornamental figureheads. . . .
>
> The political executive is the proverbial man in the middle.[2]

This last may be a thumbnail sketch of the whole matter. Recognition of a mixed intermediate group may be necessary to an understanding of the essential interactions within the national government and also to a comprehension of the public's need to supplement its participation in elections with direct pressures upon specialized administrators and assistant departmental secretaries.

While the term *political executives* is probably the designation most used for this intermediate group, restraint should be exercised in relation to the adjective *political*. Many of these officials may be more scientist, economist, or other professional specialist than politician in the partisan or presidential sense.

Erwin C. Hargrove, also, explains the tendency of the cabinet to divide into two distinguishable groups:

Not all departments are the same in their composition, internal politics, external alliances, and relationships with the President. . . . The inner cabinet, consisting of the departments of State, Defense, Treasury, and Justice, is more responsive to the President than the outer ring. They are less client-oriented departments; in fact, the President is their chief client. Any President must deal directly and frequently with the heads of these departments because their business is the highest on his list of concerns of national security and economic policy. . . . The outer cabinet is composed of the domestic policy departments, several of which are actually umbrellas over bureaus with long previous histories and often with conflicting missions. . . . The problems of command and control over such loose collections of bureaus exist at both the Presidential and secretarial levels.[3]

This shows that the division of presidential appointees derives from basic forces, particularly the specialized diversity of the administrative operations and of the politico-economic constituencies into which the national society is subdivided. The White House may be the number one special-interest pressure group, but it is only one of many. Accordingly, one general type of presidential appointee serves the President as his own constituency, and the other general type serves administrative constituencies. This is in line with the views of several political science analysts of the national government that the executive branch is essentially a political arena in which there are a number of competing forces and that the President achieves more through persuasion than through command.

Thomas E. Cronin is more specific in identifying the two cabinet groups. First in a 1970 article and then in his 1975 book on the presidency, he considers the heads of the Departments of State, Defense, Treasury, and Justice to constitute an inner cabinet. These references to an "inner" and "outer" cabinet do not mean that either is an entity in itself, meeting or otherwise acting as a unit. The point is, simply, that these cabinet members are likely to be substantially closer to the respective President than are the other department heads. Moreover, the four seldom if ever advise the President as a group. The secretaries of state and defense come together in the National Security Council and may meet informally with the President at the same time, but they are otherwise more apt to appear individually. Cronin describes the manner in which there are two such groups:

> A pattern in the past few administrations suggests strongly that the inner, or counseling, cabinet positions are vested with high-priority responsibilities that bring their occupants into close and collaborative relationships with presidents and their top staff. . . .
>
> The outer-cabinet positions deal with strongly organized and more particularistic clientele, an involvement that helps to produce an advocate or adversary relationship to the White House. . . .
>
> White House aides and inner-cabinet members may be selected primarily on the basis of personal loyalty to the president; outer-cabinet members often are selected to achieve a better political, geographical, ethnic, or racial balance. In addition to owing loyalty to their president, these people must develop loyalties to the congressional committees that approved them or those that finance their programs, to the laws and programs they administer, and to the clientele and career civil servants who serve as their most immediate jury. . . .
>
> Invariably, the White House staff suspects that outer-cabinet executives accentuate the interests of extragovernmental clientele over the priorities of the president.[4]

These observations touch upon a number of operational relations or essential interactions within the national government. They indicate again that the President's cabinet is not likely to bring much unity to the multidepartmental executive branch, and, in fact, may even tend to strengthen its subdivided character. They also show that the larger outer group of cabinet members is intended to have loyalties to political forces in addition to that to the President. A further factor is the probability and even necessity for the department heads' associating closely with the attitudes and objectives of career administrators within the respective departments. Cronin's statement touches upon another unofficial division within the presidential appointees, which we will consider shortly, that is, the repeated conflict between White House staff and departmental officials.

The focus upon the cabinet and the executive departments in this analysis does not mean that the independent agencies do not involve the division of presidential appointees. In fact, they are such clear examples of opposing loyalties, constituencies, and objectives that we take their separation for granted. For years political scientists have pointed out instances of regulatory commissions' and banking boards' differing on particular policies or in general attitudes from Presidents and their Executive Office advisers. We are giving more attention to the cabinet and the departments because there may be a common belief that they bring unity to the executive branch.

We are particularly concerned with evidence and recognition of division within the body of presidential appointees in the top levels of executive positions. This is not new. Leading political scientists have called attention for some time to separation within that elite group. Stephen K. Bailey wrote in 1956 that "rarely in our history have the visible political executives in the federal bureaucracy been solely and continuously 'the President's men.' Even when they started out as 'his' men, personal fealty has often been weakened or destroyed by lateral pressures from Congress, by subterranean pressures from clientele groups, or from within the bureaucracy itself; by the corrosive acid of personal ambition; or by the honest differences over what was best for the country or the party. And many of our political executives have not even started as 'the President's men.' "[5] In 1967 Professor Grant McConnell explained the dilemma facing an incumbent president: "Appointments to office —patronage in a sense, but at a high level—are essential devices of the political art. The difficulty is that the ends of bureaucratic control and of acquiring political support are often mutually exclusive. A political appointee to the Department of Agriculture, say, recommended by a large farm organization that has supported the President cannot be readily removed or expected to be simply the President's man in the executive. He is a political officer in his own right, rather as if he had won office by election."[6]

Many political-science specialists have commented upon the rivalry between the presidential appointees at the White House and those in the departments. Stephen K. Bailey in 1956 asserted: "With the exception of two or three department heads, the most powerful top side policy determiners and co-ordinators in Washington are not found at the departmental level at all but in the White House Office and in the other constituent units of the Executive Office of the President."[7] Louis W. Koenig later said that collectively the White House staff "tends to be more powerful than all other groups in the executive branch, including the cabinet and the National Security Council."[8] William E. Mullen explains that because "cabinet secretaries have so many masters to serve, the president cannot always count on them, and he soon learns to count on his aides instead."[9] A public administration specialist, Robert Presthus, draws similar conclusions: "Members of the President's White House Office staff occupy positions of special importance for executive control. Inside observers have estimated that only two or three Cabinet members rival the 'President's Men' in influence and authority."[10]

Two 1979 analyses of the presidency present comparable views. Robert E. DiClerico says that "even those who serve at the pleasure of the President may not always be thoroughly supportive of his policies" and that the responsiveness of cabinet and sub-cabinet officials to nonpresidential constituencies "have frequently prompted White House aides to charge that Cabinet officials 'go off and marry the natives.' " Richard M. Pious declares: "Secretaries and subcabinet officials are wasting assets whose value to the president depreciates during his administration. Their limited loyalty to him diminishes steadily as they are 'captured' by the permanent government."[11]

Another cause of White House–cabinet rivalry is the multiple pressures encountered by department heads from units of Congress, judicial institutions, party or group factions, career-service contingents, and other sources which tend to draw them away from the White House presidency. Richard F. Fenno, Jr., in 1959, described these conflicts in his landmark study of the President's cabinet. One of his key statements is: "Department secretaries live in a world which has many extra-presidential dimensions."[12]

Thomas E. Cronin has found specific evidence of separation when interviewing both presidential assistants and departmental officials. Few on either side "are easily pleased," he reports. "White House aides usually come in expecting that people in the departments will do what they are told"; but they learn that, as one said, even political appointees in the departments within a year "get captured and taken in by the agencies." Cronin also notes the opposing dissatisfaction. "Departmentalists believe that White House meddling in department affairs is often disadvantageous for everyone involved." He notes a deeper sense of alienation among the heads of the more

specialized departments: "Interviews with the domestic cabinet members yield abundant evidence that most of them felt
removed from the White House." He gives a clue to the causes:
"As tension builds around whether or to what extent domestic
policy leadership rests with the departments or with the Office
of Management and Budget or the White House, and as staff
and line distinctions become blurred, the estrangement between
the domestic department heads and the White House staff
deepens."[13]

A number of political scientists have recognized, in varying
degrees, a threefold pattern of executive policymakers. Professor Robert C. Fried, in a 1976 analysis of the American bureaucracy, identifies three classes of administrative personnel
without expressly indicating the counteraction among them. He
says that the President has "three kinds of staff: (a) his personal staff in the White House and the Executive Office of the
President; (b) his staff of political executives heading the departments and bureaus; and (c) his staff of federal employees,
both civilian and military, all of whom work under his ultimate
direction and supervision."[14] Yet he does acknowledge that the
President may have limited control of the executive branch.
"Being chief administrator is not the most important of his
jobs, compared with formulating American defense and foreign
policy and providing Congress with legislative leadership. Presidential reputations are made in policy and political leadership,
rather than in managing the executive branch," he explains.

Fried's analysis points out that "great administrators," such
as James Polk and Herbert Hoover are seldom rated among our
"greatest presidents." He admits that poor administrative performance may have unmade the reputations of Presidents
Grant, Harding, and Nixon. President Nixon's acknowledged
achievements in foreign policymaking, he states, "may eventually be clouded over by what he allowed and encouraged his
subordinates to do."[15] But we may interpose that this difficulty
concerned only one of the three classes of executive officials,
that is, the White House staff and other members of the inner
circle of the presidential executive branch. Nixon's fall did not
result from the separate existence of the career and noncareer
administrative branches.

The existence of the secondary separation within the partisan
appointees of the President, as well as the primary separation

between noncareer and career personnel, is more than implicit in this descriptive observation of Professor Richard E. Neustadt:

The Presidency's character shapes what there is of unity in the executive establishment. Every agency is headed by a presidential appointee (Senate consenting). These appointees are not immune to the old charge of Charles G. Dawes that "members of the Cabinet are a President's natural enemies." But they and their immediate associates do have some things in common with each other and the President which their career subordinates do not: temporary tenure and a stake in his success. Our terminology acknowledges their semblance of community; we speak of them collectively as "the administration," something wider than "the White House," looser than "the Presidency," but different from "officialdom," *an intermediate layer neither truly presidential nor wholly bureaucratic.*[16] [Emphasis added.]

Later in his discussion Professor Neustadt explains that "most Cabinet officers, . . . and their immediate associates are caught between a burgeoning White House staff . . . and ever more entangled departmental jurisdictions consequent upon the outpouring of laws in Johnson's time."[17] The division of presidential appointees continues. "In the first months of the Carter administration," Richard M. Pious says, "battles had already broken out between HUD and HEW, on the one hand, and the White House on the other, over projected spending levels for the departments."[18]

Two other political scientists also accord separate identity to the intermediate executive group and seem to treat it as a constitutional development. Kenneth M. Dolbeare and Murray J. Edelman, in their penetrating general explanation of the national government, make this comment upon current developments:

The Constitution, as we have seen, scatters official power across a wide spectrum of positions within the governments of the United States. First, it divides power in important ways between the national government and the various state governments, and further fragments the power of the national government among the three major branches. Subsequent developments have extended this fragmentation well beyond the Framers' intentions, so that significant portions of the capacity to govern are today located (through a combination of tradition, necessity, and aggrandizement) in, for example, the committees of the Congress, the Joint Chiefs of Staff, or the middle ranges of the executive bureaucracy.[19]

This recognizes separate identity as well as power in the "middle ranges" of policymakers and also indicates that it is an enduring constitutional development. Likewise, the authors' analysis of decision-making elites acknowledges a threefold classification of officials identified in part by length of tenure. They assert that "a pattern of circulation appears to be developing in which decisionmakers are neither pursuing lifelong careers in government service nor close associates of the President. Instead, they are people who move back and forth between the upper echelon of business or law and government."[20]

The threefold pattern of the executive system is recognized by Professor Thomas E. Cronin in his recent analysis of the state of the presidency. He finds identifying criteria in the time frames of the different groups:

> A significant factor in promoting conflict between the departments and the presidential staff is their different perspectives on time. A president and his staff think in terms of two- and four-year frames, at the most. . . . Career civil servants, on the other hand, are around after the elections regardless of the outcome. . . . The work incentives for most careerists are slanted toward doing a thorough, consistent, and even cautious job, rather than toward any hurried dancing to the current tunes of the White House staff. The time frames of subcabinet officials fall in between: some seek to impress the president; others, the agency's permanent interest groups, congressional committees, and department professionals.[21]

Actually, the subcabinet officials may have a shorter average tenure than the Presidents. Yet their attitudes are likely to be intermediate between those of the White House contingent and the career executives. They are a distinguishable and conceptually separate aggregation. There may be a number of causes of such a horizontal division among the presidential appointees. Professor Cronin mentions that "the growth of the White House staff is in part a direct response to the increased number of intradepartmental controversies."[22] But that, in turn, may be one consequence of the presidential attachment to particular decisionmaking with his White House staff rather than to general policy development with his cabinet.

Hugh Heclo recognizes some of the identifying characteristics of the intermediate executive officials. His book on the subject of executive politics in Washington concerns the lower levels of political executives and the higher grades of civil servants. His description of presidential appointees in the departmental managements is most interesting. He deems them to be strangers to one another as well as to the White House and to the continuing career officials. That characteristic may deny them unity, but it enhances their separation from the presidential forces and also explains their dependence upon the permanent administrators in their respective units.

Heclo seems primarily concerned with relationships between the political executives and the bureaucrats or career civil servants, but he does recognize and identify gaps between the presidential appointees in the departments and those in the Executive Office. For instance, he observes that one "well-worn channel of conflict on political appointments is between the White House and its own top appointees in departments."[23] Other statements which suggest a division of presidential appointees are: "Political appointees out in the departments and agencies can expect to remain in their twilight zone. . . . Since there is only one chief executive but many sources of political support and inspiration, top political appointees do not necessarily hang separately if they fail to hang together. *E unibus plurum.*"[24] Heclo also explains a principal cause of their plight: "The single most obvious characteristic of Washington's political appointees is their transience." They are not likely to be in any one position for very long; and, in fact, Heclo calls them "Birds of Passage."[25]

The constructive aim of Heclo's book is, apparently, to bridge the chasm between the political executives and the supergrade civil servants. He claims that enlargement of either group might make matters worse and proposes a more unified middle force. "Both horns of the dilemma can be avoided," he states, "by establishing a group of high level officials who are more changeable and mobile than bureaucrats but more institutional and enduring than political appointees."[26] He would place all executive officers in GS 17 and 18 of the General Schedule and in Level V of the Executive Schedule in a Federal Service of about 1,800 positions.[27] The service would be a rotating pool with executives transferable from one bureau or office to another.

That might well lessen the immediate gap between the Federal Executive and General Schedule officials but at the same time might equally cause gaps above and below the new group. The Civil Service Reform Act of 1978 established a Senior Executive Service of as many as 8,000 positions drawn largely from the supergrade levels: GS 16, 17, and 18 of the General Schedule and the equivalent in some of the other merit systems. The Act also gave the higher political executives more carrot-and-stick authority over these senior officials, and it facilitated some transfers between departments and bureaus.[28]

Any such rearrangement cannot eliminate the need for middle-level officials who are permanent in place as well as in tenure. If the supergrade executives become a changing group, there would be increased dependence upon the regular-grade officials who remain in the particular bureaus. The need of the higher come-and-go executives for the information and knowledge of the career bureaucrats seems inescapable. Analyses of the presidency continue to attest to this.[29]

Roger Hilsman, in his 1979 explanation of the American national government, supports Heclo's objective of trying to improve the quality of political executives. Hilsman had several years of experience in the State Department and other government institutions. He stresses the need for high-caliber appointees in federal executive positions, noncareer supergrade assignments, and excepted policy and confidential positions under Schedule C of the civil service. His analysis gets to the basis of the difficulties in the relationships of the White House contingent and the departmental managements. Most noncareer executives, he says, try to persuade and prod the bureaucracies into doing what the President wants, but "political appointees also face up and out—*up* to the White House and inside the government, and *out* to Congress, the clientele constituencies, special interests, and attentive publics." He concludes that "political appointees are rarely the representatives only of the president who appointed them."[30]

In sum, the recognition by various political scientists of the White House–departmental separation attests to the underlying divisions of presidential political appointees. This is not limited to cabinet and subcabinet officials but concerns also many specialized administrators. The Watergate-related exposures made Americans aware of the high degree of autonomy exercised by the FBI and the CIA. Monetary and tax problems throw light on the independent power of the Federal Reserve Board and the Internal Revenue administration. Administrative policymaking in vehicle safety, grain exports, and energy also suggest a distinct executive force between the White House and the career civil service. We will examine its scope and nature.

The Dimensions of the Emerging Fifth Branch

Most of the policy-making executives who are not within the actual realm of the presidential government and are above the continuing government seem to be in four general levels:

1. Those departmental secretaries and general undersecretaries who are not in the presidential inner cabinet.
2. Specialized undersecretaries, military secretaries, substantive assistant-secretaries, general counsels of the departments, and members of independent boards and commissions.
3. Administrators of the principal bureaus, services, and agencies, whether departmental or independent, as well as administrative assistant-secretaries of the several departments.
4. Those supergrade officials of the civil service and other merit systems who have temporary or noncareer assignments and are substantially responsive to the prevailing partisanism of the departmental managements.

The scope of discretionary authority, as well as the degree of political orientation, is in general largest in the first group and decreases progressively in the succeeding categories. The first and fourth groups tend to be boundary zones with memberships fluctuating according to circumstances. The two middle groups are the most definite components of the changing administrative force that is emerging as the "fifth branch." We will look more closely at each of the four levels.

The secretaries at the head of the executive departments have mixed roles. The majority are more departmental than presidential. Each is a member of the cabinet, but that membership is more a symbolic and political-image relationship than an

administrative or managerial one. When a member is consulted
by the president on policy issues, he serves more as a staff officer than as a line executive. When he functions as head of his
department, he is drawn away from the White House. This may
happen in lesser degree to a member of the inner cabinet. Yet
each must expend time and effort in defending departmental
positions and interests before the sessions of various congressional committees. Each is the primary spokesman of the respective department in its relations with the White House. A
cabinet member may defend presidential causes in public debates, but in governmental relations he must support the departmental position if he is to have standing as an administrator.
The general undersecretaries usually are the alter egos of the
secretaries, and we may treat them together. Thus, the top level
of the fifth branch is identified by types of functions as much
as by titles of relevant officials.

The assistant secretaries of the departments, along with the
specialized undersecretaries in the State, Defense, and Treasury
Departments, seem to be the most crucial class of political executives. Among them we are likely to find the greatest variance
in policy-making authority and opportunity. Likewise, among
them we may find the widest differences between actual and
potential performances. This is the level at which ideals and
actions most need to be reconciled and at which there may be
the most failure to do so. The ratio of political and professional
orientation differs among departments and even within departments, but by and large this is the level at which crucial opportunities may be seized or lost. In fact, many presidential decisions are basically those of an assistant secretary which the
White House takes over, formally or substantively, because of
their critical character. For instance, the conduct of relations
with China is primarily the task of the assistant secretary for
Far Eastern Affairs rather than of the secretary of state, the
special assistant to the President, or the chief executive himself.
The same may be said of shuttle diplomacy in the Near East
or of monetary affairs. This last is the primary responsibility of
the undersecretary and assistant secretary of the Treasury for
monetary affairs.

A president may involve himself in such a middle-level policy
decision when it reaches headline intensity or when it holds
exceptional promise for his political and perhaps historical pres-

tige. A particular crisis is likely to have a combination of causes, but often an added factor is the lack of experience in Washington legislative and executive processes among the come-and-go executives in the relevant department or agency. Moreover, the efforts of a deputy or assistant secretary to get on top of a rising crisis may serve professional and departmental goals more than the political well-being of the President. An instructive case of White House takeover occurred during the gasoline-oil crisis of 1979. President Carter became more and more disturbed at the performance of the Department of Energy, and he increasingly shifted the top decisionmaking to the domestic policy staff of the Executive Office of the President.[31] This is more evidence of the underlying division of presidential appointees between those in the departments and those at the White House.

While the assistant secretaries may differ considerably in the degree to which they are administrators, policy revisionists, or program developers, the next level of departmental political executives is more definitely and strictly composed of administrators. They include the commissioner of Internal Revenue (Treasury), the commissioner of Immigration and Naturalization (Justice), the administrator of Rural Electrification (Agriculture), the director of the Bureau of the Census (Commerce), the Federal Highway administrator (Transportation) and the administrator of Veterans Affairs. There are, of course, many others, with varying degrees of public impact, each heading a semiautonomous operating subsystem. That may be one measure of the effective fragmentation of the nonpresidential executive branches.

The supergrade civil servants are a boundary group by their very place in the executive arrangement and also because a quarter of them may have assignments that are noncareer, limited, or probationary rather than career. Viewed for substance, most of the supergrade group is an elite policy-making force that may be as mindful of the alternating partisanship of their immediate superiors in the departmental and agency managements as of the routine legalism of the mass of career personnel. At times the supergrades with career assignments may be a group intermediate between the presidential establishment and the regular merit service. Moreover, we have seen that one-tenth of the supergrades may have noncareer assignments on appointments from outside the government and that still others of this elite group may be on temporary assignment in presidential-appointee positions because of the difficulties of finding proper persons for such posts.[32]

Another difficulty in classifying supergrade civil servants is that among the upper-level merit-system officials there are some come-and-go professionals or technicians, such as lawyers, economists, mathematicians, or scientists specializing in one or another type of regulation, analysis, experimentation, data processing, and so on, who leave the government after a few years for similar but more promising positions in the private sphere.[33]

The foregoing discussions of the general types of officials within the fifth branch of noncareer, away-from-the-White House executives concerned departmental policymakers, because that is where most of the problem may be in recognizing the lines of separation between continuing, presidential, and changing classes of officials. While the independent agencies may be a motley aggregation from the view of formal structure, they present a clearer case of presidential appointees becoming nonpresidential in their operating attitudes. Congress placed these agencies outside the departmental system for the very purpose of increasing their independence of the White House.[34] This is particularly true of the independent regulatory commissions, the banking boards, and the government corporations. But it is also the case with those agencies which are headed by single administrators, such as the Veterans' Administration and the General Services Administration. Congress has special interests in keeping them beyond the spell of the White House.[35] Accordingly, the emerging fifth branch of intermediate policymaking officials includes not only the political or noncareer administrators of the cabinet departments but, even more, the various commissioners, board members, administrators, and other executive personnel of the independent agencies.

Having sketched the dimensions of the fifth branch, we will now examine the potentials and problems it presents, including the difficulties of bipartisan guidance and public control.

The Potentials of Specialized Activism

Whether we view government to be the articulation of our expectations or the attainment of more social harmony, the principal source of controversy in our political system is the pace of activity toward our socioeconomic ideals. The participating electorate is divided in large measure between those who want categorical programs and those who accept incremental changes in these fields. At times, of course, we feel forced to give prime attention to national security; but since the 1930s and 1940s when social security and civil rights took over the headlines in domestic politics, basic differences between the presidential candidates and their respective followers have concerned the extent to which they are liberal or conservative in relation to various types of public welfare and social adjustment.

The American political spectrum is divided in one political science text on the national government into five "perspectives," which are designated *Radical Left, Liberal Critics, Centrists, Conservative Critics,* and *Radical Right.*[36] What they differ on most is how much social change the government should undertake to achieve. The focal point of their differences is, most of all, the choice of a President; and the Democrats much more than the Republicans favor a candidate with an activist stance, as we have noted in the chapter on presidential government. Once in office, Democratic Presidents Kennedy, Johnson, and Carter were virtually forced to devote a majority of their time to foreign affairs; but in comparison with Republican Presidents, they were on the side of social reform and welfare activism.

Progressive liberals in socioeconomic matters, such as those concerning the problems of the low-income families in the large cities, place heavy emphasis upon positive activism in the presidency, and their disappointments of the past ten years have not altered their viewpoint to any substantial degree. Their frustration is likely to continue. All recent Presidents, even those who gave domestic matters priority in their campaigns, have become absorbed in national security and diplomatic matters because of their scope and urgency. All Democratic Presidents of this century were drawn away from their primary interest in domestic welfare; and from Truman on, successes have been limited largely to the realm of foreign affairs. During the forty years since Franklin Roosevelt's success with the New Deal recovery program, Congress has approved presidential welfare programs only in the years 1964–65. Then President Johnson

had not only his own skill but also a special regard for the
memory of John Kennedy in gaining congressional approval.
Yet even he encountered another source of frustration: the
Poverty program, especially the Community Action project,
floundered in application and provoked criticism that caused
Congress to repeal parts of the endeavor.[37]

This record casts doubt upon the proposition that we need
activist presidents to achieve socioeconomic reforms. Many
Democrats and others may still look to the White House for
such purposes, perhaps in desperation, because the only visible
alternative is the Congress, and that holds little hope for initia-
tive and attainment. We may need to look to the less visible
forces of the government. Among the appointed officials, those
with the most potential may be the assistant secretaries of the
departments concerned with domestic matters. They are in a
position to mediate between political and technical standards
and between general and special publics, and they may have
sufficient closeness to an area of operations that they can antici-
pate critical situations and deal with them by preaction rather
than reaction. However, their contribution now is often meagre
or spasmodic; because, for one reason, their average terms are
short. It is probably true that behind all the publicity focused
upon the President and the departmental secretaries, the assistant secretaries may contribute more than is commonly recognized; but in such positions there are probably the greatest
opportunities for increased contributions, particularly in the matter of specialized activism and program innovation or revision.

The primary educational task here seems to be to develop
awareness of the positions of assistant secretaries and their potential for specialized activism and responsibility. The first step
may be mere identification. Those positions in State, Defense,
Treasury, and Justice Departments tend to be technical or governmental in character. The Department of State usually has
about eight assistant secretaries, including six with geographical responsibility, such as European Affairs. The Department
of Defense has a number of assistant secretaries on technical
matters. Each of the three military departments (Air Force,
Army, and Navy) has four assistant secretaries: for research and
development, installations and logistics, manpower and reserve
affairs, and general financial management. The Treasury has assistant secretaries for tax policy, enforcement, international af-

fairs, economic policy, and fiscal affairs. And the Department of Justice has eight assistant attorneys general for fields of law, such as antitrust and civil rights, as well as a solicitor general. Each department also has an assistant secretary for administration and some for congressional affairs and public relations.

The assistant secretaries for the more specialized departments concern fields that are less governmental than sociological. They could have a direct impact upon the general and special publics. They deal with subjects that cause liberal-conservative conflicts among many voters and, hence, are more relevant to the problems of responsiveness and responsibility. For instance, the Department of Interior has three assistant secretaries who relate to substantive matters: energy and minerals; land and water resources; and fish, wildlife, and parks. The Department of Labor has assistant secretaries for labor-management relations, manpower, employment standards, and occupational safety and health.

In the specialized domestic-economic departments, there are about twenty-five positions of assistant secretary in substantive areas. Some of these now have administrative functions, but potentially they could be positions of specialized activism in the innovation or revision of particular programs. Their meagre contribution thus far may be due considerably to unfavorable conditions. Whether a longer, protected tenure, proper salaries, and direct public responsiveness would have beneficial consequences may be a debatable matter; but the chances of improvement over the present situation are sufficient to warrant a try in some of the better known areas, such as education, resources, housing, and transportation.

Prospects for More Neutral Administration

The events of the past decade, particularly the Watergate disclosures of White House relationships with certain agencies, have raised anew the issue of the extent to which specialized administrators above the career levels should be the President's men. The answer depends much upon the alternatives. No one contends that they should be merely the Senate's men or the Congress's men. Likewise, they should not be strictly their own men. Most political scientists who have examined the matter indicate that the presidency and the houses of Congress, each in its own way, share both the authority and responsibility over administrative operations. Political scientists differ on how much administrators are and should be guided by their own professional standards.

Legal and judicial controversies are more concerned with the right to remove officials than with the supervision of them. Presidential appointment after Senate approval suggests that the administrators should be acceptable to both. That is consistent with the right of the president to remove a political executive who does not abide by presidential policy. The Senate should not be able to force the retention of such a cabinet member or agency head. Yet, if the Senate comes to disapprove of a department or agency head, it must take indirect means, such as a harsh response to appropriations or legislative requests. By that kind of action, the Senate, as well as the President, may procure removal. In effect, each has a mutual negative, and that is the essence of the more basic arrangements of authority distribution.

Whether political executives below the cabinet level should be equally the President's men seems less clear. The Supreme Court in 1926 held that a President could remove a postmaster for policy reasons, but the opinion of Chief Justice Taft seems to assume a much higher official.[38] Moreover, in his 1915 lectures on the presidency, the former chief executive indicated that only the top-level executives need be so removable. He asserted that presidential selection of departmental officials should be limited to the secretary at the head, who is ex officio a member of the cabinet, along with "a political under-secretary." The latter would act for the former on occasions. "All other officers in the departments, including the Assistant Secretaries and the Chiefs of Bureaus, should have a permanent tenure and not change with each administration," the ex-President said.[39] If that means our raising civil service status to the subcabinet level as the English do, it would seem neither possible nor desirable.

More recent suggestions tend to center upon an intermediate, semicareer and semipolitical service for supergrade officials and, to some extent, for the lower level of the Executive Schedule. Presidents seem interested in making the higher career officials more amenable to supervision by presidential appointees. Both President Nixon and President Carter proposed separate arrangements for supergrade officials.[40] But the principal cause of inefficiency in the executive branch seems to be the short tenure of the presidential appointees. No President is likely to propose a longer term, such as ten years, for political executives in general, because that might increase their separation from the White House. Yet longer tenure might attract knowledgeable professionals who would be willing to adjust their attitudes as the parties in the White House change.

Watergate and related events of recent years have brought new reasons for strengthening the specialized administrators and what is commonly called the bureaucracy. Foremost, is the idea that middle-level officials may serve as a check upon excesses in the White House. Thomas E. Cronin, when considering ways of "braking" the presidency, works the problem down to difficulties in developing career personnel. That seems implicit in these comments:

> During the 1960s civil servants in most domestic departments did not consciously obstruct most of the Kennedy-Johnson objectives. . . . The most frequent difficulty was that for such significant new departures as antipoverty agencies, reforms in criminal justice, or environmental protection efforts, no competent federal civil service organizations existed at the time. Time was required to create effective organizations, which were made up mostly or wholly of outsiders. . . . In short, far more attention should be paid to the question of how to create and sustain large pools of talented public executives.[41]

Cronin may be thinking largely of career administrators, but there may be an even greater need for developing a stronger force of officials at the administrator/director level of presidential appointees. We may need to look specifically at the various bureaus and agencies and consider ways of developing the potential of the specialized administrators for a more neutral operation, as well as endeavoring to increase their efficiency and responsiveness.

Noncareer positions below the cabinet level tend to be unattractive because they are nonprestiguous and the salaries may be inadequate. Salaries for members of Congress and top appointed officials are renewed quadrennially. Sizable adjustments were made in January 1977, but within two years there were new inadequacies.[42] The alternative of making positions such as that of assistant secretary more prestiguous might be preferable to raising the whole salary pattern.

The inexperience of political executive appointees from assistant secretaries down, in their particular administrative situations, makes for weak departmental hierarchies. This may account for the durability of the unofficial control systems, such as the hundreds of issue networks and action triangles dominated by small congressional blocs, group representatives, and unit administrators. Logically, this suggests a need for longer, fixed terms. But there is no assurance that such terms would make the positions more attractive to qualified public administrators or professional advisers, particularly in view of the political and economic uncertainties and the prospect of more inflation in future years. Moreover, there seems to be no legislative trend toward fixed terms for departmental executives. A ten-year term was urged for the head of the FBI,[43] perhaps as much to show disapproval of the forty-seven-year reign of J. Edgar Hoover as to prevent rapid turnover. Presidents and many members of Congress are not likely to favor increasing the autonomy of various assistant secretaries and other departmental officials. Whether such a change would make the persons in these positions less responsive to special interests and more accountable to the general public may depend upon how much direct involvement the concerned public is willing to undertake.

Prospects for Bipartisan Guidance

The working disassociation of fifth-branch officials such as assistant secretaries and specialized administrators from both the electoral legitimacy of the presidency and the technological legitimacy of the regular-grade civil servants prompts questions of how we can increase the chances that these middle-range policymakers will be responsive to the public interest.

This approach assumes that we wish to go beyond the ideological belief in a monolithic executive pyramid and the theory that it should and can be controlled entirely from the top. That simple approach places utmost faith in the related notions that the President represents the entire nation and that the White House can and will cause the whole executive structure to serve the public interest. But that is a fond belief which allows us to blame special-interest actions upon politicians and bureaucrats. "The president as advocate of the public interest," William E. Mullen says, "is a myth closely related to that of the president as the representative of the entire people."[44]

The belief that the executive structures can be controlled from the top level is probably the greatest obstacle to a sound understanding of the administrative operations and the control methods at work in the United States government. We observed that most political scientists agree that presidential control of the executive branch is considerably limited. Also, we saw that presidential prestige does not rest upon the role of chief administrator but rather upon actions in military and diplomatic situations and upon dramatic or symbolic decisions in a few crises of headline intensity.

When we extend our thoughts beyond the simple ideological belief that the President is an omnicompetent chief administrator and recognize the diversity of internal and external forces which bear upon the executive operations, we find the organizational hierarchy composed, most essentially, of distinguishable levels of officials with varying degrees of discretion and differing mixtures of legislative, executive, and judicial functions. For the purpose of analysis, we have assumed six general levels: presidential, secretarial, assistant-secretarial, noncareer-administrative, supergrade-career, and regular-grade career. The political/administrative ratio changes as we proceed down the several levels. We find, also, much interaction at various levels with corresponding parts of the congressional hierarchy, such as party leaderships, major committees, numerous subcommittees, unofficial blocs, and so on. In addition, there are comparable patterns of relationship with judicial institutions and with various unofficial forces, including parties, general and special groups, and individual participants.

The place of fifth-branch officials in this complex system of interactions is not readily evident, but their roles may be crucial in any effort to make executive operations more responsive to reasonable concepts of the public interest. The middle-level policymakers may be the principal means through which public-interest organizations may surmount the highly fragmented autonomy of hundreds of issue networks and action triangles that now comprise much of the operational structure of the national government. Guidance and restraint through consumer and other general-area pressure groups seem to be necessary supplements to the electoral process.

The first step in an educational analysis of middle-level controls seems to be recognition that the nonpresidential realms of government are inevitably specialized and fragmented and that enhancement of public control almost necessarily involves multiple institutions or channels. For purposes of explanation, we will examine two such means. This section will look at the prospects of more bipartisan guidance by the official committees of Congress, and the next section will consider the forces of specialized public involvement.

The potential of congressional subcommittees in this matter stems from the apportionment of their membership between the two major parties. The majority party tends to have the upper hand, but there is an appreciable degree of bipartisanism in the operation of most committees. Moreover, they are about the only regularly established institutions in Washington that provide any reasonable opportunity for increasing bipartisanism. The main line of development would seem to be fuller and more regular interaction between middle-range executive officials and corresponding subcommittees.

A further possibility is the use of joint committees composed of members from both parties and from both houses and having a specific area of jurisdiction. There are now such committees for atomic energy, the budget, certain internal revenue matters, and defense production. Congress may have too many committees now, but joint committees could have an integrative effect, tending to reconcile differences between the two houses as well as between the two parties. They might give administrative officials a better opportunity to view the opposing positions of several forces.

The official bipartisan committees might be helpful in countering unofficial blocs and in raising the level of public responsiveness among the administrative branches, but their effectiveness is most probable in domestic affairs. The current trend among political scientists seems to question the foreign/domestic dichotomy, but there is still substantial difference between the two realms. The President, congressmen, and journalists still distinguish between them in many situations. President Carter has had more success in projects relating to Panama or the Near East than in those concerning domestic economy or mixed programs such as energy. On difficult foreign affairs issues, Congress eventually defers to the President; for example, it could have stopped the Vietnam War at any time, but it did not do so.[45]

The War Powers Act of 1973 imposed some limitations upon Presidents, but its effect is uncertain.[46] In his 1980 book on the presidency,[47] Robert J. Sickels discusses several difficulties of the shared control of foreign and military affairs, such as the beliefs of many Presidents that circumstances required action before getting approval of Congress. The National Security Council could probably reduce the singlemindedness of the White House in such policy decisions if its functions were more obligatory and if not all of its members were the President's men.

The belief that responsibility must be singular may not be as strong as it was before Vietnam, Watergate, and the Nixon pardon. We have little difficulty in placing blame for those misfortunes, but a little dispersion of responsibility might have prevented them. Bipartisan guidance and control, of course, will not solve all problems. In fact, the two parties together may represent the views of only 70 percent, more or less, of the electorate; but that is better than the one-party perspective that characterizes the presidency and the singlemindedness that has pervaded the White House in recent decades. Whatever the developments of bipartisanism in the congressional or presidential units, guidance and restraint of the main flow of executive operations necessarily entails public participation in processes that are in addition to and more direct than the electoral system.

Potentials of Public Control

"Every free government is necessarily complicated." That quotation from Daniel Webster, used by Francis Lieber in his 1853 book on civil liberty and self-government, seems to be a fitting approach to the problem of public control.[48] Concentration of power may simplify the identification of responsibility, but the whole antimonarchical history of representative constitutional democracy calls for rejection of the idea of association between the American government and the single personality in the Oval Office. We need a pattern of responsibility to match the pattern of shared power. Such an adjustment would involve three principal types of factors. The first concerns the limited and special character of presidential government, the second relates to the division of the government into five coordinate branches, and the third pertains to the degree of fragmentation in the actual control mechanisms.

The activity of a President is often ceremonial or symbolic.

This is more personification than representation. Public forces, as well as governmental and political forces, allow a President to speak and act for them. Concerned segments of the social system exert upon the person in the Oval Office an almost constant pressure that their preferred ideals and expectations be affirmed. Presidential leadership may be, in considerable measure, a matter of sharing feelings and anxieties and of criticizing those aspects of life that irritate the voters. It may take the form of proposed legislation to reform or to correct, or it may be "simplistic populism" and "quick shots at stock villians." Whatever its form and degree, such activity is a response to public demands. The various media insist that the President engage in dramatic appearances and that he produce headline answers to headline anxieties. The White House staff keeps alive the belief of presidential omnipotence and omniscience. In the various efforts of President Carter to improve his public image and his approval-poll ratings, the White House advisers and assistants were increasingly prominent.

Ideological symbolism extends also to the popular conception of the Constitution. The image of three-branch government, with the executive branch headed by an elected President in full control, permits Americans to believe that they have public democratic control of the whole administration of government. Yet the regular-grade civil servants and a goodly share of supergrade officials may have, collectively, as much autonomy in the actual operation of the government as the presidency and the Congress. They constitute the continuing government, which other branches endeavor to guide and control. The noncareer executives—assistant secretaries, bureau administrators, and nonpermanent supergrades—may constitute a more amorphous collective than even the regular civil service; but their very disassociation from more legally constituted structures, such as the Executive Office of the President, permits them to achieve, if they have the inclination, a substantial degree of autonomy. Moreover, given the complexity of the government and the vagueness or ambiguity of many laws, orders, and rules, their combined policymaking authority may exceed that of other branches in the regular operation of the government. Their potential power is greater than their actual power, but the latter is far beyond that commonly recognized.

A number of political scientists assert that the bureaucrats are more representative of the American society than are the elected officials.[49] This seems to concern socioeconomic identity, that is, the geography and class pattern of their origins, more than their policy attitudes in actual operations. Persons of comparatively humble origin who gain middle-class status are not necessarily sympathetic to the underprivileged and may even be less charitable in spirit than are the wellborn. On the other hand, the general public's opinion of bureaucrats is apt to be based upon impressions of particular actions, inactions, or reactions rather than upon sociological background or other facts about the civil servants.

There appears to be constitutional propriety and even necessity in allowing the appointed executives in the third, fourth, and fifth levels of the national government to have a policy-making, as well as operating, status coordinate with the institutions of elected officials, the members of Congress as well as the President. Peter Woll, who has been writing about the national administration for a number of years, points out in his 1974 analysis of public policy that the autonomy of the bureaucracy as a coordinate branch has become essential to responsible government:

> Among other things, the Watergate scandals illustrated that an independent bureaucracy is necessary for the maintenance of a system of governmental responsibility. The powers of the executive branch are far too extensive to be controlled by any one of the primary branches of government without upsetting the delicate balance of powers in the Constitution. The bureaucracy must be maintained as a semi-autonomous fourth branch of the government to check any potential excesses on the part of the president or Congress.[50]

Seemingly, we now are at the point where we not only cannot be sure that the elected officials will control in a proper manner the appointed officials but also where we may need to rely upon the often scorned bureaucracy, or a major part of it, to restrain our elected representatives in the White House and on Capitol Hill. The burdens of representative democracy now extend beyond the election of top officials and the maintenance of channels of communication with them. Public control now involves direct relationships with the appointed political executives in the middle ranges of government management. That brings us to the specialized government and the fragmentation of control mechanisms.

We have seen in preceding chapters that the effective control power of the presidency over regular operations of the government may not extend beyond the second level of policy-making officials, so that autonomy of the middle range of political executives may be an autonomy of perhaps fifty units of government. Accordingly, direct public control would need to have that degree of specialization. There is now, of course, much greater fragmentation. The unofficial control mechanisms that bring together for particular areas of operation one or more members of Congress, the relevant agency administrator, and representatives of the affected special-interest groups number in the hundreds—let us say three hundred. Thus, an official specialization of fifty, or even seventy-five, units would be a substantial improvement. But, first of all, we need to recognize that the idea that the executive branch is or can be a single pyramidal structure is a mythical abstraction and that trying to achieve it merely preserves the greater fragmentation.

Certainly the task of public control of the administration is far more complex than a dialogue with the President or the Congress or both. The election process and the presidential office are each a limited channel of communication from the concerned publics to the operating units. The election procedure can transmit only a single message, such as A over B, no matter how specific candidates may be on various issues. An elected official cannot be sure which of his positions the electoral plurality actually favors. Then the President is virtually forced to limit his interests to the major public anxieties. If the concerned publics wish to keep the full, regular flow of executive decisions responsive to national ideals and interests, they may need to develop direct relationships with the specialized administrators, particularly those in the middle levels of the more crucial areas of operation.

Figure 2 shows the extent to which the administrative branches are government-wide in their function and need extended control beyond that which can be given by the presidential establishment.

Two political science analysts of the national government point out the need for more penetrating citizen involvement in the administration of specialized units. Eugene Lewis explains

LEGISLATIVE FUNCTIONS   EXECUTIVE FUNCTIONS   JUDICIAL FUNCTIONS

Congressional Branch

Presidential Branch

Judicial Branch

Changing Administrative Branch

Continuing Administrative Branch

that professional bureaucrats dominate much of the policy-making process because of their expertise and the scarcity and dispersion of outside attention. He asserts that:

> If great numbers of nonbureaucratic political actors concentrated their energies on a single issue or set of issues, then the power of professionalized bureaucrats would, in my view, be diminished. The normal situation is the opposite: Attention to single issues by large numbers of people in the political system is an extraordinary event. Because of the diversity and complexity of important matters, discrete publics tend to focus attention very briefly on any single matter.[51]

Thus attention to a given problem is scarce and "prolonged attention is extremely rare." In fact, there is a fragmentation of attention even in the bureaucratic subsystems: "The division of labor is also the division of attention." Lewis argues that lack of public attention to an issue is no assurance that the matter is unimportant or noncontroversial. He points out that during a twenty-year period (1953–74) the "Defense Department obtained an average 90 percent plus of their budget requests"; and he contends that this happened "only because they never reached a point where those capable of effectively disagreeing could make their voices heard."

William L. Morrow, in his analysis of public administration and politics, describes the recent increase of public-interest groups and citizen participation in specialized areas of government in contrast with the traditional dominance of special-interest organizations:

> Contemporary politics, however, has been marked by a revolution seeking more direct participation by citizens in policy-making. In contrast to the tendency for institutions to represent organized interests, this resurgence of participatory democracy seeks direct citizen access to decision centers and involvement in decision-making regardless of any connections or affiliations that the participants might have with organized interests. In fact, the participation movement has stressed representation of unorganized publics that have been given only casual concern in policy areas.
>   . . . The most popular defense of the renewed stress on participatory democracy is that it represents a profitable learning experience for the citizen participants. They become more educated, more tolerant, more compassionate people. They have

the satisfaction of knowing they contributed policies affecting not only their lives, but the larger community.[52]

Much of the citizen participatory effort has been directed at local governmental processes. That, of course, has a convenience and, perhaps, a more direct relationship. But public control of the national government requires involvement in the national policy-making processes. There are national government offices in many localities, but the top policy is most often made in Washington. Citizen involvement there almost necessarily requires some form of organization, such as the public-interest groups that operate on a general and broad level.

CHAPTER SEVEN

THE ESSENTIAL INTERACTIONS
OF FIVE-BRANCH GOVERNMENT

THIS BOOK deals with the simple imagery of geometric patterns in the political science explanation of the United States government. Americans generally idealize the triangular model of separate legislative, executive, and judicial branches; and basic university courses in our national government usually make the three-power doctrine an introductory highlight. This is a seductive approach. It is a common starting design for the Constitution, the institutions, and the functions of our government. Yet many political scientists also make that tripartite formula the point of departure for penetrating and often deviating analyses of the various governmental processes.[1] Accordingly, we have undertaken to appraise the three-branch model and to examine the propriety of a more inclusive pattern.

We began by looking at the general character of constitutional distribution. We examined three views of the Constitution. The first features the vesting clauses at the start of Articles I, II, and III. These clauses suggest a three-institution, separate-function pattern with limited applicability. The second concerns the main body of the Constitution and the multiplicity of specific provisions. The underlying principle is checks and balances or shared functions; and it seems to have broad, flexible applicability. The third view recognizes the open-endedness of the document and the authority of Congress to enact laws necessary and proper for carrying into execution the powers of the government. Congress has established an increasing number of departments and agencies to undertake the specialized legislative, executive, and adjudicative functions which now make up most of the operating activity of the government.

We concluded that each of the three patterns of distribution has fundamental legitimacy and an integral place in the total constitutional system of limited government. Each serves the objectives of preventing undue concentration of power and of assigning authority according to a rational pattern. Each conforms to the proposition that the separation of institutions is preliminary to the more ultimate goals of interdependence of functions and the shared duty to cooperate in achieving and maintaining a workable government.[2]

The Constitution, we observed, expressly authorizes three classes of executive officials, distinguishable both by the level of the position and by the political identity of the appointing official. The first is a superior type of officer, with presidential appointment subject to senatorial consent; the second and third are inferior types of officer, one class appointed by the President alone, the other by the heads of departments as Congress may stipulate.[3] These provisions furnish a constitutional basis for some inner separation of executive officials and for the resulting counteractions among the executive forces themselves and with other branches of the government.

The chapter on the general character of the executive branch gave particular attention to its congressional basis, its diverse functions, its administrative politics, departmental disunity, and the levels of executive policymakers. We concluded that the constitutional principle of checks and balances operates inside as well as outside the executive branch.[4]

The principal reasons for considering a geometric pattern of the United States government which recognizes more than three branches are the numerous assertions of political scientists that the executive branch is divided between major types of appointed officials. A common contrast is made between the presidency and the bureaucracy, and more specific distinctions are made between noncareer or political executives and career or merit-system appointees. These designations reflect not only differences in tenure but also conflicts of supporting constituencies.[5]

Several political scientists suggest that the administrative bureaucracy constitutes a fourth branch of government that is presumably coordinate with the three better-known branches.[6] Others divide the executive officials between the presidential government and the permanent government.[7] Definitions of the terms entail a horizontal boundary that cuts across various types of institutions. Two chapters undertook to ascertain the dimensions of the permanent or continuing government and the presidential government. We concluded, with respect to the upper limits of the former and the lower limits of the latter, that a considerable body of executives is excluded from both much of the time. The preceding chapter examined the emerging fifth branch of changing administrators and its actual and potential characteristics.

This chapter will undertake to explain the five-branch approach to the United States government, with particular emphasis on ways in which the expanded pattern of essential interactions makes us aware of the full measure of constitutional checks and balances.

We may form a general pattern of essential interactions by perceiving the lines connecting the five points of a combination pentagram and pentagon such as shown in Figure 3 below.

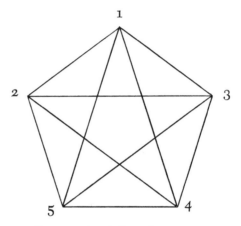

1. Congressional Branch
2. Presidential Branch
3. Judicial Branch
4. Continuing Administrative Branch
5. Changing Administrative Branch

Figure 3.

The five-branch pattern has greater educational utility and more public-control relevance than any model of a different number of branches. A three-power model of legislative, executive, and judicial powers disregards the semiautonomous character of the administrative forces and their specialized legislative and adjudicative functions. A four-branch model of congressional, presidential, judicial, and administrative forces does not recognize the division among presidential-party appointees as well as that between such officials and the career-merit appointees. Moreover, it does not call attention to the opportunity of the two administrative branches to challenge and constrain each other, or to the importance of direct relationships between public-interest groups and specialized administrators.[8]

There may be some argument for a six-branch pattern with separate identities for the Senate and the House of Representatives. Bicameralism is one type of check and balance, and the Senate has a few special roles. But both houses are elected assemblies representing geographical units, and they are basically similar in most of their relationships with the other branches. The addition of a sixth branch would intensify considerably the scheme of inner channels without substantive improvement to the educational usefulness of the geometric model

In short, the five-branch pattern has particular advantage, because it focuses attention upon the two basic types of administrative policymakers and their relationships with the other three branches. It also shows a direct means by which the general or public-interest groups may develop checks and balances in competition with the special groups.

This separate identification of five branches of officials does not deny the semiofficial power of the press, the parties, or the groups which some observers call fourth or fifth branches.[9] These forces are coordinate, not from their separate roots, but from their unofficial penetration. For instance, the press and the presidency, despite their displays of opposition, thrive upon each other. A President is continuously prime material for headlines and, in turn, is increasingly a public-relations personality moving from one media event to another.[10] Hence, the press is less a separate branch than a partner to the presidential branch.

Similarly, the major political parties are integral parts of the elected institutions, particularly the Congress. The central organizations of the two houses are institutions of the majority and minority parties, with leaders, policy committees, and conferences. Then the official legislative, appropriative, and investigative committees also have dual-party membership.[11] Congress is the national bi-party or duo-party organization, if we have one.

The interest groups, whether special or general, are powerful, not because of their separate identities but because of their association with the particularized subunits of Congress and the administrative system. Thus, the groups are less a separate branch than unofficial allies of the legislative and administrative subgovernments.

The Character of the Five Branches

We will begin the examination of essential interactions within the United States government by reviewing briefly the character of each of the five coordinate branches.

The Congressional Branch (1). Most basically, Congress consists of 535 political personalities. Each of the 100 senators and the 435 representatives has a personal electoral constituency. The grass-roots essence of American democracy is the representation of particular states and districts. Although many forces influence the policy-making decisions of the members of Congress, in the last analysis they need only to be responsive and responsible to the active voters of their respective electoral constituencies, because the voters determine whether they will continue in public office.

There are many ways to conceive of the congressional branch. We may think of it as one entity, as two houses, as two party-organizations in each house, as more or less twenty committees in each chamber, or as more than a hundred subcommittees in each house. We may also conceive of Congress as a few hundred informal blocs. These blocs reflect the particular interests of senators and representatives arising from the requests of their electoral constituencies and from the expertise they acquire in committee and subcommittee assignments. The specialized expertise accumulated over the years may enhance the general standing and power of a member of Congress.

Each of these different concepts of the Congress tends to be a level of relationship with the policy-making officials of the executive and administrative branches. Formally, the legislative process is the consideration and enactment of public laws; but informally, it involves an almost continuous interaction between the specialized subunits of the houses of Congress and comparable elements of the executive/administrative complex. The houses increasingly have their own professional experts, but in considerable measure they depend upon those of the departments and agencies in the official executive branch.[12]

The Presidential Branch (2). Concepts of the presidency range from a single personality to the whole executive branch. Here we are concerned with identifiable and meaningful divisions of policy-making officials and their interactions. The chapter on presidential government concluded that from such a viewpoint, the presidential branch consists of from 50 to 100 top assistants and advisers mainly in the Executive Office of the President but also including a few department and agency heads who have a special relationship with the particular President.[13]

We also saw that the President has supragovernmental roles in international relations and domestic public relations, that the American public tends to mythologize the incumbent President, that the short tenures and alternating partisanship of the Presidents are limiting factors upon the control of and influence over many of their own political appointees, and that White House participation in administrative operations is confined to a few selected issues that, actually or potentially, have headline character.

The traditional ideology of three-power government, which we can derive from the initial vesting clauses of Articles I, II, and III of the Constitution, places the presidency in a subordinate position; that is, it indicates that the role of the President is to execute the laws enacted by the legislators.[14] The five-branch pattern recognizes that policymaking in the execution of laws is undertaken mostly by semiautonomous subunit administrators, while the President is in effect an elective monarch who is engaged mainly in maintaining relations with the strategic electorate and in performing such monarchlike roles as commander in chief, chief diplomat, chief legislator, and chief citizen.[15]

The Judicial Branch (3). Various persons conceive of the judiciary in different ways. Some assume that the Supreme Court is the judicial branch. Others include the courts of appeals and the district courts. Still others take the special courts into account. Then the administrative tribunals located in the executive branch might also be added, because in many instances appeals may be taken directly to the appeals courts without a trial in the district courts. Whatever the approach, the judicial system is not entirely unified or symmetrical. The Constitution prescribes the Supreme Court, but Congress decides the number of justices and may limit its appellate jurisdiction. Congress has established eleven circuit courts of appeals, nearly one hundred district courts, a few special courts, and more than a score of administrative tribunals.[16]

The general courts—the Supreme Court, the courts of appeals, and the district courts—form a pyramid, but the Supreme Court is not a typical appellate court. It is more like a representative-legislative body than most courts. Socioeconomic factors may enter into the selection of new judges. The Court may or may not give full review to many appeals; and, when it does, all nine justices generally enter into the decision. Over a period of time, the Supreme Court justices tend to form right, left, and center blocs. The Court's selection of appeals involving new constitutional issues makes it a high-level legislature.[17]

The special courts relate only to a few subject areas—the military, customs, patents, money claims, and taxes—but not to most areas of government. The administrative tribunals include some independent regulatory commissions and a number of agencies within departments. Their specialized adjudicative activity is one reason for the existence of administrative branches apart from the presidential establishment.

The Continuing Administrative Branch (4). The idea of career officials in the executive departments goes back to the Confederation government that preceded the Constitution. For instance, Joseph Nourse served as registrar of the treasury from 1781 to 1829.[18] The change of presidential parties with Thomas Jefferson in 1801 and Andrew Jackson in 1829 brought about the immediate replacement of almost one-tenth of the civilian employees.[19] The spoils system is often associated with the Jacksonian brand of presidential partisanship. Subsequent excesses led to the statutory establishment, beginning in 1883, of the civil service and other merit systems.[20] The noncareer/career distinction increased, and recently the unionization of large bodies of employees has added to the quasi-independence of the civil service.[21]

"A measure of conflict is instinct in the relations between a permanent bureaucracy and a temporary political executive."[22] In the American system "the bureaucrat is not only permanent in tenure but permanent in place";[23] that is, careers are in particular bureaus. The greater know-how, professionally and politically, gives the career administrator an advantage over a political superior. Presidents and others have sought to reduce this advantage by lessening the permanence of the senior civil servants, particularly their permanence in place. The devices of excepted positions, probationary and noncareer assignments, and the pooling of administrators have made the upper boundaries of the permanent or continuing administrative branch an irregular and uncertain matter.[24] Nevertheless, there is a sizable body of career policymakers in the executive departments and agencies. The chapter on the dimensions of continuing government concluded that the fundamental determinant of continuity may be a working harmony with congressional subunits.

The Changing Administrative Branch (5). The chapters delineating the continuing and presidential governments found that a considerable number of specialized executives and other policymakers are not definitely within either the career service or the presidential force. They range from excepted appointees of the civil service to heads of some cabinet departments, but they hold positions mainly in the intermediate levels, such as assistant secretaries of the departments, top executives of bureaus or agencies, and members of boards or commissions.[25] The lower and upper boundaries are irregular and uncertain and may fluctuate from time to time, but there is a distinguishable group of middle-range policy-making officials with the common attributes of being separated from both the career service and the presidential establishment. These officials may lack a sense of common identity, but their opportunity to challenge both the continuing administrative branch and the presidential branch gives them in reality the quality of a separate force. Recognition of them as a coordinate branch might increase their sense of responsibility to the concerned publics. Short tenures make many of them unprepared to dominate their subordinates, who are mostly career administrators with both professional and political know-how in the inner workings of Washington. The plight of these political executives is described by Hugh Heclo:

> The number of political executives is small vis-à-vis the bureaucracy but large and fragmented in relation to any notion of a trim top-management structure. . . . Political executives

have no common culture for dealing with the problems of governing, and it is seldom that they are around long enough or trust one another enough to acquire one. . . . They must be able to move in two worlds—the tight, ingrown village life of the bureaucratic community and the open, disjointed world of political strangers. A public executive in Washington needs the social sensitivity of a villager and the political toughness of a city streetfighter. It is an increasingly unlikely combination. . . . Political appointees in Washington are substantially on their own and vulnerable to bureaucratic power.[26]

This last indicates that political executives in the departments and agencies, even though appointed by the President with party and subparty politics in mind, tend to separate from White House circles. Dr. Heclo does not assert an open chasm, but he suggests a lack of closeness and articulates the gradual process of "going native" in the bureaucracy. "Even the most presidentially minded executive will discover that his own agency provides the one relatively secure reference point amid all the other uncertainties of Washington."[27]

One of the most basic causes of such difficulties is the short tenure of such political executives—the average is less than three years.[28] Presidents and their supporters are not inclined to suggest fixed, longer terms for such officials. The request that the new head of the FBI serve ten years is an exception.[29] Presidential proposals, including those of President Carter, are directed rather at lessening the permanence of the top career administrators.[30] One means of achieving this goal is to make them assignable to other bureaus or agencies. This would seem to decrease their capacity to contribute without a compensating increase in the capacity of their superiors.

Triangular Patterns of Essential Interactions

We will now examine the checks and balances within the five-branch structure of the United States government by analyzing each of ten threefold sets of branches and their basic interrelationships.

Congressional (1), *Presidential* (2), *and Judicial* (3) *Branches.* These are the branches of the traditional ideology; the common concept of them tends to reduce them to their most visible personalities. "Though the President, congressmen, senators, Cabinet members, and Supreme Court justices often appear in the headlines, what they do rarely has a direct effect on people's everyday lives."[31] This observation by a pair of political-science specialists in the American politico-governmental system indicates the tendency of both public and press to overrate the few higher officials.[32]

Each of these branches now has the power to be rather selective in its choice of issues for consideration; each has considerable discretion to choose the pressures to which it will respond. In contrast, the administrative branches must deal with the broad scope of regular operations.[33]

The checks and balances within the three traditional branches are now not so much the interactions of legislative, executive, and judicial functions as the counteractions of three types of representation. Congress represents legally 50 states and 435 districts and politically the more vigorous of the general- and special-interest groups. The presidential branch represents legally the entire nation and politically the majority of the winning presidential party. The President may depend most upon certain factions, and the cabinet members tend to represent other elements of that spectrum. The Supreme Court represents socioeconomic segments and the spectrum of politico-moral ideals.

Congressional (1), *Presidential* (2), *and Continuing Administrative* (4) *Branches.* These three forces give rise to more persistent conflicts than any other trio of branches. The President, the senators, and the representatives are often rivals in elections and political antagonists in legislation. Together they are the officials most directly responsive and responsible to the active voters. In contrast the career civil servants are chosen by invisible professionals according to complex procedures and supposedly objective standards.

Various congressional committees or blocs and the presidential forces compete for control of the continuing administrative units. "Separation of powers makes the American bureaucracy serve two masters," one political science analyst of the American bureaucracy asserts;[34] and another explains: "The executive branch has not one but two managers—the President and his rival, Congress."[35] Still another analyst explains that competition between those two branches may defeat efforts to control the bureaus. He states that the administrators "play the president off against the Congress" and that in their frustration, "Congress and the President struggle against each other for the control of the bureaucracy—and therefore of policy; but bureaucracy escapes."[36] A fourth observer states that, because of the inability of presidential, congressional, and other forces to control the bureaucracy, alliances have to be worked out.[37]

There may be times when the presidency and the bureaucracy join forces against Capitol Hill, but at other times Congress and the administrators may join in association against the White House. Louis W. Koenig gives this picture of such essential interactions during the regime of President Nixon:

> In the Nixon era, characterized by running conflict between the President and Congress over domestic programs, the legislators, typically, championed the bureaus against the president's budget cuts and impoundments of funds, and the depredations of department secretaries, who, reflecting Nixon, interpreted program intent restrictively and even contrary to legislative mandates that often were drafted by the bureaus in the first place.[38]

Other political scientists point out the capacity of the career service to check and balance the elected officials. Peter Woll and Rochelle Jones set forth this conclusion:

> In order to perform properly within our political system, the bureaucracy must maintain at least as much independence as Congress and the President. As an agent of each, it must be able to check both. The separation of powers would be violated if it came under the domination of either. Moreover, the professional character of the administrative branch demands a degree of independence and continuity. Only at the very top levels should it be subject to partisan political influence. The President is a partisan figure, and so is his staff.[39]

Thus, presidential-administrative separation may have a basic constitutional function; that is, it may serve to provide a broad foundation for constitutional checks and balances. The continuing administrative branch seems to have a coordinate position similar to that of the other branches, with relationships of independence as well as dependence, in a total pattern of interdependence.

Congressional (1), *Presidential* (2), *and Changing Administrative* (5) *Branches.* These are the most patently partisan forces of the national government. The members of Congress and the President are, of course, elected by the active voters of their respective constituencies; and most of the members of Congress, as well as the President, have been nominees of one or the other of the two major parties. The fact that they represent different constituencies adds political force to the functional checks and balances specified in the Constitution. Congress and the presidency compete in several fields of shared power, including legislation, appropriation, communication, and supervision of the administrative bureaucracy. Both have developed their own staffs of specialists in several fields. For instance, both Congress and the White House have separate budget agencies. But the longer tenure of members of Congress gives them many advantages over the President and his political-executive appointees in establishing continuing sources of information and professional advice among career officials in the administrative units.[40]

The changing administrative branch consists largely of officials selected by the incumbent President, with much consideration given to their party affiliation and their identification with particular segments of the party.[41] Both the presidential and changing administrative branches are characterized by alternating partisanism, in contrast with the two-party structure of Congress and its official committees and subcommittees. The decline of major-party unity and the increase of constituency politics during recent years has resulted in even more political antagonisms among these three branches.[42]

Congressional (1), Judicial (3), and Continuing Administrative (4) Branches. These are, comparatively speaking, the continuous branches. They have substantially more permanence than do the presidential and changing administrative branches. The average tenure of a President has been six years, and since 1960 it has been four years. The political executives who comprise the changing administrative branch have an even shorter average tenure.[43] Representatives have a two-year term, but there is no limit upon re-election; and members of Congress in positions of power, notably the committee chairmen, frequently have ten, twelve, or more years of experience in Congress and even in specialized committee work. Most senators also have longer periods of service than do the Presidents.

The judges of courts established under Article III of the Constitution have lifetime appointments. Moreover, members of the Supreme Court, like those of the houses of Congress, change gradually, so that the institutions have substantial continuity in contrast with the almost complete change within the presidential and changing administrative branches when the White House shifts from one party to the other or even from one President to another.

The continuing administrative branch is composed largely of career appointees and, hence, has a high degree of permanence. Its replacements, too, tend to be gradual.

Yet these more continuous branches differ in their degree of permanence. Judges seem less likely to change position than do administrative officials, and both may have longer career records than does an average member of Congress. Recently, there has been a higher percentage of new and younger members in the Congress. The differences among these three branches in political and professional roots, as well as in functional specialties, make for a considerable interplay of checks and balances.

Congressional (1), *Judicial* (3), *and Changing Administrative* (5) *Branches.* The interactions among these three branches would seem to be mainly in the upper-middle range of policymaking. The congressional and judicial branches, which would appear to be at a high level when interacting with the presidential establishment, are at more middle levels when in confrontation with the administrative branches. Another probability is that their relationships with the changing administrative branch are a bit higher than those with the continuing administrative branch just discussed. The three executive-system branches have different elevations, and the changing administrative branch holds the middle position. This may affect its relationships with the congressional and judicial branches.

These three branches probably determine more of the policy for regulatory functions of the government than any other trio of branches, because many members of the regulatory boards and commissions are in the changing administrative branch. The extent to which these three branches determine official policies generally is difficult to assess, because the contributions of the political executives in the changing administrative branch vary considerably. Their potential is much greater than their actual contribution.

The interactions among the three branches arise from differences in objectives, standards, and constituencies. Congress is a mixed political bag; the judiciary is a more limited and consistent source of policy development; and the changing administrative branch has the potential to be more activist than the others and closer to the prevailing political plurality.

Congressional (1), *Continuing Administrative* (4), *and Changing Administrative* (5) *Branches.* These are the branches in which the whole is less than the sum of the parts. Each branch is a conglomeration of subunits more or less corresponding to general- or special-interest groups in the politico-economic society. There is a substantial parallel between the congressional subcommittee structure and the administrative organization.

We noted in the chapter on the dimensions of the continuing government that one of the more fundamental bases of continuity is the relationship between specialized administrators and corresponding subcommittees or informal blocs in the congressional branch and that this continuity is strengthened further by informal ties with interest-group spokesmen. There are hundreds of such iron triangles; they tend to characterize operations at the middle and lower-middle levels of policy-making.[44]

The political executives of the changing administrative branch may be less involved in these triangles than are the career officials of the other administrative branch. Yet we saw that this is due largely to the inexperience of the higher political executives, since they have short tenure and a high turnover. But we also saw that, as they become more familiar with the ways of Washington, they tend to work more closely with career bureaucrats and corresponding specialists in Congress and in the interest-group system.[45]

Checks and balances operate among these three branches too; because, among other reasons, one consists of elected officials, another of bureaucratically appointed officials, and the last of partisanly appointed officials.

Presidential (2), *Judicial* (3), *and Continuing Administrative* (4) *Branches.* These three branches probably have more distance between them than any other set. The presidential branch has the highest elevation in the minds of the public, and it operates much of the time in external roles: in either foreign diplomacy or domestic public relations.[46] The judicial branch is more independent and standoffish than any other branch. The continuing administrative branch is largely the career civil service and similar appointees under other merit systems. Most career officials prefer to be partisanly neutral, and they try to carry on their administrative politics with low visibility.

The interaction among these three branches is apt to be more formal and less competitive than are other interbranch relationships. The governmental activities of the presidential branch are more likely to involve the congressional and changing administrative branches than the judicial and continuing administrative branches.

The administrative bureaucracy often is said to be under joint or competitive control of the presidency and Congress,[47] but the judiciary may have the greatest impact and influence upon the continuing administrative branch.[48] The specialized administrative officials often initiate much of the new legislation,[49] and what they do not initiate, they may formulate or reformulate. Yet the most important interpretation of legislation is that of the courts, and a final judicial opinion is the most definite key to the meaning of relevant portions of the law. Likewise, many particular decisions and orders of career administrators are appealed to the courts, and decisions in such cases are determinative of the procedural as well as substantive rules of operation.

Presidential (2), Judicial (3), and Changing Administrative (5) Branches. Here we have three general types of presidential appointees. In each, party identification is usually a factor in the selection. The recognition of congressional party wishes differs. In selecting officials for executive-branch positions, a President generally gives only secondary consideration to Capitol Hill desires. Senatorial consent, where necessary, comes rather easily. But for judges, the practice is otherwise. Members of Congress virtually nominate many lower court judges, and the Senate scrutinizes closely presidential nominees for the Supreme Court.

Presidents usually have different political standards for White House assistants and for departmental chiefs. Personal loyalty is primary for the former, whereas capacity to represent different segments of the President's political party is often important for departmental executives in clientele areas such as the Interior, Commerce, Labor, Agriculture, HHS, HUD, and

Transportation. The relationship of the political executives in the changing administrative branch to the general- and special-interest groups is, as we have noted before, a matter in which there is a good deal of flexibility and not much uniformity.[50]

Most of the policy-making officials of these three branches are presidential appointees, but the impact of an incumbent President upon them differs considerably. The person in the Oval Office tends to dominate those in the presidential branch, but the executive officials in the changing administrative branch have several masters. Presidential influence upon the judiciary depends upon the number of appointments, and the effect of a particular selection is usually delayed and uncertain.

Presidential (2), Continuing Administrative (4), and Changing Administrative (5) Branches. These three branches constitute the officialdom of the formal executive branch. The *United States Government Manual* lists the executive institutions in three categories: the Executive Office of the President, the Executive Departments, and the Agencies (often called Independent Agencies). The classification in this book is less of institutions than of officials. The boundaries between the major groups are largely horizontal, and they cut across the institutions, including those of the Executive Office. Each major type of institution has career civil servants as well as noncareer political executives. The control and influence of the President differs considerably among the three groups. A President has most control over his White House staff and least over the lower category of career civil servants. Presidential control or influence over the middle group is apt to be either formal or occasional, as circumstances determine.

The political ideology of full presidential command and executive-branch unity may be contrary to developments with respect to the responsibility of subordinate officials for illegal or unjust actions. The War Crimes trials tended to reject the defense that the deed was ordered by a superior. The issue arose also in the impeachment hearings and court actions concerning Watergate events. Inferior officers were tried, found guilty, and punished. That seems contrary to the doctrine of monocratic administrative responsibility and full presidential control of a monolithic executive branch.[51]

This is related to the proposition that checks and balances extend to the interior operations of the executive branch and that inferior officials may provide some limitation or restraint upon their superiors, even a President.

The powers of administrative officials to check a President against possible excesses differ among the three executive branches. Directness of relationship helps, but lack of bargaining independence may weaken the position of those close assistants and advisers who do not have political bases of their own. On the other hand, the autonomy of the career or semicareer administrators is offset by remoteness of place or situation.

The basic differences in the position of the presidential group, the continuing administrators and the changing administrators, shows the value of the five-branch pattern for purposes of understanding governmental operations and of strengthening methods of public control. The idea of five branches is not a prescription but rather an identification of the most basic of the types of conflict and counterbalance within the government. The existence of constituency competition as well as shared functions among the executive structures is recognized by most political-science authors of general explanations for the university course in American national government.[52]

Recognition of the three executive/administrative branches also aids the comprehension of other developments, such as the increasing independence of the presidency during recent decades. The elevation and externalization of the presidency resulted not only from the enlargement of foreign-relations problems and responsibilities but also from the heavier emphasis by the several Presidents upon public and media relationships within the country. The more a President moves toward the people and the more frequent are his press conferences and grass-root visits, the more he moves away from less visible administrative activities.

Judicial (3), Continuing Administrative (4), and Changing Administrative (5) Branches. These branches are composed entirely of appointed officials, but very few of those with policy-making discretion are appointees of a President alone. The judges require Senate approval; the officials of the continuing administrative branch are appointed under procedures of the civil service or other merit system; and most of the political executives of the changing administrative branch are subject to approval by the Senate.

The difficulties encountered by the congressional and presidential branches in supervising the administrative subunits make checks and balances among these three appointed branches an important matter.

The check of the judicial branch upon the administrative officials is limited but strong. It is exercised mainly by published decisions, and costs of the judicial process tend to restrict it in volume or scope.

Where checks and balances have the greatest opportunity to exercise guidance and restraint is in the relationship of the two administrative branches to each other. We have seen that political executives in the changing administrative branch often are unable to maintain their positions of superiority in an effective manner because of their short tenure. The consequence is that career administrators, even though in lower-level positions, may determine much of the policy and method of the bureaus or offices nominally headed by noncareer presidential appointees. This situation is a frequent object of reform proposals, but the usual plan seems to reduce the strength of career executives more than to increase the power and position of noncareer political executives.[53] Public-interest groups seeking to counteract special-interest groups might find better allies if noncareer executives in the departments had more definite tenure and more continuing relationships.[54]

The Duty to Share Responsibility

The idea of five distinctive and coordinate branches—that is, three executive branches in addition to the congressional and judicial branches—is not a license for functional independence among the administrative units of the executive branch. Rather, it is a recognition of the institutional identity and the operational interaction of the major classes of executive officials. Like the congressional and judicial branches, the presidential, continuing administrative, and changing administrative branches have different roots and goals in the total operation of the politico-governmental system. Our analysis of the principles of constitutional distribution shows that independent institutions are a preliminary to dependent functions. The initial vesting clauses of the Constitution may suggest separate functions, but we saw that the keystone principle is functional interdependence. Either there is an inherent dependence among essential processes, or the Constitution prescribes mutual dependence.

The interrelationship of the two doctrines of separation and balance is recognized and perhaps suggested by the formula of separated institutions sharing powers advanced by Richard E. Neustadt. Political scientists increasingly accept the Neustadt concept of constitutional distribution. It is akin to emphasis placed by the Supreme Court upon interdependence with separateness and reciprocity with autonomy.[55] The Court pointed out that some functions, such as the presidential veto and the congressional override, are not shared. But they are technical or procedural actions. When powers or functions are conceived more broadly, such as the authority to legislate in a specified area, there is, in fact, widespread dispersion, with repeated Supreme Court approval of congressional delegation and administrative legislation.

The functional interrelationship of the governmental branches is evident also in the multiplicity of roles. None of the branches has a single, exclusive function. Each has several functions, such as the congressional processes of appropriation, investigation, communication, representation, surveillance of administration, and legislation. At the same time, each branch participates in a different way in the processes of making law and exerting influence over the application of the law.

The three executive/administrative branches, likewise, share in general functions of directing operations. Each participates in its own way in making policy, legislatively or adjudicatively, and in exercising managerial discretion. Their manner of participation differs because of a number of institutional and functional characteristics, such as those relating to source of power, method of appointment, condition of removal or replacement, degree of political and professional discretion, and distance from the immediate fortunes of the electoral process.

The recognition of the three executive/administrative branches also helps to explain the different degrees of presidential involvement in operational policies and operations. The President spends the most time with officials in the presidential executive contingent, the least with career civil servants, and an intermediate amount with fifth-branch political executives.

This is related to the division of executive actions between the presidential few and the subunit many. The latter are apt to involve iron-triangle support; that is, administrative policy decision may have the backing of concerned members of Congress and relevant interest groups. These numerous subgovern-ments, whether iron triangles or issue networks, often seem to work against the incumbent President; but that may be in large part because opposition to the White House draws more attention than does support.[56] A President is actively concerned with only a few areas of conflict, but in those situations the White House may be eager for interest-group approval. In fact, President Carter had a special assistant assigned to enlist the support of such organizations for White House projects.[57]

The growth of public- or general-interest groups may pro-vide a new and more effective way of counteracting the special-interest pressures and bringing the fifth branch of changing administrative officials into active and consistent response to the public interests. This is the means of direct relationship with the specific issues and the particularized administrators. For instance, in mid-1979, in the issue of the safety of DC-10 aircraft, the Airline Passenger Association obtained a court in-junction against the use of the planes when appeals to the White House and Congress had brought no such stern action.[58] This may be an example of the inadequacy of "overhead democ-racy"[59] in many situations and of the potentials of "lateral democracy" in those instances. Moreover, public-interest groups may help to restrain special-interest pressures. Both types of organizations approach the government laterally, but the former proceed at a higher and broader interest level and thus may bring a wider public interest to bear upon such controversies. Moreover, the direct inputs from general-interest groups to the less publicized executives of the fifth branch might stimulate a stronger and more integrated sense of responsibility to the gov-ernment and the public.

The Acceptability of the Five-Branch Pattern

The reactions of political scientists and Americans in general to the constitutional pattern of a five-branch government with three executive branches—presidential, continuing, and chang-ing—as well as the congressional and judicial branches, probably reflect practical more than legal considerations. Some people will continue to believe that there must be some way to bridge the gap between the presidency and the different levels of spe-cialized administrators. Executive unity is a comforting myth.

It makes the complex government seem neat and orderly, and it wraps all that is good and all that is bad into a single personality. Other persons may welcome the five-branch model because it gives overdue recognition, symbolic as well as empirical, to the persistent divisions within the executive arrangement. Presidential complaints of the autonomy of administrative units go back at least to Franklin Roosevelt's accounts of the intractability at the Navy Department. Then, too, there is Harry Truman's well-known comment on the disillusionment that Dwight Eisenhower would have if he were to bring his military sense of command to the White House. Political scientists have a long record of describing and explaining the disunity in the executive hierarchy. They seem eager to accept Neustadt's conclusion that presidential power is the power to persuade and not the power to command. There is also some acknowledgment of the next step. That is the presidential practice of surmounting the task of persuading men of political and professional standing by establishing a nonpolitical, personal White House staff with such a degree of loyalty that they do not need to be persuaded. There is perhaps a little recognition of the further factor that the demands of the press and the public for sovereign reaffirmation of our preferred ideals and interests has virtually forced recent Presidents into the business of being a national personality image. This tends to mean that the President need not be concerned with the regular course of administrative operations and can give the impression of strong leadership by means of dramatic reactions to headline crises and other selected issues.

The belief in full executive unity is kept alive by repeated suggestions of devices to aid the presidency in effectuating complete command. Most sweeping among these are the reorganizations, such as the departmentalization of independent agencies. The Department of Health, Education, and Welfare was established in 1953 to bring unity to these fields; but after a quarter of a century diversity remains. In fact, in 1979 education became a separate department. Other suggestions for achieving presidential command are different types of cabinets and cabinet memberships, such as more businessmen or more professors. The proposals include a supercabinet, a new style Vice-President, a chief administrator, and so on.

These are no more likely to succeed than the panacea of the past three decades, that is, the loading of the White House with special assistants and advisers. A President who tries to develop managerial consensus among his cabinet members, as candidates often say they will, would probably receive a low rating in the more wanted role of dramatic personality. A Vice-President can rarely assist a President administratively to any appreciable degree, because he too has a partisan orientation, a short term, and an image responsibility. Also, his political outlook may differ a bit from that of the President, and he is not subject to policy replacement as a cabinet member is. A special administrative Vice-President selected by the President would have many of the same deficiencies, such as short tenure and partisan point of view. Civil servants would respond with the same cold respect they give to a President.

This study has concerned the political-science propriety of a five-branch model for explaining the legitimate functional structure of the United States government. It is not a normative model but a descriptive one. The study explained that there are constitutional and empirical bases for an educational approach which recognizes the existence of continuing and changing administrative branches in counteraction with the congressional, presidential, and judicial branches.

The national government has changed much since 1789.[60] It is vastly larger, its organization is far more complex, and its aims and objectives are much broader and more positive than the constitution makers of the founding period could have imagined. The executive personnel are now mostly specialized, with both political and professional specialties increasingly involved in particularized legislative and adjudicative functions. The continuing or permanent force greatly outnumbers the presidential appointees, and many of the latter have trouble keeping in touch with the White House. The system of checks and balances among distinct branches, in order to provide in the present situation the safeguards envisioned at 1789, needs more than three counterbalancing forces. The evolving division of the vastly expanded executive branch into three branches, potentially checking and balancing each other as well as the legislative and judicial branches, is basically in harmony with both the realities of the present government and the traditional constitutional principles of coordinate branches engaged in counterbalanced action toward common objectives.

The five-branch guide to essential interactions recognizes the expanded use of constitutional authority, but the necessary complexity of the pattern may work against its public acceptance as an educational tool. Many persons prefer the three-power model, despite its inappropriateness in many situations, because of its transcendent symbolism and simplicity. Some Americans limit their concept of government even more; they focus upon the social philosophy enunciated by the headlined personalities. In fact, there is a wide tendency to assume that the President is the government. That premise is much reinforced by the practices of the mass media. There is a common tendency to disregard the operating arrangement of the specialized institutions and officials with the simple assertion that it is all a vast mass of bureaucratic red tape.

Acceptance of the idea of a five-branch system entails the thoughtful consideration of several lesser-known facts about the government. These include such facts as the crucial distinction between criminal-law and noncriminal-law processes, the constitutional principle of shared functions, the congressional authority over administrative structures and operations, the extent to which administrative officials engage in specialized legislation and adjudication, the scope of the presidential spoils system, the substantive difference between the career and noncareer bureaucracy, and the division of political executives between the White House and the departments. To be considered above all is the fact that government activity centers in the hundreds of informal, semiautonomous triangles or networks that are dominated by the interactions between particular members of the Congress, group representatives, and administrators with a common specialization.

One of the principal obstacles to acceptance of the concept of five-branch government may be the belief that it calls for constitutional changes in governmental arrangement. Actually, it is a descriptive summary of the underlying allocation of officials and functions. The pentagram-pentagon design is offered as an empirical aid in comprehending the existing system, and the only normative or prescriptive factor is the suggestion that if Americans wish to make the governmental administration fully responsive to the public interest, they will need to supplement their actions at the elections with much more participation in public-interest organizations. In short, it will be necessary to engage in lateral democracy as well as in overhead democracy.[61]

Recognition of the educational utility of the five-branch approach involves a considerable awareness of the idea of a system, and a complex system at that. We may find this difficult in the present state of our mass-media divertissements. We are more accustomed to simpler modes of thought: those we find in the moral drama, with its hero/villain dichotomy, and in the confrontation debate, with its assumption that choices are limited to polar alternatives. Public control of the administration is a many-sided affair: we need to think not of an ideal plan but of a combination of practices.[62]

One merit of the five-branch pattern is its relative complexity. Its educational value is less in its acceptance than in its use. It is a means of testing an empirical proposition: that there are as many as ten interbranch triads of checks and balances within the government. If we keep this in mind when we read, hear, and think about particular operations, we may learn not only the types of situations which do not conform to the three-separate-power model, but also the extent to which the five-branch pattern of essential interactions is most helpful to an understanding of the total constitutionality of our governmental system.

CHAPTER EIGHT

THE FIFTH BRANCH IN CIVIL SERVICE REFORM

THIS BOOK has explained the executive branch of the United States government not as a simple unity engaged in a single type of function under full control of the President but, rather, as a multiplicity of institutions and officials engaged in legislative and adjudicative, as well as executive, activities and involved in essential interactions with various official and unofficial forces. We depicted major separations within the executive branch by differentiating presidential, continuing administrative, and changing administrative branches. This conception of government is, of course, considerably more complex than the view held by most persons. Those observers or commentators who do recognize any division or conflict within the executive branch are likely to deem it a hero/villain dichotomy in which an activist President is pitted against a do-nothing bureaucracy.

These contrasting views of the executive branch are involved in the proposal and adoption of the Civil Service Reform Act of 1978 on the one hand and in its application on the other hand.[1] This law is a comprehensive measure which makes scores of changes in the civil service statutes. The campaign of the Carter administration for its public and congressional acceptance was developed around the common ideological belief that bureaucratic inertia frustrates the efforts of the Presidents and others who have good intentions.

The proposal of the President most publicized to end this governmental weakness was to give the heads of agencies more power to demote or dismiss the inefficient and to reward the few with exceptional performance records. That idea appealed to persons who had been frustrated or bewildered in their dealings with governmental bureaucrats. But how is it likely to fare in application if we consider the actual working structure and operation of the national government as we have analyzed it in the preceding chapters of this book?

The agency heads who are to discipline their career subordinates are largely in what we have called the *fifth* or *changing administrative* branch. They are the spoils-system appointees of the President and the department heads. Their average tenure is less than three years, and their inexperience often makes them dependent upon their career subordinates. Despite appointment by the incumbent President, many soon find themselves separate from and in conflict with the presidential establishment at the White House. Those who go native are likely to side with the career civil service, and those who do not are apt to be deemed come-and-go political opportunists. Will they make the civil service more efficient or more political? Or are they so lacking in relevant experience that they will not do either? The first question surfaced a bit in the debate on the legislation, but the second question appears to have been overlooked. We may see more definitely what was involved by inquiring into the character of the campaign of the Carter administration for enactment of the bill.

The crusade for acceptance of civil service reform entailed a number of tactical decisions. There seem to be four factors relevant to our analysis.

First is the usual tendency to claim that the proposed legislation would achieve much more than could reasonably be expected.[2] Such a promotional effort was needed to overcome the apathy and inertia of the public in general and the intensified opposition of those who felt improperly damaged in particular. Without such exaggeration, enactment would have been unlikely.

Second is the merchandising of the reform proposal. It was directed at the large number of persons who hold a hero/villain view of the presidency and bureaucracy, rather than at the small number who recognize the separations and fragmentations within the executive branch as the normal condition. Much use was made of the common belief that civil servants never do much work because they can never be fired. The President's statement transmitting the legislation to Congress acknowledged that most employees are dedicated workers, but the general tenor of the selling campaign drew upon the conviction that more bureaucrats should be dismissed or otherwise disciplined for inefficient and frustrating ways.

A third tactical decision seems to concern the identity of the agency heads who were to receive the increased authority over

career personnel. They are, as we have seen, appointees under
the presidential spoils system. Augmenting their power could
lead to charges that they would politicize the civil service, even
though most of them do not have the inclination and the capacity to do so. They are called *political executives*, and most are
replaceable by the incumbent President for policy reasons.
Maybe not many of them would wield a partisan whip over civil
servants, but a few might try. The proposed legislation and
the White House promotion efforts did not disclose their political connections and tended to leave the impression that the
relationship between agency heads and their career subordinates is similar to that which obtains in most private business
corporations.

This leads to the fourth tactic: to be prepared to meet any
charges that the increase of authority in agency heads would or
could result in politicalization of the civil service. The proposed
legislation included an extensive restatement of the principles
protecting employees against partisan pressures and other unfair or improper practices. The 1978 Act also established separate institutions to hear grievances of employees and to protect their rights. These developments may have the most lasting
effect.

The merchandising of the proposed legislation eventually
overpowered the pockets of opposition. Most members of Congress took the popular view. The mass media almost outdid
the White House in effusive endorsements. Editorially the press
heralded a new era of good management.[3] The opposition was
small but equally dramatized. One national news magazine
said editorially that the proposed legislation would enable any
future political dictator to take the whole organization captive.[4]

The purpose of this chapter is not to determine which of the
bipolar contentions is correct. Rather, the aim is to ascertain
how far both may be wrong, considering the inexperience and
short tenure of the agency heads. In this analysis and review,
we will look at the general character of the reform law, the
complexity of the executive operations, and the different meanings of politicalization; we will then examine the new Office of
Personnel Management and the new Senior Executive Service.
Finally, we will appraise the means of protecting the rights of
employees and of concerned public groups.

General Character of the 1978 Reform Act

The legislation proposed by President Carter and enacted by Congress in 1978 was "the single most comprehensive revision of the Federal personnel system since 1883,"[5] the year in which the civil service laws were first adopted. There have been many piecemeal changes since then.[6] The 1978 Act added to or replaced seventy-five sections of Title 5 of the *United States Code,* as well as revising many others. Prior to the 1978 law, the civil service portion of the *Code of Federal Regulations* covered about 460 pages; now, with the new legislation, it covers approximately 590 pages.[7]

The reform was both structural and substantive. The 1978 Act and a companion reorganization plan replaced the Civil Service Commission with a Merit Systems Protection Board and an Office of Personnel Management. The legislation had seven substantive subjects: (1) merit system principles for the protection of employees against improper practices by agency executives; (2) standards and methods for appraising performance; (3) staffing procedures (the Act sought to streamline hiring and firing methods and to limit veterans' eligibility preference); (4) establishment of a senior executive service in which top career administrators would be more responsive to political executives; (5) pay increases, particularly conditions for incentive awards, bonuses, and in-grade adjustments; (6) research programs and demonstration projects in personnel management; and (7) federal service labor-management relations. This last included an extensive codification of regulations with respect to union representation and the establishment of a Federal Labor Relations Authority to assure some degree of collective bargaining and a considerable measure of arbitration for aggrieved employees.[8]

There was more to the comprehensiveness of the President's reform legislation than the diverse, specific provisions. Its sheer inclusiveness added a moral and psychological dimension that made it a much more salable item; it also enhanced the captivating power of the title *Civil Service Reform.* For many citizens and some representatives, the more reform of the bureaucracy the better. Each house of Congress gave the law almost unanimous approval. The way in which it was designed and sold was an outstanding demonstration of the capacity of the Carter regime to merchandise new-hope packages.[9]

A key factor in the selling campaign was concentration upon a particular public anxiety, that is, upon the gnawing conviction that too many bureaucrats do too little and stay too long. President Carter, in his transmittal message, said many persons suspect "that there are too many government workers, that they are underworked, overpaid, and insulated from the consequences of incompetence." But he also pointed out that such criticisms are "unfair to dedicated Federal workers who are conscientiously trying to do their best." He concluded that the "only way to restore public confidence in the vast majority who work well is to deal effectively and firmly with the few who do not."[10] The stress laid upon firing bureaucrats is likely to be particularly satisfying to those persons who have been frustrated or mystified in their relationships with administrative operations.

The merchandising focus is evident in an examination of statements about the number of employees fired and the difficulties of the adversary proceedings for that purpose. In urging enactment the President stated, "Last year out of about 2 million (Federal civilian) employees only 226 people lost their jobs for inefficiency."[11] This is a very special statistic. It gives no indication of the total separations from government service or even of the number of persons discharged. We saw earlier that annual separations number about 600,000; that half are not resignations, deaths, or retirements but rather terminations, reductions-in-force, suspensions, and discharges.[12] The rate of turnover is higher among lower-grade employees and among more recent appointees; but the civil service is not a static force even at the higher grades, and a substantial number are forced out by direct or indirect means.

The Civil Service Commission issued a news release explaining the President's statement.[13] The release showed that during the year in which 226 persons were ousted for inefficiency, a total of 17,157 employees were dismissed. Many were in temporary or probationary status, but about 6,000 had acquired the right to legal appeal.[14] The figure of 226 combines three limiting conditions: (1) it relates to employees with appeal rights, (2) it pertains to dismissal after full use of adversary proceedings, and (3) it concerns only those cases in which the ground for dismissal was inefficiency in performance. There were 3,164 dismissals through adverse actions for some type of misconduct, and 418 by such procedures for "suitability reasons." In addition, 2,287 employees with appeal rights resigned after adverse action had been commenced or threatened. The commission classified these last as dismissals rather than resignations, and that would seem to conform to the substance of the matter.[15]

The commission's news release appears to defend emphasis upon the special statistic by contrasting discharges for "misconduct" with those for "unsatisfactory performance." But those familiar with dismissal proceedings, I believe, would consider an act of misconduct much easier to prove than inefficiency in performance where both grounds are available. The commission's release also suggests that appeal procedures are too burdensome, because dismissals among probationary and temporary employees are much larger than among those who had rights of appeal. The principal cause for that would seem to be that the latter are a select group: they have passed through the probationary or other temporary period, as well as having done well on competitive entrance tests. If the rate of dismissal were not much smaller among selected employees, there would appear to be need for reform in the hiring or testing processes even more than in the firing procedures.[16]

The public media seems not to have given much attention to the full picture of employee dismissals and other separations. Newspaper editorials used the 226 figure without explanation of its special character and without other indication of the total record.[17] We may assume that public information is inadequate and unbalanced.

The legislation may have general and specific merit despite the character of supporting presentations, but we may expect the consequences to be less than many of its advocates indicated. The President's stress upon inefficiency in performance as a ground for adverse action may lead agency heads to choose that particular path of dismissal even though other grounds, such as misconduct, are available and are easier and quicker to establish. An increase of number in the inefficiency-dismissal category during future years might suggest that the 1978 statute has been a success; but that statistic alone would hardly be a proper gauge by which to appraise its results.

The 1978 legislation eliminates some uses of the term *civil service* and makes new uses of the term *merit system* in its broader sense.[18] The statute sets forth *merit system principles* and applies them to employees under the civil service proper as well as under other plans.[19] The new law replaces the Civil Service Commission with two new institutions: the Merit Systems Protection Board and the Office of Personnel Management.[20] The first title recognizes the plurality of the merit systems.[21] These institutional changes do not mean termination of the civil service system. One of the express responsibilities of the director of the Office of Personnel Management is the execution and enforcement of the "civil service rules and regulations." Part I of Title 5 of the *United State Code,* which was formerly entitled "The United States Civil Service Commission," is now entitled "Civil Service Functions and Responsibilities."[22] Accordingly, the civil service system as developed since 1883 is continued despite changes in structures and procedures. The 1978 law adds or replaces at least seventy-five sections of the code, but in several instances the new section is similar in subject matter to the prior one. The new statements of standards place greater stress upon efficiency of performance, but changes of rhetoric do not always alter executive-employee relationships.

Many aspects of the 1978 Reform Act will depend upon the manner of application. The statute increases the authority of agency heads over career executives; but other political appointees, such as assistant department secretaries, are likely to be almost as important. It seems necessary to analyze and appraise the whole contingent of political executives and their relationships with career officials.

"The Executive Melange"[23]

The scope of difficulties which may affect application of the Civil Service Reform Act of 1978 is evident when we recall the complexity of governmental operations described in the preceding chapters. That explanation extended from mixed principles of constitutional distribution to essential interactions among the five major types of policy-making officials. The primary reforms are directed at the authority of officials in the changing administrative branch over those in the continuing administrative branch, but the latter are responsible and responsive also to the congressional and judicial branches, as well as to their superiors in the executive hierarchy. Moreover, the interbranch relationships concern the many specialized subunits even more than the branch as a single entity.

The primary source of this complexity is, of course, the Constitution itself.[24] Its essence is not the simplicity of three institutions with separate powers but the mixture of shared powers among conflicting forces. The broad congressional authority to enact laws necessary and proper for carrying into execution the powers of the government and any department or officer gives Capitol Hill initial and final control of the administrative operations.[25] Congress has established and maintains at least thirteen departments and fifty agencies.

The official classification of executive institutions is threefold: the Executive Office of the President, the Executive Departments, and the Agencies.[26] The first consists of six to sixteen agencies loosely connected. Most of the departments are conglomerates. The remaining agencies often are called independent for a number of reasons: they are outside any department, many are headed by bipartisan boards or commissions, some have quasi-judicial responsibilities, and a few have special relationships with Congress.

Congress has compounded the complexity of specialized agencies, bureaus, and departments by authorizing many administrative units both outside and inside the departments to engage in legislative and adjudicative functions in many particular areas.[27] The consequence is that many administrators feel obliged to serve Congress and the courts as well as the President. This accentuates the interactions among the several levels of executive policymakers and results in many types of checks and balances within the executive branch.[28] The increasing specialization among government programs makes for more and more fragmentation and for informal working relationships among official and unofficial forces with common interests. In many ways the government is actually a few hundred subgovernments.[29]

The manner of appointing officers is another source of complexity. The Constitution specifies three ways of appointing executive officials: (1) applies to superior officers and involves both the President and Senate, (2) and (3) apply to inferior officers and involve appointment by the President alone or by the department heads. Historical practice has developed a broad distinction between the appointment of noncareer or political executives and the appointment of career personnel. Congress has fortified and extended this categorization by establishing the civil-service and other merit systems. Congress has further classified the ranks of civilian personnel by different types of salary schedules. We have seen that there are eleven levels or grades of officials in the executive category. The five levels of the Federal Executive Schedule form an upper group of less than a thousand, the supergrades (GS 16, 17, and 18) of the merit services comprise a middle group of roughly 10,000, and the high regular grades (13, 14, and 15) hold a lower group of executives numbering about 75,000.[30]

The principal distinguishing quality of the three groups of executives is the amount of experience and continuing interest in their immediate positions. The upper group consists largely of noncareer officials who come and go with the presidential regime, if not more often. The middle class is mixed, but appreciably more hold career than noncareer positions. Most of the lower group of executives have career status, that is, legally protected tenure.[31]

The upper level consists mainly of political appointees in the top ranks of the departments and agencies in the executive branch. Their various decisions, as well as those of the White House, produce the presidential-party policies. A newly elected President endeavors to have persons of the same party in most of these positions as soon as feasible. But many such appointees lack experience in the executive branch; most are new to their particular situations. When the presidential party changes, there is an almost complete turnover within a comparatively short time. Most of the political officials in these top positions serve less than four years, and many leave within thirty months.[32] The short tenure and wholesale turnover when there is a change of presidential party give the upper class of executives the distinctive quality of alternating partisanism. As a result government differs from private business, where anything like a complete turnover every few years is a rarity.

The fact that most of these political executives are affiliated with the presidential party does not mean that they are a unified group. Their party roles may be more diversifying than unifying. Each party is a conglomeration, and a President is likely to represent less than the full spectrum. Many cabinet members are chosen to represent other segments of the party, like agriculture or labor. Such actions broaden political appeal but may weaken the administrative force. President Carter's mid-1979 cabinet shuffle, which had the net effect of replacing two Washington insiders with a Deep South ex-mayor and a Far West mayor, coincided with a determined effort to rebuild popular prestige by stressing outside viewpoints as contrasted with inside management relations. Several political science specialists have pointed out the disunity in presidential-departmental administration.[33]

We may depict the general pattern of this divisiveness in two ways. One is to consider the distance of the officials from the Oval Office. In this picture, there are roughly six areas: (1) the White House staff, (2) the other presidential-policy assistants in the Executive Office, (3) the cabinet members in the more general departments (State, Defense, Treasury, and Justice), (4) the cabinet members in the other departments, (5) the top officials of the single-headed independent management agencies, and (6) the members of the commissions and boards of the banking, regulatory, and other independent agencies. The other general way of marking the divisions within the presidentially appointed contingent reflects horizontal levels rather than vertical contours. For instance, the top rank of the departments includes the secretaries and the general deputy or undersecretaries; the next rank are specialized deputy secretaries and the substantive assistant secretaries; while the third tier includes the administrative assistant secretary and the several bureau or agency administrators within the department.[34]

These and other fragmentizing forces may cause the presidential-party policies in the departments and agencies to differ in varying ends and ways from those of the White House.

The Meanings of Politicalization

There is one statement in the Civil Service Reform Act of 1978 which logically could be an admission that politics is not all bad. The statute says that the Senior Executive Service should be administered so as to be free of, among other things, "improper political interference."[35] If the word *improper* is not superfluous, the law recognizes at least indirectly that there

can be "proper political interference." But probably there was
no such deliberate intention. In general, the designers of the
1978 legislation, as well as most of its advocates and opponents,
accepted the common public assumption that *politics* is a synonym for *bad* or *evil*. The official proponents called attention to
the various measures against *political* abuse but did not acknowledge the possibility that the *political* executives might use
their increased authority to convince career administrators to
accept the prevailing presidential-party policies.

The political-science discipline may be less disturbed by any
inadequacy in the 1978 law than by the more pervasive fact
that the word *political* has such a range of meaning that it
has no capacity to communicate definite ideas. For much of the
public, *politics* is simply a matter of self-interested party manip-
ulation. The political-science idea that politics is a process of
conflict resolution[36] hardly enters the public consciousness. Most
citizens do not recognize that, in addition to electoral politics,
there are types of operational politics, such as those concerned
with the budget, the proposal of legislation, the response to
investigations, and the course of administrative adjudication.
Thus, the public and the political-science profession react quite
differently to the assertion that the Reform Act of 1978 may
politicize the career administrators.

The political-science use of the term is itself not always consistent. Some analyses divide appointed executives between
political and *career* groups, even though those terms are not
categorical opposites. That division is often offset by broader
assertions that there is no sharp or complete distinction between
politics and administration.[37] Most political scientists assume
that the executive branch is a varying mixture of administration
and politics. One leading analyst says that the national executive branch is best described as "a political arena."[38] That, of
course, is not the popular idea or even the view of most of the
mass media. The more prevalent idea is that the executive
branch is an extension of the presidency and that, while the
President may be a politician in electoral matters, the executive branch, the President included, is not political in its handling of governmental operations.

There are many types of politics at work throughout the
executive branch, but they differ in kind and degree among
the eleven ranks or grades of executive officials. Presidential

appointees in the White House and in many cabinet positions are much concerned with electoral politics and continued voter support of the President. Other presidential party appointees without legally protected tenure are deeply concerned with specialized policies of the presidential party.

The middle level of executives is a more continuing force. About three-fourths have legally protected tenure, while others are excluded or excepted from merit-system limitations.[39] The lower group of executives is almost entirely in a type of career position. The middle and lower executives have little concern with party welfare, but they are involved in the policy- and decision-making politics of specialized operations.[40]

There is a range of meanings for *politicalization* that we may illustrate by identifying, in particular, three types of politics relating to the operation of the executive branch.

The first type concerns the official or overt *spoils system.* This embraces positions the winning presidential party may award to persons who assisted it in the nomination and election of the President and who may help it in its governmental endeavors and in winning future elections. This spoils system includes appointments to judgeships and other positions in the judicial system, and these may help the majority congressional and presidential parties; but we are concerned here with appointments to the executive branch. These last include about 550 positions filled by the President with consent of the Senate in the top ranks of the departments and agencies. They embrace also about 2,500 positions in eight or ten pay levels or grades, starting with Level IV of the Federal Executive Schedule and extending down through several grades of the General Schedule.[41] The positions at civil service grades are excluded or excepted from certain competitive selection procedures, and they do not have legally protected tenure. They are replaceable for political or policy reasons. Their freedom to take part in political activity is limited to some extent. The Civil Service Reform Act of 1978 appears not to have increased the number of positions within this overt spoils system, and it set forth one limitation that had been only an informal practice.[42]

There is also an unofficial or covert spoils system. This results from the manner in which political executives use the discretion permitted by the civil-service or other merit-system regulations in the selection of employees. For instance, an agency head can choose from the three highest applicants on a civil service register for a particular position. An executive might take political factors into consideration in making that decision. There are also possibilities of burying preferences or biases in job descriptions for the more specialized kinds of positions.

The chances of rewarding or favoring party loyalists are, of course, limited by the rules of proper practice, such as the merit system principles in the 1978 Act and by the institutions for enforcement, such as the Merit Systems Protection Board. But the difficulties of using such procedures and the reluctance of many employees to engage in such litigation mean that there will not be complete restraint or detection of such improprieties.

Some covert politics has always been a danger in governmental management. Will the 1978 Reform Act increase that danger? It enlarges the authority of agency heads and streamlines the discharge and demotion procedures. Inevitably there will be more opportunity for abuse. One stated objective of the 1978 law is to make control of the career administrators more flexible,[43] and that necessarily widens the area of discretion. That phenomenon may not be entirely offset by increased use of protective principles and institutions. It is, in other words, an element of bad that goes with the good. This is not an argument for denying the enhanced authority but rather an explanation of why we need to have public-interest pressures directly in relation to the specialized executives. We cannot leave all of the vigilance to Congress. In short, the constitutional principle of checking power with power is deeply relevant to the relationships of concerned publics and appointed officials. Wider and stronger use of general-interest pressure groups seems to be a constitutional necessity.

The third general type of politicalization does not so much concern the giving of positions to party workers as the imposition of party policy upon continuing (or career) executives. This involves the relationship between the President's Senate-confirmed political appointees and the middle level of executives. These last are at least three-fourths merit-system officials.

The relationships between the higher come-and-go political executives and the supergrade civil servants in the middle level of policy executives are inherently difficult. The one group is superior in legal authority but lacks relevant experience, while the other group has much relevant experience but is inferior in rank. A typical observation calls attention to "the feeling on the part of every new Administration that the career bureaucracy is not responsive to or sympathetic with the policies and goals that were articulated during the presidential campaign."[44]

The gap between the White House and the continuing administrative force is often blamed upon the inertia of civil servants and upon the idea that career officials are uncooperative or unproductive or both. A more fundamental reason, however, may be the complexity of the American political and governmental system. We need to keep in mind that there is no single continuing set of approved policies. There are at best four sets of party policies, that is, those of the majority and minority congressional parties and those of the majority and minority presidential parties.[45]

The policies and goals of the majority congressional party are at least as much approved by the electorate as those of the majority presidential party. They are often not the same, even when Democrats (or Republicans) are at the top of both branches. There has been activist unity between the White House and Capitol Hill during only about five years in the last fifty.[46]

Merit system officials properly should respect the policies of the majority congressional party as much as those of the majority presidential party. The Constitution gives Congress power over executive authority. Many political scientists have pointed out that Congress, as well as the President, is constitutional master of the administrative structures and operations.[47]

Should career policymakers give proportionate weight to the policies of the minority congressional party and the minority presidential party? Usually the minority party receives from 40 to 49 percent of the two-party vote. That is a substantial portion of the public. The tenets of constitutional democracy in the United States do not support absolute majoritarianism; rather, they demand reasonable respect for minority opinions. The second party in the houses of Congress enters officially and importantly into the legislative process. The minority presidential party has little or no official place in the government, but logically neutral career officials should give the policies of the defeated party at least 40 percent weight and those of the White House no more than 60 percent weight.

Most of the departmental and agency heads whose carrot-

and-stick authority is increased by the 1978 legislation are spokesmen for only one of the four policy parties which make up the representational pattern of our governmental system. That suggests the need for increased amounts of counteracting vigilance by congressional committees and public-interest associations.

Political Aspects of the New Personnel Management

The 1978 Civil Service Reform Act divided the functions of the Civil Service Commission and gave them to new institutions. The director of the Office of Personnel Management now has the executive and legislative functions, and the Merit Systems Protection Board has the adjudicative responsibilities. The new protection board, like the old Civil Service Commission, has three members, no more than two of whom may be adherents of the same political party. Each member has a seven-year term and may not be reappointed. A member may be removed only upon notice and hearing and only for misconduct, inefficiency, neglect of duty, or malfeasance in office. Hence, the board has the structure of a quasi-judicial independent commission. In contrast, the new Office of Personal Management, like the General Services Administration, is an institution with a single head even though it, likewise, is an "independent establishment." The director and deputy director of the office are each appointed by the President with the consent of the Senate. Neither has a fixed term, and each is removable or replaceable for policy or nonlegal cause.[48] Each position is political in the manner of the head of a department or independent agency.

Most political-science analysts believe that a single administrator might be more amenable than a three-man commission to political-party or presidential pressure, but they equally believe that a single head is more likely than a plurality of executives to be innovative and activist.[49] The preference for a single executive goes back to the Constitutional Convention of 1787, when delegates decided early against a threefold presidency. A few political analysts have suggested a cabinet government in lieu of a single presidency,[50] but this has been largely a temporary reaction to intervals of overreaching or imperialism.[51] Most political scientists support a strong presidency. Even the Watergate affair did not alter the general views of social analysts.[52]

When an executive institution is headed by a single political appointee there is some opportunity for covert use of a spoils system. Such danger is apt to exist throughout the executive branch. This is a situation where the good of activism or efficiency may outweigh the bad of limited political abuse. Again, we see the need for general-interest groups as well as congressional units to exercise the specialized critical review which political analysts often call "legislative oversight."

Critics of the new Office of Personnel Management assert that there is too much possibility of politicalization of the continuing civil servants. The charges relate to legislative authority of the new office more than to executive responsibilities. An amendment was introduced in the Senate to leave the legislative functions with the Civil Service Commission, but it was not adopted. The Merit Systems Protection Board was authorized to review the rules and regulations adopted by the Office of Personnel Management. These changes caused a reversal of position by a leading critic, Bernard Rosen, a former executive director of the Civil Service Commission. After the revisions, he said he was satisfied with the new structural arrangement.[53] This need not mean an absence of danger. Wherever there is discretionary authority, abuse is possible. Vigilance by congressional subcommittees and by public-interest associations is a continuing requirement.

The final law changed the presidential proposal in a number of ways that to some extent lessened the discretion of both the Office of Personnel Management and the agency heads in hiring and firing. Some of the original proposals indicate an intent to strengthen presidential party appointees in the high levels, but the most controversial provision involved a mixed political posture. This was the recommendation of a substantial reduction in the statutory preference for veterans in the selection of civil service appointees. Veterans opposed the presidential proposal and found strong support in Congress. Feminists and other minorities backed the White House position, but the final action of Congress was a victory for the veterans.[54]

The President also sought to increase management discretion in the selection process. The long-established rule is that an agency head, in filling a position under the civil service competitive examination procedures, may select from among the three highest rated applicants. The presidential reform pro-

posal sought to widen the choice to the highest seven. This
would have allowed more opportunity to choose a party favorite
as well as to avoid a veteran. Congressional committees dis-
approved, however, and the rule of three remains.[55]

Other presidential proposals would have increased managerial discretion in the procedures for discharging and suspend-
ing an employee. In some instances this shifted the burden of
proof from the government to the employee; in others, it shifted
the employee right to a hearing from a pre-termination period
to a post-termination period. In general, Congress reduced the
extent of such changes. However, the net effect is that the final
legislation increased the discretionary authority of the agency
heads, so that the need for vigilance by Congress and by special-
and general-interest groups is increased.

The more analytical and, perhaps, scientific approach to the
issue of politicalization in the new arrangement for personnel
management would seem to be, not *whether* there will be political aspects in its operation, but rather *how much* there will
be and *how* improper political action can be kept to a pragmatic
minimum. First, we may consider how much difference there
is between a single executive and a triumvirate with bipartisan
membership. The idea of two-party representation may be attractive, but the two major parties are loose organizations.
Each covers a large part of the political spectrum. There may
be little difference between some Democrats and some Republicans. Moreover, a President of one party selects the ad-
herent of the other party. If the Republican party chose the
Republican member to be appointed by a Democratic President, the bipartisanism might be more meaningful. But, with
the present method of appointment, a three-member board may
be little less political than a one-person directorship. The principal advantage of a triumvirate may be in its continuity. That
concerns its general efficiency more than its political attitude.
If the single head is changed every three years, which seems
to be the average for presidentially appointed bureau chiefs,
we may expect that most of the administrative policymaking
will be done by subordinates with continuing tenure. In other
words, we are confronted again with difficulties which arise
from the inexperience and short tenure of political executives.

The most interesting fact about the new Office of Personnel
Management is that it is an independent establishment and is

not in the Executive Office of the President. Hugh Heclo proposed in 1977 that there be such an agency in the Executive Office; and his comments on the 1978 legislation indicate that a President would have difficulty influencing a personnel management unit with the status of an independent agency.[56] In general, the new office would seem to present an old set of problems, that is, the inadequacy of the presidential and congressional channels of public control and the need for more direct pressure by concerned citizens upon specialized administrators through general-interest organizations.

The division of the civil-service administration between executive and adjudicative functions has a wider significance. It is a partial application of the separate-power doctrine. It is not complete for want of a separate assignment of legislative functions. The 1978 law places that responsibility primarily in the Office of Personnel Management and gives the Merit Systems Protection Board review authority. That is not meeting the full separation theory. We would not accept the elimination of Congress on the proposition that the judiciary could review the legislative actions of the executive. Why did Congress accept the limited allocation? Perhaps they viewed the legislation in general and not in specific terms; also, members of Congress often seem more interested in administrative adjudication than in administrative legislation. The former is more likely to involve their particular constituents and supporting groups.

The Federal Trade Commission and several other agencies have mixed powers and plural managements. Should their functions be separated and the executive functions transferred to a new office with a single head? There might be benefits from such a change. Most of the regulatory agencies tend to be too unresponsive to presidential and public anxieties.[57] A single presidential appointee in charge of their executive responsibilities might be an improvement.

The Political Aspects of the Senior Executive Service

The foremost target of politicalization in the 1978 Reform Act has been the plan which gives presidential appointees in the upper level of departmental and agency executives carrot-and-stick authority over career administrators in the middle group of executives. The law makes some of the compensation of

members of the new Senior Executive Service depend upon
bonus-award decisions of superior political executives.[58] The
express statutory goal is more efficient performance, but many
political executives will see the possibilities of making career
officials more responsive to departmental and agency policies
of the prevailing presidential party and less sympathetic to
policies of the congressional parties and other public groups.
The plan will inevitably result in more politicalization of some
kind.

The Senior Executive Service is legally a volunteer force. Eligibility is limited by pay rank and type of position. It is not open
to presidential-senatorial appointees, but it is open to those in
Levels IV and V of the Federal Executive Schedule who are
appointed by department and agency heads. Most of those
positions do not have protected tenure. The service is open
to the much larger numbers of supergrade positions under the
General Schedule or its equivalent.[59] Most of the supergrades
have legally protected tenure, but about a half of Grade-18, a
third of Grade-17, and a sixth of Grade-16 positions are political,
excepted, or noncareer appointments.[60] Senior Executive Service positions must also be executive in character, but that
requirement is defined broadly.[61] There may be 10,000 persons
who meet these general tests, but the law excludes members
of the Foreign Service and the intelligence organizations.[62]
These exclusions reduce the number of eligibles by about 1,000.

There are both career and noncareer appointments to the
new service. Also, there may be emergency appointments (maximum of eighteen months) and limited-term appointments
(maximum of one three-year term). No more than 10 percent
may be noncareer appointments.[63] At least a third of the positions will be reserved for career appointments.[64] This may induce
career civil servants to enter the plan. The White House probably will expect department and agency heads to place positions of the proper level and type in the executive service
category.

The eligible career officials are apt to vary in their attitudes
toward the less protected positions. Cautious persons prefer
familiar settings and may not wish their working conditions to
depend upon the wide discretion of political superiors. They
might be less hesitant about career-reserved offices, particularly
if they have been occupying the posts and if they feel assured

of receiving the bonus every second year. (Only half of the senior executives in an agency can have the bonus during one year.) In contrast, other persons might be willing to risk non-career positions if they see an opportunity for a higher grade and larger salary. Some government employees seem to make a career of noncareer jobs.

Career officials also may differ in their willingness to be associated closely with a partisan contingent. That might put them at a disadvantage when the next partisan group takes over. In some instances, civil servants may have private preference for one party or the other. Early reports indicate that more than 95 percent of the nearly 9,000 eligible executives chose the new service and that it began with a total membership of approximately 8,500 senior executives.

The most crucial relationships are apt to be those between the lowest political executives and the highest career administrators. The degree of coordination may depend upon the extent of common specialties and tends to vary with place and time. The status of the presidential regime may also enter the picture. When a President is in the learning period, the political and career executives also may be seeking a working accommodation. If newly appointed managers are too demanding, the senior career officials, whether in the Senior Executive Service or not, may cause political superiors to alter the mode of operation. Likewise, when a presidential regime is in the lame-duck condition of its last two years, career officials may withdraw from the Senior Executive Service, so as to avoid taint by association with the old regime when the new administration comes in.

Will the Senior Executive Service become a junior political force and a willing servant to the prevailing presidential regime? This problem may be self-resolving, but not in a simple way. In many areas experienced officials are highly important and lower-level political executives may "go native"—that is, they may defer in large measure to the continuing administrators. In other situations, executive decisions may be more policy- and politics-oriented. There the subordinate executives may be willing to work closely with the presidential and departmental party appointees. Thus, the new service may tend to divide between career and political segments in much the same manner as supergrade officials divided under the previous arrangements.

The idea of a pool of transferable executives reflects an emphasis upon generalists without permanence in place in contrast with specialists with permanence in place as well as tenure. This last has characterized the American civil service,[65] but it may be somewhat in decline.[66] Part of the current preference for generalists may be an admiration of the administrative class of the British civil service. That began as an elite group recruited from the cream of Oxford and Cambridge and trained for careers at the top of the continuing officialdom.[67] It has now lost some of its uniqueness because of recruitment from general civil service and the need for high-level specialists in the new complexity of government. Yet the British system still differs substantially from the American civil service. In large part, this derives from the dissimilarity between the two systems of governmental party leadership.

The major British parties are more unified and constant than are their American counterparts. Then, too, British party leadership is the same for the executive and legislative realms under the parliamentary-cabinet form of government.[68] There is also much more continuity in the leaderships. The minority party has a "shadow cabinet" of parliamentary leaders who will become the nucleus of the executive cabinet when the party gains power. With both party leaderships constantly in visible competition, career administrators find it easier to be neutral. The party in power is also more willing to accept their neutrality.

The British equivalent of the American political executive group rarely goes below the level of our deputy secretaries. The total force is about 100, in contrast with 550 or more in the United States. As a consequence, the British civil service extends to a definitely higher level than does the American system.[69] Moreover, British legislative committees are less specialized than ours,[70] so there is less need for specialists in the top ranks of the civil service.

If we wished to have a senior executive service comparable to the British administrative class, we would probably need to adopt some of the conditions that account for the top-level generalists in Britain. These might include the English type of party leadership and the continuity of cabinet membership from minority to majority power. Most of all, it would seem to require that about two-thirds of our presidential-senatorial appointments in the executive branch be converted to career or semicareer status.

The 1978 Act also seeks to make some of the compensation of the lower-level executives more dependent upon acceptable performance.[71] This concerns about 72,000 managers and supervisors in Grades 13, 14, and 15 of the civil service or their equivalent.[72] The law provides for a merit pay system, but that applies not to grade promotions but to within-grade step increases. Previously the law made these raises dependent upon two conditions: one was the passage of time (varying from one to two-and-a-half years), and the other was a determination by the agency head that the employee "is of an acceptable level of competence."[73] In practice the within-grade increases became virtually automatic. The 1978 Act tries to change this by specifying a more elaborate standard with stress upon acceptable performance. Will a change in statutory language bring about a change in managerial attitude toward legal standards? There would seem to be need for something else that would change the response of management to statutory conditions. The results may tell us something about the relative force of statutory language and managerial realities.

Protection of Employee Rights

The second primary objective in President Carter's message transmitting the 1978 Civil Service Reform bill is to "ensure that employees and the public are protected against political abuse of the system." The President explains that the protection process for employees is costly and time-consuming and that a "speedier and fairer disciplinary system" will create a better climate for managers and workers as well as bring about a more rapid hearing.[74]

The Reform Act and the related reorganization do three things in general with respect to employee protection. First, the new law sets forth merit system principles as a basis for identifying prohibited personnel practices. This is partly a restatement of various principles previously enunciated, but its comprehensiveness is welcome. It covers several areas prone to discrimination, favoritism, and inequality. Relevant to this analysis, it prohibits "arbitrary action, personnel favoritism, or coercion for partisan political purposes."[75] The statutory codification of these principles provides advocates of the new law with a quick answer to charges of politicalization. But actual effectiveness will depend upon how the principles are invoked by the employees and applied by the protective institutions.

The second major change is the establishment of the Merit Systems Protection Board to undertake the quasi-judicial functions formerly exercised by the Civil Service Commission. The concentration of adjudicative responsibilities may offset the stronger arrangement for executive-legislative functions in the Office of Personnel Management. The protective force of the new board will rest considerably with the special counsel. The counsel has a five-year term and is removable only for legal cause.[76] The position seems a bit less political than that of a district attorney.

The 1978 law seeks to protect a "whistle blower" by authorizing the special counsel to take such steps as the stay of a personnel action which would have "a substantial and adverse economic impact on the employee." Originally this part of the reform bill applied only to disclosures of "information concerning a violation of any law, rule, or regulation"; but Congress broadened the applicable grounds to include "mismanagement, a gross waste of funds, an abuse of authority, or a substantial and specific danger to public health or safety."[77] This may be wide enough to permit a threatened employee to counter the superior with charges of impropriety. Conflicts between upper-level officials often involve differences of management policy and the possibility that a threat of adverse action may turn into a whistle-blower case could cause the superior official to hesitate. Congressional amendments to the law also require that the agency's report on an informant's allegations be sent to Congress. The prospect of a Capitol Hill investigation also might lead a manager to resort to less coercive measures. Many times the practical probabilities are more determinative than the legal possibilities.

The third major change for the protection of employee rights is part of the comprehensive codification of labor-management regulations. Title VII of the 1978 Act sets forth the basic principles of Federal Service Labor-Management Relations, including the rights and duties of labor organizations.[78] Previously these principles were stated only in executive orders or administrative regulations. Employee unions may benefit from this more permanent enunciation.

Unions composed of national government employees do not have many of the collective bargaining rights of the major industrial unions. The rights retained by agency managements are broader than those reserved by private employers. But, from the viewpoint of individual employee rights against abuse, the statute permits an employee grievance procedure. This may involve compulsory arbitration and could be one of the most important aspects of the 1978 law.

The Reform Act and the companion reorganization provide for a Federal Labor Relations Authority. This is an independent establishment within the executive branch. It is composed of three members, no more than two of whom may belong to the same political party. It took over functions previously handled by a unit in the Department of Labor and is comparable in its field to the National Labor Relations Board. The 1978 law may be the Wagner Act for the government employee unions. The new authority is like the Merit Systems Protection Board in being a quasi-judicial agency. The statute also authorizes a general counsel to serve as an investigating and prosecuting attorney for the authority.

The growth of employee unions during recent decades may be the most important development with respect to the administrative bureaucracy of the national government. The benefits are not measured merely by the number of members; because a union, with exclusive right to represent, may aid nonmember employees in the affected units. The percentage of government employees covered by union representation authority varies. During 1976 the percentage was 83 in the trades and labor fields and 51 under the general schedule.[79] Union protection may gradually make career status less important to government employees, but it may increase the difficulties of political executives in their management efforts.

The Protection of Public Interests

The 1978 Civil Service Reform Act focuses upon the operational relationships of superiors and inferiors. To political executives in the upper levels of departmental management it gives more discretion to reward and discipline subordinates; to employees it gives more definite procedures against political abuse of managerial power. The President's transmittal message mentions protection of the public from political abuse of the civil service system, but that is about the limit of direct reference to the public interests. There is a specific objective of providing incentives and opportunities for managers "in order to improve the efficiency and responsiveness of the Federal Government."[80] That may indicate a newborn hope that career officials will be more in line with presidential party policies. But there is much more to relationships of the continuing administrative officials and the public welfare of the national citizenry. The relevant factors include political divisiveness of the executive branch, diverse types of politics in administrative relationships, the extent to which institutions and functions are fragmented, practical limits on presidential and congressional control, the scope and force of lateral pressures upon specialized policy actions, and the inadequacy of citizen participation in the representational opportunities of public-interest associations.

The bill may have been designed for the popular belief that the executive branch is a monolithic pyramid with the President at the top in full control through his appointees in the upper levels of the departments and agencies. That, of course, is a simplified myth.[81] The executive branch is not only a political arena, it is a plurality of battlefields. There are two major gaps in the control hierarchy: one is between the political appointees at the White House and those in the departments; the other is between the political and the career officials. The Presidents contribute to these separations by their concentration upon external relations, notably upon international diplomacy and electoral politics. Presidential prestige rests much more upon the roles of chief of security, legislative innovator, and national citizen than upon that of chief administrator. Also, the White House staff is more important than the cabinet in the maintenance of the public standing of the President.[82]

The cabinet in its turn is often much more a set of party segments than an administrative unit. The majority of cabinet members are selected less for their previous loyalty to the President than for their ability to be policy specialists in an area of political debate. Many are chosen less for their managerial experience and capacity than for their potential contribution to the public image of the presidential party. Moreover, in presiding over their respective departments, they need to serve other masters in addition to the President. These include four or more congressional committees, the relevant citizenry, and the continuing personnel of their units.[83]

The operation of a department is a complex mixture of administration and politics. We have seen that there are eleven pay ranks of executives. In each level or grade, there is some kind of functional politics. At the top ranks this is most likely to be presidential-party politics, while at the lower levels the primary concern tends to be operational politics. Operational politics involve such matters as budget appropriations, legislative revisions, constituency pressures, and congressional investigations.[84]

President Carter's proposal of increased authority in agency heads may have grown out of his early preference for cabinet government and the idea that a line of command emanates from the White House, to the department heads, to the next levels, and then to the career-executive levels. But there is much evidence that gaps persist in the political-executive contingent of presidential appointees. All Presidents for the past two decades have experienced division between their White House staffs and the departmental contingents. Such a schism began to surface within a half year after Jimmy Carter entered the Oval Office.[85] Another persistent gap occurs within the departmental and agency hierarchies. It is not always at the same level. Only half of the highest civil service grade (18) are career officials. Those who are not may be closer to their political superiors than to their career subordinates. In other situations the lower level of presidential appointees may go native and work more closely with top career officials than with their political superiors.[86] We noted above that the new Senior Executive Service may divide informally between the career-minded and the political-minded, and that such a division would vary from time to time and place to place.

Will the increase in authority granted in 1978 to political executives make the administrative bureaucracy more responsive to the public interest? It may be a bit ironic to expect party appointees to protect the common good. It may be even more curious to expect inexperienced superiors to dominate experienced subordinates. Is giving more control power to the partisan officials like putting foxes to guard the chickens? Perhaps in some instances, but more often the appropriate analogy is that of assigning foxes to guard the hounds. Moreover, many of the foxes are new to the game, whereas most of the hounds have been at it for several years.

The managerial difficulties encountered by Presidents and their cabinets arise not merely from the conflicts between political appointees and career officials. Even more, the troubles derive from the vast extent of operational specialization within the national economy as well as within the government.[87] The social and political fragmentation are institutionalized in at least three systems: (1) the special-interest groups protected by the First Amendment, (2) the congressional system of committees and subcommittees, and (3) the semiautonomy of the specialized administrative subunits.

The three types of institutions for a particular specialty often form an unofficial unit of decisionmaking. At its simplest, it may be an understanding among a member of Congress, a group spokesman, and an administrator. There are hundreds of such triads. Political scientists call them "iron triangles" because of their impregnability against pressures from above. The ad hoc triangle has become a symbol of particularized and often invisible government. But it may not be the only form of fragmented policymaking. Hugh Heclo asserts that the basic unit is more aptly an "issue network" composed of a larger number of policy specialists in a less rigid arrangement.[88] He points out that executives are becoming more concerned with policy issues as more implementation is assigned to private contractors. Yet such networks by their very nature may augment still more the difficulties of presidential-cabinet supervision.

Congressional fragmentation, which enhances administrative particularism, has been increasing in recent years because of the weaknesses of the parties, the larger number of subcommittees, and the tendency of elected representatives to keep closer to their constituencies than to the general legislative process.[89]

The multiplicity of complex issues facing the country may be the principal reason that continuing specialized officials rather than the President and the Congress make most of the less publicized policy decisions. A President has his choice of the whole vast executive panorama, but he can act effectively on only a few selected matters.[90] Actually, a President who wishes to decide a particular issue himself must take time and effort to master the specialized details. Decisions based upon staff-prepared summaries which present action alternatives are likely to be image projects more than fundamental determinations. President Carter repeatedly reduced his field of concentration, as, for example, in his shift of design in July 1979. Throughout, he devoted much attention to a few matters, most notably the Panama Canal Treaty, Near East diplomacy, energy, SALT, Iran, and Afghanistan. These were important, of course, but so were many other less dramatized matters.[91]

Congress can cover many more fragments than the President, because it has 535 elected members and more than two hundred subcommittees. We may lose sight of this fact because the President is a much publicized personality, whereas to most persons Congress is either a mystifying abstraction or a few uncooperative figures with rather poor public images. The press and other mass media also focus upon the tip of the policy-making iceberg. Only the concerned groups may be aware of the vast invisible government. They find, sooner or later, that the electoral system provides a disturbingly limited channel of communication and control. Increasingly they are learning that they must supplement action at the polls with participation in those general-interest associations which exert direct influence upon specialized fragments of executive operations.

Many persons are apt to say that civil service officials should serve the public interest and not the views of a political party or an interest group. That has a certain appeal. But how should officials determine what public interest is in a particular situation? Does the electoral process give the answer? The White House and Capitol Hill may not agree. Does the congressional election with its 535 voter decisions provide a more accurate composite of the public interest than does the single electoral action which determines the identity of the President?

Should merit-system administrators look beyond the political parties and their office-holding spokesmen in the determination of what is best for the country? Are there nonpolitical expressions? Should officials adopt the results of polls on public issues? That might allow control of the government to pass to those persons who feed data into a computer. The idea of public interest has a captivating appeal which often stops further thought, but any attempt to find what it means in a specific circumstance is likely to put us back into the political arena of counteracting forces.

What *is* clear is the inadequacy of the existing system of control. The process of electing representatives, including the President, furnishes only a partial means for public guidance of administrative operations. General public opinion is as limited as the mass-media drama. If the pressures of the special-interest groups are to be offset, there will need to be a greater increase in general-interest associations. In fact, the democratic duty of individual citizens now includes participation in applying direct public pressures on specialized administrators as well as in voting at public elections.

APPENDIX

THE CHARACTER OF CONSTITUTIONAL DISTRIBUTION

THESE ARE EXCERPTS from political science texts for the basic university course in American national government. The excerpts provide a cross section of views of political scientists concerning the essential character of the constitutional patterns for the allocation of functions among governmental institutions, with particular attention to indications that those principles are flexible in application and that they have the capacity to embrace a distribution model of more than three branches.

1. "The Founding Fathers wanted to establish a government that would guarantee freedom by making sure no one could exercise unchecked power. They banked on the selfishness of each set of political officeholders to offset that of others, rather than on the good intentions of any one. . . . They established an open system and assumed that policy would emerge only after it had been hacked away at by many governmental warriors and whatever private ones cared to try a jab or two." Charles R. Adrian and Charles Press, *American Politics Reappraised: The Enchantment of Camelot Dispelled* (New York: McGraw-Hill, 1974), p. 158.

2. "The list of checks and balances could be continued, but the general idea is clear: each of the three branches may act alone in view of somewhat autonomously exercised powers, but each department is checked by the others. It is in this sense that the executive authority of the United States government is both enormous and restricted, a seeming paradox that is part of the American political system and its philosophy." Donald T. Allensworth, *The U.S. Government in Action: Policy and Structure* (Pacific Palisades, Calif.: Goodyear, 1972), p. 22.

3. "The internal intrabranch aspects of the separation of powers doctrine appear also to have increased as government has grown in size. This is particularly true regarding the executive and legislative branch, but especially so regarding the latter." Theodore L. Becker, *American Government—Past—Present—Future* (Boston: Allyn and Bacon, 1976), pp. 120–21.

4. ". . . this entire system of checks and balances had served the republic well and in a generally positive way for a full century; and parts of it had grown through time during that century of development. But as the twentieth century approached and industrialization proceeded apace, this venerable system became more obstructionist than developmental." Roderick A. Bell and David V. Edwards, *American Government: The Facts Reorganized* (Morristown, N.J.: General Learning, 1974), p. 88.

5. ". . . the separation of powers is without purpose unless it results in checks and balances, and for that to happen the powers must be shared, at least to a limited extent." Martin Birnbach, *American Political Life: An Introduction to United States Government* (Homewood, Ill.: Dorsey Press, 1971), p. 156.

6. "The principle of limited government is also carried out through the previously described devices of separating powers among different branches of the federal government and through its corollary principle of checks and balances." Blanche D. Blank, *American Government and Politics: A Critical Introduction* (Chicago: Aldine, 1973), p. 63.

7. "We have a 'government of separated institutions *sharing* powers.' . . . Not only does each branch have some authority over the actions of the others, *but each is politically independent of the other.* . . . The framers were also careful to arrange matters so that a majority of the voters could win control over only part of the government at one time. . . . Presidential power is doubtless greater today than ever before. It is misleading, however, to infer from a president's capacity to drop an H bomb that he is similarly powerful in most other policy-making areas. The more analysts study policy developments over time and engage in revisionist treatments of past presidents, the more it is clear that presidents, in fact, are seldom free agents in effecting basic social change. We have seen that as priority-setter, politician, and executive a president must share power with members of Congress, bureaucrats, and interest-group elites, among others." James MacGregor Burns, J. W. Peltason, and Thomas E. Cronin, *Government by the People*, 10th ed. (Englewood Cliffs, N.J.: Prentice-Hall, 1978), pp. 26, 301.

8. "One of the most widely quoted phrases used to describe the American government is 'a separation of powers.' This means that one branch has a distinctive role to play in one of these areas: legislation (passing the law), execution (enforcing the law), and adjudication (interpreting the law). This works well in theory, but

in practice it is often quite difficult to isolate these various roles, as they tend to merge or are so closely interconnected that separation is all but impossible. When the complexities of these three branches are increased by the problems of a bureaucratic system, some real idea of the difficulties of governmental analysis is revealed." David A. Caputo, *Politics and Public Policy in America: An Introduction* (Philadelphia: J. B. Lippincott, 1974), p. 111.

9. "*Separation of powers.* . . . In a very real sense, 'separation of powers' is a misnomer; the powers given to national government are blended and fused. *Checks and balances* (*politics*). This oft-cited term captures the ideological gyroscope of our constitutional system. Division of power among governmental units might prevent autocracy but invite political paralysis. To bring the units together in harmonious relationship, so-called checks were placed in the Constitution. In fact, it is hard to pinpoint a phase of significant governmental authority left *exclusively* in the hands of any one branch. The intent was to create a *balance* of political power—for the three constituent agencies with national jurisdiction to lie on the same plateau of coercive capability. For those who judge political processes by their problem-solving *efficiency*, this scheme is forever doomed to be a disappointment. Friction among the competing power centers is inevitable, and this was entirely intentional." Ira H. Carmen, *Power and Balance: An Introduction to American Constitutional Government* (New York: Harcourt Brace Jovanovich, 1978), p. 19.

10. "Critics see the separation of powers and system of checks and balances as a needlessly complicated and unwieldly method of governing. . . . Defenders point out . . . that while social changes may have been slowed by the separation of powers and system of checks and balances, it has not prevented them; and that invariably the three branches act in concert in time of national emergency. Besides, they say, the separation of powers and system of checks and balances, by helping ensure that change will be orderly and measured, helps guarantee that social change will indeed come and that social gains once made will not be easily lost." John P. Carney, *Nation of Change: The American Democratic System,* 2d ed. (San Francisco: Canfield Press, 1975), p. 67.

11. "Fragmentation of power remains the primary feature of our governmental institutions. . . . All the original checks and balances laid out in the Constitution remain in force. The *unwritten constitution*—traditions, laws, procedures that have developed around

the Constitution—has added countless more." CRM Books, *American Government Today* (Del Mar, Calif.: Ziff-Davis, 1974), pp. 36–37.

12. "Although the Constitution established institutional checks and separated powers, the United States is also a government of *shared powers*. The branches of the government are separated, but their powers and functions are fused or overlapping. The Constitution provided many ways in which the three branches would interact. . . . Clearly, the President is involved in the legislative function. Similarly, Congress is involved in the executive process by its watchdog functions and through its power to create federal executive agencies and to advise on and consent to the appointment of high-level federal officials. . . . among the three branches (as among human beings) there is a never ending tug of war for dominance, a process that Alpheus T. Mason has called 'institutionalized tension.'" Milton C. Cummings, Jr., and David Wise, *Democracy under Pressure: An Introduction to the American Political System*, 3d ed. (New York: Harcourt Brace Jovanovich, 1977), pp. 47–48.

13. "The Framers also tended to believe that in addition to serving as a check on despotism, the partitioning of authority would make some positive contributions. The existence of multiple centers of power, none of which would be wholly sovereign, would help (might indeed be necessary) to tame power, to secure the consent of all, and to settle conflicts peacefully. . . . Because constant negotiations among different centers of power would be necessary in order to make decisions, citizens and leaders would perfect the previous art of dealing peacefully with their conflicts, not merely to the benefit of one partisan but to the mutual benefit of all the parties to a conflict." Robert A. Dahl, *Democracy in the United States: Promise and Performance*, 3d ed. (Chicago: Rand McNally, 1976), p. 74.

14. "In short, the separation of powers is a rather fragile device, requiring good sense and moderation. The public generally, and presidents, judges, and legislators in particular, must respect the separate jurisdictions of the branches despite, indeed because of, the difficulty of drawing boundary lines. It must also be remembered that separation of powers is an organic part of a subtle constitutional system, needing other parts of the system for its own operation and itself in turn necessary to their functioning. For example, . . . separation of powers is closely linked to bicameralism. Similarly, separation of powers depends upon the multiplicity of interests which lessens the likelihood of majority factions. . . . At

the same time, the very existence of independent branches tends to foster the necessary multiplicity. The forming and reforming of diverse groups for immediate, limited purposes is encouraged by the differences in times and manner of election, sizes of constituencies, and kinds of power that characterize separation of powers." Martin Diamond, Winston Mills Fisk, and Herbert Garfinkel, *The Democratic Republic: An Introduction to American National Government*, 2d ed. (Chicago: Rand McNally, 1970), p. 111.

15. "What the separation of powers does is to assure that the power of government is placed in several hands, each with a distinctive constituency. The probability is high that the several constituencies represented will not share the same values or priorities, and that conflict will result over all but the most innocuous questions. Although many people in government belong to the same political party, the fact that they are associated with different institutions and respond to distinctive constituencies leads them to disagree with each other. . . . Separation of powers in effect assures internal conflict among both majority and minority officeholders in the national government, and encourages attempts at temporary alliances between like-minded elements across party lines." Kenneth M. Dolbeare and Murray J. Edelman, *American Politics: Policies, Power and Change*, 3d ed. (Lexington, Mass.: D. C. Heath, 1977), pp. 228–29.

16. ". . . the constitutional separation of powers has been augmented by *political* checks and balances. While the Presidency has evolved in this century as a natural representative of the centralizing, metropolitan, cosmopolitan aspects of our society, Congress has tended to reflect the more particularized, decentralized, parochial elements." John C. Donovan, Charles H. Sheldon, Everett C. Ladd, Jr., Harry Lazer, and Robert S. Gilmour, *Democracy at the Crossroads* (New York: Holt, Rinehart & Winston, 1978), p. 319.

17. "The Constitution utilizes both the concept of *federalism—division of power* between the national and state governments—and *separation of powers*—the checks and balances existing among the three branches of the national government. In reality, the term *shared powers* is more accurate. Power is neither completely divided nor completely separated. Both the national and state governments have some powers in common, such as taxation, road construction, and education. And within the national government, overlap exists among the executive, legislative, and judicial branches, even though they are independent of each other. . . . The average American bene-

fits from these many centers of governmental power because they allow *multiple access points* to government. . . . To illustrate, the National Association for the Advancement of Colored People (NAACP) has worked through the courts at local, state, and national levels as well as through the legislative and executive branches at all three levels of government. Its earliest successes were in the national judicial branch before the U.S. Supreme Court, . . . but more recently it has been successful in influencing other 'access points.' " Charles W. Dunn, *American Democracy Debated: An Introduction to American Government* (Morristown, N.J.: General Learning, 1978), p. 57.

18. "During the nineteenth century, there were two further important though unintended antimajoritarian developments—the rise of standing committees in Congress, each capable of blocking legislation, and the creation of bureaucratic agencies, each able to initiate and shape legislation independent of executive instruction." Dushkin Contributors, *American Government '73 '74 Text*, Issac Krammick, ed. (Guilford, Conn.: Dushkin, 1973), p. 35.

19. "In the democratic world, two principal models of executive power have been developed historically: the *cabinet* model, characteristic of European and Asiatic democratic countries; the *presidential* model, used in the United States and copied, if ineffectively and incompletely, by the Latin Americans. The cabinet model is based on a *union* of executive and legislative powers, with the cabinet acting, at least in theory, as an agent of the legislature (in reality, the cabinet often acts as the leader of the legislature, or even its superior). The presidential model is based on a *separation* of executive and legislative functions. In such a system, the executive and the legislature are somewhat independent and are deliberately placed in positions that can readily lead to conflict. Such conflict is considered desirable because it hampers the exercise of power and restricts the development of overwhelming governmental authority over the governed. . . . The separation of powers in our system is incomplete, however, and the executive function overlaps the judicial, and legislative function." Thomas R. Dye, Lee S. Greene, and George S. Parthemos, *American Government: Theory, Structure and Process*, 2d ed. (Belmont, Calif.: Duxbury, 1972), pp. 27/-78.

20. "Thus, the concept of 'separation of powers' is really misnamed, for what we are really talking about is a sharing, not a separating, of power; each branch participates in the activities of every other branch." Thomas R. Dye and L. Harmon Ziegler, *The*

Irony of Democracy: An Uncommon Introduction to American Politics, 4th ed. (North Scituate, Mass.: Duxbury, 1978), p. 49.

21. ". . . it is clear that there is no rigid separation of powers in American Government. The President is chief executive, chief legislator, and through the power of judicial appointment, a major force in determining the constitutional positions taken by the judicial branch. Congress, through its powers of appropriation, investigation, and confirmation, goes far beyond a mere legislative role to intervene in the administrative side of government." William Ebenstein, C. Herman Pritchett, Henry A. Turner, and Dean Mann, *American Democracy in World Prospective*, 4th ed. (New York: Harper & Row, 1976), pp. 66–67.

22. ". . . so the Constitution limits the ruling power in our system to guarantee that no one level, and no one branch within any one level, can dominate the others. But all these limits are so complicated, and all these pieces are so jumbled, that things rarely work in practice exactly as we have outlined them in theory. Thus, the task of governing—or "guiding the ship of state"—is complex, and the way it is done is always controversial." David V. Edwards, *The American Political Experience: An Introduction to Government* (Englewood Cliffs, N.J.: Prentice-Hall, 1979), p. 15.

23. "The makers of the Constitution settled for 'divide and survive.' The framers of the Constitution were not content merely to set up a large centralized government to offset the power of the state legislatures, for they also had to worry about the potential oppressiveness of their own creation. They therefore constructed the presidency, the two houses of Congress, and even the judiciary in such a way that these branches would be in almost continual conflict with each other." Peter K. Eisinger, Dennis L. Dresang, Robert Booth Fowler, Joel B. Grossman, Burdette A. Loomis, and Richard M. Merelman, *American Politics: The People and the Polity* (Boston: Little, Brown, 1978), p. 35.

24. "Separation of powers is a cardinal feature of American democracy, but it has many critics. Some think that one, or more than one, of the branches can acquire too much influence. . . . Another group of critics decries separation as frustrating leadership and producing stalemate. . . . The fact is that separation is intended to assure critical interaction between the branches. How else can fearful people be sure that political power is properly checked? Furthermore, there are unifying forces, the most important of which are the political party, mass news media, and the need of modern

governments for strong leadership." John H. Ferguson and Dean E. McHenry, *The American Federal Government*, 13th ed. (New York: McGraw-Hill, 1977), p. 45.

25. ". . . the most typical centrist view of the realities of the American system is that power is limited and diffused. . . . Thus we have an elaborate structure of checks and balances, severely limiting the power concentrated in Washington. . . . To complement the constitutional balance, then, we have a group balance. So, through the separation and division of powers in the Constitution, the courts, the media, the parties, and the interplay of groups, centrists maintain that we have a system of *pluralism*, or many sources of power. The majority does not run things directly. Leaders (elites) in government and private organizations carry out most of the decision making." Leonard Freedman, *Power and Politics in America*, 3d ed. (North Scituate, Mass.: Duxbury, 1978), pp. 14, 15, 16.

26. "As scholars have pointed out, the Constitutional Convention of 1787 did not really create a government of 'separated powers' but a government of separated institutions sharing powers. The Executive is part of the legislative process, and so is the Judiciary. Congress has a role to play in the carrying out of the laws, and so do the courts. . . . The government, finally, was one of *balances* and *checks*. Different branches of government were given different powers. But each branch was also given authority to involve itself in what were the primary responsibilities of the other branches. . . . The government was also balanced—and safeguarded against the fluctuations of public passions and the 'tyranny of the majority'— by the way in which the different branches were selected." Roger Hilsman, *To Govern America* (New York: Harper & Row, 1979), pp. 7, 51.

27. "The President cannot always rely on his formal authority in situations that call for presidential leadership. . . . The president is not only unable to compel action on the part of individuals not under his authority; he even finds it difficult to compel action on the part of executive branch officials who are. The president is at the top of a vast bureaucracy with millions of people, each responsible to his immediate supervisor. Presidential commands may be misunderstood or simply disobeyed, and the president may not have knowledge of the noncompliance. Senior members of his staff may initiate programs without his knowledge or consent. . . . The use of the authority to remove a cabinet officer is not indicative of strong leadership, but of a failure of leadership. It suggests that the presi-

dent has been unable to persuade the cabinet officer to do what the president thinks should be done." Thomas G. Ingersoll and Robert E. O'Connor, *Politics and Structure: Essentials of American National Government*, 2d ed. (North Scituate, Mass.: Duxbury, 1979), pp. 32–33.

28. "The dominant view of the eighteenth century was of a universe in neat if delicate balance, governed by the laws of physics demonstrated by Sir Isaac Newton's work on the forces of gravity. With such a view of the natural laws of the universe, the idea of a mixture of opposed forces, each affecting the others, and all held in place by the interaction, had powerful appeal. Hence the idea of combining contrary views appeared to be in harmony with the natural laws governing the entire universe. *Separation of powers* among decision-making agencies and the exercise of *checks and balances* were thus viewed as desirable principles in their own right. The tasks of decision making—rule making, application of rules, and settlement of disputes—were accordingly given to separate bodies (separation of powers) and each was given some control over the others' use of powers (checks and balances). . . . So committed were the delegates to the concepts of separation of powers and checks and balances, that they spent far more time debating procedures and structure of government than they did governmental powers. . . . Although basically separated along functional lines—Congress makes policies and the president applies them—legislative and executive powers were also deliberately mixed to insure that each branch could check the other in the interest of the same sort of balance Newton saw in the universe." Marian D. Irish, James W. Prothro, and Richard J. Richardson, *The Politics of American Democracy*, 6th ed. (Englewood Cliffs, N.J.: Prentice-Hall, 1977), pp. 84, 85, 86.

29. "Despite the two-century hold the theory of the separation of powers has upon the minds (and emotions) of Americans, such separation has fortunately never been achieved in practice. . . . Congress has often by statute declared a policy and left to the President or some administrative authority the duty of promulgating rules and regulations (a legislative power) to carry that policy into effect. In like manner, Congress has frequently clothed administrative bodies with powers essentially judicial—for example, the power to pass upon small claims against the United States for property damage or personal injury. In a realistic view of the total process of government there is such a blending of powers, functions, and

duties that the lines separating the three branches grow dim."
Claudius O. Johnson, Daniel M. Ogden, Jr., H. Paul Castleberry,
and Thor Swanson, *American National Government*, 7th ed. (New
York: Thomas Y. Crowell, 1970), pp. 46–47.

30. "The separation of powers within the national government
is spanned by the system of checks and balances that was designed
to affect the operations of that government as well as the relationships among the national government, the states, and the people.
Various means were provided to enable inspection and restraint of
one part of the system by another, to keep the government operating in its proper channels. The principle permits all participants to
frustrate in some fashion the activities of other groups in government. It seems to guarantee that widespread agreements among
groups will precede action. Within government, the system of checks
and balances implies that a degree of cooperation among the separated branches is necessary, but provides that such cooperation
shall be ensured only at a cost." Harvey M. Karlen, *The Pattern of
American Government*, 2d ed. (Beverly Hills, Calif.: Glencoe Press,
1975), p. 79.

31. "Contrary to the intention of the framers—who attempted to
distribute the legislative (policy making), executive, and judicial
functions of government among separate branches of government,
with the three responsive to different constituencies but sharing the
functions of government—the contemporary presidency has substantially absorbed many of the powers of government." Ira Katznelson
and Mark Kesselman, *The Politics of Power: A Critical Introduction
to American Government*, 2d ed. (New York: Harcourt Brace Jovanovich, 1979), p. 260.

32. "The precise relationship between the three branches of government is a matter of continuing controversy, as can be seen
from the debate over the president's power to conduct an unde-
clared war in Southwest Asia. On the one hand, it is argued that
the president derives his authority from his powers as commander-
in-chief; on the other hand, it is argued that only Congress has
the power to declare war. . . . Although the Constitution is not
very clear as to who should control the executive establishment,
it is worth noting that Congress is in a strategic position in this regard. It can create an agency or abolish it and it can give or take
away the money for making it effective. It can place the agency
under the president's control or altogether outside the executive
establishment. It can decide the powers and duties of the agency,

and in many instances it is up to the Senate to ratify executive appointments. Yet the president is also not without authority since the general executive power belongs to him. Control over the executive establishment is therefore divided." Robert L. Keighton with Martin P. Sutton, *One Nation* (Lexington, Mass.: D. C. Heath, 1972), pp. 44, 225.

33. "In creating the three branches of government, the Constitution did not give one branch exclusive control over the bureaucracy. It vested substantial controlling powers in Congress, which can create, reorganize, and terminate administrative agencies and regulate their conduct through its power of appropriation. The Senate must give its consent to major administrative appointments. But the Constitution also vested the executive power, the commander-in-chief power, and other authority and duties in the President. Thus in effect the Constitution made the two political branches competitors for exerting dominion over the executive branch. But the judiciary was not left out. Constitutional amendments, particularly the Bill of Rights, require that the national bureaucracy observe civil liberties, subject to the monitoring eye of the courts." Louis W. Koenig, *Toward a Democracy: A Brief Introduction to American Government* (New York: Harcourt Brace Jovanovich, 1973), pp. 247–48.

34. "A model based on the notion that 'separation of powers' and 'checks and balances' mean that Congress has all the power to make law but no other power, that the President has only the power to administer the laws, that the Supreme Court has all the power to decide certain individual cases under law but no other power, and that no one else has any power at all, does not fit the facts of any government the framers ever knew, of the one they set up and served in, or of any government the world has seen since. Thus, the simplistic model must be abandoned for more complex ones which take full account of both the multiplicity of political actors and the complex overlappings in their spheres of activity, which the framers obviously envisioned and which actually occur." Louis W. Koenig, Glendon Schubert, Lloyd D. Musolf, Laurence I. Radway, and John H. Fenton, *American National Government: Policy and Politics* (Glenview, Ill.: Scott, Foresman, 1971), p. 17.

35. "Institutions in government are centers of power. There are three power centers expressly established in American national government by the Constitution: Congress, the Presidency, and the Supreme Court. But, in the nearly two centuries since the Philadelphia convention, several other power centers have evolved through

extraconstitutional or nonconstitutional means. These institutions have developed in good part to meet certain needs that the formal, named institutions could not or would not fulfill. . . . The federal bureaucracy is another power center. Although the Constitution, in retrospect, seems to hint at this institution by reference to executive departments, its emergence as a center of power together with its vast size are certainly beyond the scope envisioned by the framers. Milton A. Krasner, Stephen G. Chaberski, and D. Kelly Jones, *American Government: Structure and Process* (New York: Macmillan, 1977), p. 9.

36. "In applying the doctrine of the separation of powers, the founders established separate institutions which *share* the authority of government. The fact of sharing authority was made explicit in the concept of 'checks and balances,' which is usually listed as a twin concept along with the separation of powers. . . . The President's power of decision—his ability to launch nuclear war, for example—seems the ultimate power. But his days are actually spent in coping with the separation of power system. The Constitution encourages each branch to encroach upon the authority of the others." Karl A. Lamb, *The People, Maybe*, 3d ed. (North Scituate, Mass.: Duxbury, 1978), pp. 211, 214.

37. ". . . the system has come to operate in ways that the framers could hardly have dreamed of. Presidential supremacy in policy initiation versus the intended role of Congress as the seedbed of legislation represents one of these adaptive patterns of operation. . . . If the extraconstitutional checks and balances are coupled with the constitutional ones, it can be readily seen that the political system interlocks in countless ways. Many of these checks and balances are explicitly built into the constitutional system, and others are implicit because of the separation of powers and federal principle. This will become more apparent as we delve more deeply into the pressure group and political party aspects of the American political system." Erwin L. Levine and Elmer E. Cornwell, Jr., *An Introduction to American Government*, 4th ed. (New York: Macmillan, 1979), pp. 40, 42.

38. "The key to the constitutional system is not the principle of separation of powers but the principle of checks and balances. The principle of checks and balances implies an intermixture of powers. . . . The separation of powers means that the President *shares* powers with others who are involved in making and administering public policy." John C. Livingston and Robert G. Thompson, *The Consent*

of the Governed, 3d ed. (New York: Macmillan, 1971), pp. 159, 388–89.

39. "The doctrine of the separation of powers was more rhetorical than real, but its value as a symbol against arbitrary government compelled Madison to elaborate on the notion in the *Federalist* papers. Ironically, as with federalism, Madison had started out, in the Virginia Plan, with a scheme of government as far removed from the separation of powers as possible. The executive was to be chosen by the national legislature, which was also to choose the members of the national judiciary. . . . In many respects, the contemporary realities of separation of powers bear a remarkable resemblance to the Madisonian conception and little likeness to the formalistic and rigid notion of it which subsequently developed. The key to the problem lies in the word separate. For, although each of the branches owes its existence to a different mode of selection, neither Montesquieu nor Madison meant them to be separate in a functional sense. For both Montesquieu and Madison the central idea was not to separate power but to diffuse it, that is, to make the effective exercise of power depend on mutuality of agreement and at the same time prevent each center of power from subverting the other. Louis Loeb and Daniel M. Berman, *American Politics: Crisis and Challenge* (New York: Macmillan, 1975), pp. 360, 362.

40. "The principle of the separation of powers is nowhere to be found explicitly in the Constitution. But it is clearly built upon Articles I, II and III in the following manner: (1) the provision of three separate and distinct departments or branches of government; (2) provision for very different methods of selection of the top personnel, so that each branch is based upon a different 'constituency'—this is the idea of a 'mixed regime' in which the personnel in each department are expected to develop very different interests and very different outlooks on how to govern; and (3) provision for 'checks and balances' whereby each department is given some right to participate in the processes of each of the other departments. Consequently, ours is not a system of separated powers but a system of 'separated institutions sharing powers.'" Theodore J. Lowi, *American Government: Incomplete Conquest* (Hinsdale, Ill.: Dryden, 1976), pp. 104–5. The final statement makes reference to Richard E. Neustadt, *Presidential Power* (New York: John Wiley & Sons, 1960), p. 33.

41. "Although the Constitution makes the President the focal point of leadership in the American system, the separation of pow-

ers makes it virtually impossible for any branch of government to maintain continuous and effective control over the bureaucracy. Ironically, the specter of a powerful and relatively autonomous Fourth Branch of government in the form of a bureaucracy is the result of the Founders' fear of unrestrained power. For it is the very constitutional fragmentation of power designed by the Founders to prevent tyranny that has made the bureaucracy incompletely controlled by any of the traditional branches of government." Fred R. Mabbutt and Gerald J. Ghelfi, *The Troubled Republic: American Government, Its Principles and Problems* (New York: John Wiley, 1974), p. 170.

42. " 'Government' as we most often visualize it has been covered in the three preceding chapters on the executive, the legislative, and the judicial organs. Traditional students of public administration made a firm distinction between politics and administration, assigning the former—policy-*making*—to these three 'political' organs (or at least the first two of them), and policy implementation, the carrying out of the political decisions, to the administrative apparatus. . . . Actually, in recent years students of administration have jettisoned this set of artificial and unrealistic categories. They now insist, properly, that the administrator makes policy every bit as much as does the elected executive or the legislator. . . . Officials all up and down the line exercise discretion in almost every action they make, and such discretion *is* policy-making. Even this perspective on the administrative role understates the full importance of that role. In a very real sense the administrative bureaucracy *is* the government in any political system. Legislatures, executive, courts, and, of course, political parties do govern, but the pervasiveness of their roles and the depth of their penetration into the body politic can hardly compare with the omnipresence, to say nothing of the sheer numbers, of the bureaucracy." C. Peter Magrath, Elmer E. Cornwell, Jr., and Jay S. Goodman, *The American Democracy*, 2d ed. (New York: Macmillan, 1973), p. 427.

43. "It is quite clear that there is not distinct separation of powers in American government. Separation of powers, as modified by the checks and balances, produces a system of three branches of government with overlapping functions. . . . The American governmental system, at times, results in confusion, lack of direction, inaction, frustration, and deadlock. It requires a great deal of cooperation, compromise, and consensus before the engine of government can move. . . . All in all, more people are satisfied with the balance

of our system promoted by separation of powers and checks and balances than are disturbed by the impediments to 'progress' prompted by it." J. Keith Melville, *The American Democratic System* (New York: Dodd, Mead, 1975), pp. 33, 34.

44. ". . . the Constitution is such that a number of conflicting interpretations can be made of many key provisions. This simple but frequently ignored fact is crucial, for it means that to a large degree the governmental structure and public policy-making processes found in the American political system today have been determined not by the Constitution itself, but by the decisions of the political system. Sometimes these decisions evolve over a period of time in the form of customs and traditions. Sometimes they take the form of acts passed by Congress or of formal decisions by the President or certain bureaucratic officials. But most often they take the form of Supreme Court interpretations, because the Constitution is sufficiently ambiguous and sufficiently open to a variety of alternative applications that many disagreements are bound to arise over the proper application of particular provisions of the Constitution." Stephen V. Monsma, *American Politics*, 3d ed. (Hinsdale, Ill.: Dryden, 1976), p. 52.

45. "Notwithstanding their desire for a stronger national government, the framers took great care to set up an internal system of checks and balances among the legislative, executive, and judicial branches to ensure that their national government could not come under the tyrannical control of one branch. . . . The consequences of this decision to opt for separate institutions, and for a sharing of power in such a way as to encourage checking and balancing, are apparent in almost every aspect of the operation of the American national government today. Richard E. Morgan, John C. Donovan, and Christian P. Potholm, *American Politics: Directions of Change, Dynamics of Choice* (Reading, Mass.: Addison-Wesley, 1979), pp. 41, 42.

46. "Separation of powers and check-and-balance arrangements are by no means matters merely of historical interest; they are part of everyday governance, as contemporary struggles over the scope of the president's war powers, the meaning of executive privilege, the impoundment of funds appropriated by Congress, and impeachment of the president bear witness. . . . This constitutional arrangement of divided powers has strongly influenced the complexion and activity of the nation's politics. . . The system of divided but interdependent powers contributes to the very limited degree of

party responsibility that prevails in the United States. It is, in other words, difficult to elect a party to office and hold it responsible for carrying out a definite political program." Robert L. Morlan, *American Government: Policy and Process*, 3d ed. (Boston: Houghton Mifflin, 1979), pp. 14, 15.

47. ". . . the framers . . . created a system in which separate institutions share power. . . . The whole matter of responsibility for the legislative process is muddled for several reasons: executive agencies often draft the bills that congressmen debate, modify and finally pass: the President or his staff often actively lobbies in Congress and stirs up public opinion for or against important proposals; and most important, bills that become law confer a great deal of discretion on the President. In sum, . . . probably the most significant function of the President in domestic affairs is to act as Chief Legislator. With congressional power shared among 535 people, usually only the President can provide effective leadership. . . . Nor is the executive branch immune from outside forces. Judges can intepret executive orders, just as they can statutes. And, in interpreting the Constitution, courts have on numerous occasions set limits to executive authority. Congress has even wider avenues of influence into administration. The Senate can confirm or reject the President's nominees for his own cabinet and several thousand other executive posts. Perhaps more important, Congress also determines the organization of all departments within the executive branch and by its control over appropriation can affect the minutest detail within federal agencies as well as the general direction of administrative policy. Indeed, many chiefs of federal offices are likely to pay more attention to the whims of senators and congressmen on the appropriations committees than to the President's policies." Walter F. Murphy and Michael N. Danielson, *American Democracy*, 9th ed. (New York: Holt, Rinehart & Winston, 1979), pp. 105–7.

48. "On the typical organization chart, the President seems to be in control because he is at the top of the structure. . . . Yet, despite the appearance of the chart, the greater share of formal power belongs to Congress by virtue of its uncontested ability to arrange the administrative machinery when it creates an agency. . . . Congress can, and often has, set up agencies that are independent of the President. . . . The Constitution has had a lot to do with the evolution of the bureaucracy, even in the absence of specific provision for it. In addition to creating the two branches of government with op-

erational authority over the bureaucracy, the Constitution created yet another source of conflict by guaranteeing individual rights against government abuse. This feature allows the courts to act as a check on bureaucratic actions. And the federal structure lends itself to decentralization in the organization of the bureaucracy. As a result, the bureaucracy is fragmented and subject to cross pressures; it reflects the diversity of the dominant elites. The bureaucracy's internal conflicts are the elite's conflicts. David J. Olson and Philip Meyer, *Governing the United States: To Keep the Republic in Its Third Century*, 2d ed. (New York: McGraw-Hill, 1978), 1978), pp. 399, 400.

49. ". . . although the Constitution places major responsibility for each of the three basic functions of government under the jurisdiction of a different branch, it also provides for the sharing of functions through the system of checks and balances. . . . Legal checks and balances, moreover, are accompanied by political checks. . . . Historian Richard Hofstadter has commented on the involved system of checks and balances. In his view, the delegates saw a well-designed government as one that would 'check interest with interest, class with class, faction with faction and one branch of government with another in a harmonious system of mutual frustration.'" Dennis J. Palumbo, *American Politics* (New York: Appleton-Century-Crofts, 1973), p. 48.

50. "In keeping with their desire to contain the majority, the Founding Fathers inserted 'auxiliary precautions' *designed to fragment power without democratizing it.*" Michael Parenti, *Democracy for the Few*, 2d ed. (New York: St. Martin's, 1977), p. 56.

51. "The Constitution embraces the principle of *separation of powers.* . . . The so-called checks and balances are variously provided in the Constitution. . . . These provisions of the Constitution do not mean that *only* Congress is involved in lawmaking, that the President does *nothing* but exercise executive powers, or that judicial powers are exercised *only* by the courts. The three branches of the national government *share* lawmaking, administrative, and judicial powers. Congress is involved in the executive and judicial powers provided in the Constitution when it creates or reorganizes the lower federal court system (the courts below the U.S. Supreme Court) or when it enacts laws establishing executive departments such as the Department of Health, Education, and Welfare or the Department of Agriculture. The President exercises legislative power when he recommends legislation to Congress or when he vetoes

acts of Congress with which he disagrees. The Supreme Court can declare an act of Congress unconstitutional if it finds that the law in question is not consistent with the meaning of the Constitution, and in doing so, the Court has a kind of veto. Beyond this negative power, when legal issues arise, the Court interprets the meaning of laws passed by Congress as they are applied to particular circumstances. Executive agencies make laws when they formulate the administrative regulations required to put policies adopted by Congress into effect. Making laws, executing them, and judging are intertwined activities of government. As a result, the constitutional principle of separation of powers, along with checks and balances, really means *sharing of powers*." Samuel C. Patterson, Roger H. Davidson, and Randall B. Ripley, *A More Perfect Union: Introduction to American Government* (Homewood, Ill.: Dorsey, 1979), p. 47.

52. "*Separation of Powers*. The nation's founders set up three branches of government; they did not intend to set up a separate bureaucracy. But the fact that they created three independent branches of the federal government made it more likely that the growing government bureaucracy would be relatively independent of the elected branches. The reason the separation of powers into three branches fosters the formation of a relatively independent fourth branch—the bureaucracy—is that bureaucracies learn to play one branch against another. In this way they enhance their independence. The examples are numerous. The branches of the armed forces are supposed to be under presidential control. The President is Commander-in-Chief of the armed forces under the Constitution. However, the armed forces have close connections with the congressional armed forces committees. They are often able to get what they want from these committees even if the President opposes them. For instance, they can procure weapons for which the President has not asked." Kenneth Prewitt and Sidney Verba, *An Introduction to American Government*, 3d ed. (New York: Harper & Row, 1979), p. 435.

53. "The Constitution doesn't say how the branches of government are to relate. Although Congress, the Presidency, and the Supreme Court remain independent of one another, their relative power has varied. . . . But each has played an important role at various times in U.S. history. In addition, the three branches haven't functioned the way the founders expected. Each was supposed to do a particular job: Congress to make laws, the President to carry them out, and the courts to interpret them. In fact, however, the three

branches share these functions. Congress does pass laws, but the executive and judicial branches play an important part in this function. The President's legislative power goes beyond his power to veto laws. Much of the legislation passed by Congress begins as part of the President's program. In the same way the Supreme Court's legislative power goes beyond its power of judicial review. In some areas the courts have laws that control citizens as much as any law of Congress, as can be seen in the case of school desegregation." Kenneth Prewitt and Sidney Verba, *Principles of American Government*, 2d ed. (New York: Harper & Row, 1977), p. 241.

54. "Fragmentation (or specialization) means that in the American national government there is no single source of dynamism that can, in all issue areas on all occasions, be relied on to provide the impetus for some sort of activity. Likewise, there is no single element that can, in all issue areas on all occasions, be counted on to promote only inaction. Instead, the cues for both inaction and action may come from any of the various subunits of the government." Randall B. Ripley, *American National Government and Public Policy* (New York: Free Press, 1974), p. 10.

55. ". . . the reader should be aware that the term 'separation of powers' is misleading and substitute the more appropriate term 'separate institutions sharing power'. . . . Congress and bureaucracy are inseparable in the American system. . . . There is a constant interchange, a continuous flow of memoranda, documents, and requests for information between committees or subcommittees and bureaus and agencies. In this way, committees and subcommittees are reminded of the importance and needs of the bureaus and agencies, thus preventing the possibility of an agency's being overlooked or ignored. Since the tenure of congressmen on committees and subcommittees usually is long, relationships that are formed tend to be long term and generally a mutual respect develops. The result is a close working relationship between the agency or department and the congressional committee." Robert S. Ross, *American National Government: An Introduction to Political Institutions*, 2d ed. (Chicago: Rand McNally, 1976), pp. 17, 145, 149.

56. "Throughout American history there has been an ongoing struggle for power particularly between the legislative and executive branches. The Framers created the Congress in a period marked by distrust of executive power. . . . In the United States, the relative importance of Congress compared with the executive has been declining since the 1930s. The forces which have been working against

legislative dominance since the thirties have been the needs of an increasingly industrialized, urbanized society which call for technical and complex decision-making. Contemporary American society is characterized by a huge economic system; the existence of a bureaucracy unprecedented in size and scope; the increase of American involvement in international affairs; and a reliance on mass communications. All of these factors dramatize and personalize the chief executive." David C. Saffell, *The Politics of American National Government*, 3d ed. (Cambridge, Mass.: Winthrop, 1978), pp. 216–17.

57. "It was expected by the Founding Fathers, and it turned out to be correct, that each branch and level of government would represent a different combination of social groups and interests. Through the bargaining among public officials, made inescapable by this fragmented structure of authority, all these groups would secure at least a part of their desires. The diversity of the nation would thus be reflected in the design of the political system and preserved by the system's operation." Robert H. Salisbury, *Governing America: Public Choice and Political Action* (New York: Appleton-Century-Crofts, 1973), p. 31.

58. "The procedures for separation of powers and checks and balances written into the Constitution were designed to curb the authority of the president. In time the growth of the federal system, the rise of political parties, and the impact of the press and other mass media were to expand both the power of the chief executive and the restraints upon the use of that power." Sam C. Sarkesian and Krish Nanda, *Politics and Power: An Introduction to American Government* (New York: Alfred, 1976), p. 110.

59. "The attachment of American constitution makers to the separation of powers and to checks and balances has several implications. First, control of programs is not given entirely to any one branch of government. Second, with a divided leadership, there can be no simple hierarchy with well-defined, superior-subordinate roles. For example, the control of bureaucrats is not the sole responsibility of the President; he must share it with the legislature and the judiciary. . . . Third, bureaucrats in charge of particular programs may receive conflicting demands from competing superiors. A House committee, a Senate committee, or the President may issue contrasting directives. Each potential superior may have his spokesman within an agency. Multiple loyalties within a department can upset the department head's control over his own agency at the same time that they inhibit clear control by either the President

or one house of the Congress. The busing controversy pitted congressional statutes against presidential directives and an ambiguous record of court decisions, with bureaucrats in the Department of Health, Education and Welfare having to decide which 'instruction' fit a particular case." Ira Sharkansky and Donald Van Meter, *Policy and Politics in American Governments* (New York: McGraw-Hill, 1975), p. 142.

60. "For convenience, the bureaucracy is often said to be in the executive branch. However, it would be better to classify it in its own—'administrative'—branch, for bureaucracy's powers are a combination of legislative, judicial and executive. The framers of the Constitution did not intend to separate the powers of the three branches of government absolutely; they simply hoped to balance the powers so that no one branch could operate free of sharp interferences from the other two. . . . All three types of powers are lodged in the bureaucracy. . . ." Robert Sherrill with James David Barber, Benjamin I. Page, and Virginia W. Joyner, *Governing America* (New York: Harcourt Brace Jovanovich, 1978), p. 423.

61. "What role can such eighteenth-century constitutional principles as federalism, balanced government, and separation of powers play in a modern industrial society? On the one hand, industrialization, economic integration, technological change, international war, and concentrations of private power encourage the expansion of national executive power. On the other hand, balanced government and separation of powers limit executive power. Congress and the courts may be unable to initiate national policy, but they can and do restrain presidential and administrative caprice." Ruth C. Silva, Edward Keynes, Hugh A. Bone, and David W. Adamany, *American Government: Democracy and Liberty in Balance* (New York: Knopf, 1976), p. 76.

62. "Many persons consider the three branches to be equal, but the Constitution clearly gives the Congress the central power if it chooses to exercise it. Nevertheless, in recent decades the President has overshadowed Congress, and the courts are a distant third as holders of power. Each branch has powers of its own and checks over the other two branches. . . . Nevertheless, the branches retain considerable independence. The classic description of the operation of the separate branches is that they provide *checks and balances.*" Max J. Skidmore and Marshall Carter Wanke, *American Government: A Brief Introduction*, 2d ed. (New York: St. Martin's, 1977), pp. 19–20.

63. "The separation of powers principle is modified substantially

in the American system, however, by formal and informal powers known as *checks and balances*. Each branch has various ways of checking and balancing the power of the other two branches. . . . In the system of checks and balances, legislative bodies have several ways to influence the other two branches. . . . After a law is passed, lawmakers have the right, perhaps even the duty to see how effectively it is being administered. This involves the process of overseeing executive agencies, a process which is carried on by various legislative committees." Charles P. Sohner, *American Government and Politics Today*, 2d ed. (Glenview, Ill.: Scott, Foresman, 1976), pp. 21, 242, 245.

64. "Federalism and the separation of powers encourage group activity. If an interest group is unsuccessful in achieving its goals at the state level, for example, it may have more success in Washington. Or if a group cannot influence the legislative branch of government, it can seek to gain the support of the executive branch or start a lawsuit in the courts to achieve its objectives." Walter E. Volkomer, *American Government*, 2d ed. (Englewood Cliffs, N.J.: Prentice-Hall, 1979), p. 114.

65. "At first, separation of powers was tied to the reduction in influence of the executive. . . . Only later was there greater concern with protecting each of the three branches from each other and in increasing the power of the executive to place it on a par with the legislative branch." Stephen L. Wasby, *American Government and Politics* (New York: Scribner's, 1973), p. 9.

66. "There is good reason to believe that the Founding Fathers provided separate constituencies not only because they wished the branches of the national government to be independent of one another but also because they wanted them to represent different kinds of social and economic interests." Richard A. Watson, *Promise and Performance of American Democracy*, 3d ed. (New York: Wiley, 1978), p. 50.

67. "Power is separated into three branches of government. But each branch checks and balances the other because each *shares* the lawmaking, administrative and judicial powers with the other two. Separation of powers really means *sharing of powers*." Raymond E. Wolfinger, Martin Shapiro, and Fred I. Greenstein, *Dynamics of American Politics* (Englewood Cliffs, N.J.: Prentice-Hall, 1976), p. 46.

68. "There is little doubt that separation of powers has encouraged the development of the federal bureaucracy, which consists

of the many administrative and regulatory agencies that enforce most government legislation. . . . The Constitution did not establish any clear lines of authority over the bureaucracy. . . . As a result, the bureaucracy is not clearly responsible to any one of the three branches. In effect the bureaucracy has become a 'fourth branch' of government often acting in a semi-independent fashion." Peter Woll and Robert Binstock, *America's Political System*, 3d ed. (New York: Random House, 1979), pp. 70, 72.

69. "*Separate institutions sharing power.* The last important device used by the Constitution to limit government is that which has come to be known as the dual principle of '*separation of powers*' and '*checks and balances.*' The phrase 'separation of powers' is an unfortunate one because it is misleading. In fact, power is not separated at the national level. What are separated are three institutions: Congress, the president, and the courts. But these three institutions *share* power. Power is limited by this arrangement *precisely because it is shared by three institutions.*" Gordon Henderson, *American Democracy: People, Politics, and Policies* (Cambridge, Mass.: Winthrop, 1979), p. 198.

70. "The Framers of the Constitution sought to create a government capable of protecting both liberty and order. The solution they chose—one without precedent at the time—was a government based on a written constitution that combined the principles of popular consent, the separation of powers, and federalism. . . . Political authority was to be shared by three branches of government in a manner deliberately intended to produce conflict among these branches. This conflict, motivated by the self-interest of the persons occupying each branch, would, it was hoped, prevent tyranny, even by a popular majority. . . . The visible struggles for political power occur within and between the presidency and Congress, but the invisible struggles take place in and among the myriad departments, agencies, commissions, and offices of government—in short, within the bureaucracy. Moreover, it is in the actions of the bureaucratic organizations that one finds the concrete expression of the policies that emerge from these struggles. The bureaucracy is a key element in both the struggle for power and the definition of values government is to serve." James Q. Wilson, *American Government: Institutions and Policies* (Lexington, Mass., D. C. Heath, 1980), pp. 40, 348.

CHAPTER ONE: *Introduction*

1. The separation of powers doctrine acquired a reputation as "the most hallowed concept of constitutional theory and practice" and as "the very character of the American political system." Karl Loewenstein, *Political Power and the Governmental Process* (Chicago: University of Chicago Press, 1957), p. 42; and Gordon S. Wood, *The Creation of the American Republic 1776-1787* (Chapel Hill, N.C.: University of North Carolina Press, 1969), p. 151.

2. ". . . the very properties that make models useful also make their use dangerous. It is very easy to confuse model and theory, to assume that a property of a model is a property of a theory or object. It is also easy to forget that models are always partial and incomplete, that some variables have been eliminated, that some relationships have been dropped, that structure has been simplified." Eugene J. Meehan, *The Theory and Method of Political Analysis* (Homewood, Ill.: Dorsey Press 1965), pp. 149–50. Twenty years ago, a foremost analyst of constitutional arrangement suggested that the separation of powers concept be replaced by a "new tripartism" based on "the distinction between policy determination, political executive and policy control." Loewenstein, *Political Power and the Governmental Process,* p. 42.

3. The basic texts in American national government are more sophisticated than such comments as the following indicate. "Although it is traditional in introductory American Government courses to say that Congress makes the laws, the President enforces the laws, and the Supreme Court interprets the laws, we know that making, enforcing and interpreting have significant elements of overlap." Victor G. Rosenblum and A. Didrick Castberg, *Cases on Constitutional Law: Political Roles of the Supreme Court* (Homewood, Ill.: Dorsey Press, 1973), p. 350. However, a survey of the introductory texts shows that they explain the mixing or sharing of functions as much as, and probably even more than, the separation of functions. See infra, app.

4. Louis Fisher, *President and Congress* (New York: Free Press, 1972), pp. 3, 255–70; and Grant McConnell, *The Modern Presidency,* 2d ed. (New York: St. Martin's Press, 1976), pp. 100, 101.

5. The similarity of the three vesting clauses indicates that they were integral parts of a common conception and that they should be interpreted in relation to each other. Chief Justice John Marshall interpreted them as a unit with interrelated limitations. He set forth the triadic formula that "the legislature makes, the executive executes, and the judiciary construes the law" in Wayman v. Southard, 10 Wheaton 1, 42, 46 (1825). The position of executive power, between legislative and judicial powers, suggests that the President is to execute what Congress has legislated. That is a highly limited view of the presidency. Significantly, the more monarchical powers of the President, such as the legislative and military roles, are set forth in specific grants.

6. Richard E. Neustadt, *Presidential Power: The Politics of Leadership* (New York: John Wiley & Sons, 1960), p. 33; (1976 ed.) p. 101. See also infra, ch. 2, nn. 21–29.

7. U.S., *Constitution*, art. II, sec. 2, par. 2.

8. In 1792 there were "about 780 employees (excluding the deputy postmasters), of whom approximately 660 were employed in the Treasury Department. In 1801 the number of employees (excluding about 880 deputy postmasters) was 2,120, of whom about 1,615 were employed in the Treasury field service." Leonard D. White, *The Federalists: A Study in Administrative History* (New York: Macmillan Co., 1956), p. 255.

9. For instance, one study of Congress lists eleven specific functions and seven general ones. John S. Saloma III, *Congress and the New Politics* (Boston: Little, Brown, 1969), pp. 22–23.

10. Fisher, *President and Congress*, p. 82.

11. Peter Woll, *American Bureaucracy*, 2d ed. (New York: Norton, 1977), p. 63. See infra, app., 60.

12. William E. Mullen, *Presidential Power and Politics* (New York: St. Martin's Press, 1976), p. 1.

13. Godfrey Sperling, Jr., *Christian Science Monitor*, May 22, August 2, 1978.

14. C. Peter Magrath, Elmer E. Cornwell, Jr., and Jay S. Goodman, *The American Democracy*, 2d ed. (New York: Macmillan Co., 1973), p. 427. See infra, app., 42.

15. Harold Seidman, *Politics, Position, and Power: The Dynamics of Federal Organization*, 2d ed. (New York: Oxford University Press, 1977), pp. 38–39, 82.

16. *United States Government Manual 1978–79* (Washington, D. C.: Government Printing Office, 1978), pp. v–vii.

17. Erwin L. Levine and Elmer E. Cornwell, Jr., *An Introduction to American Government*, 4th ed. (New York: Macmillan Co., 1979), pp. 167, 170; Robert L. Morlan, *American Government:*

Policy and Process, 3d ed. (Boston: Houghton-Mifflin, 1979) pp. 225–26; David J. Olson and Philip Meyer, *Governing the United States*, 2d ed. (New York: McGraw-Hill, 1978), pp. 401, 403; Hugh Heclo, *A Government of Strangers: Executive Politics in Washington* (Washington, D.C.: Brookings Institution, 1977), pp. 84, 113; Louis C. Gawthrop, *Administrative Politics and Social Change* (New York: St. Martin's Press, 1971), p. 24; Robert S. Ross, *American National Government: An Introduction to Political Institutions*, 2d ed. (Chicago: Rand McNally, 1976), pp. 6, 132; Louis W. Koenig, *Toward A Democracy: A Brief Introduction to American Government* (New York: Harcourt Brace Jovanovich, 1973), p. 248; John P. Carney, *Nation of Change*, 2d ed. (San Francisco: Canfield, 1975), p. 173; Richard A. Watson, *Promise and Performance of American Democracy*, 3d ed. (New York: Wiley, 1978), pp. 520, 523.

18. See infra. ch. 3, nn. 87–89.

19. Arthur M. Schlesinger, Jr., "The Limits and Excesses of Presidential Power," *Saturday Review*, May 3, 1969; reprinted as "Strengthening and Restraining the President," in *The Power of the Presidency: Concepts and Controversy*, ed. Robert S. Hirschfield (Chicago: Aldine, 1973), p. 368; Erwin C. Hargrove, *The Power of the Modern Presidency* (Philadelphia: Temple University Press, 1974), p. 238.

20. *New York Times*, May 25, 1978.

21. See infra, ch. 2, "Constitutional Basis of Specialized Structures." See also Henry J. Merry, *Constitutional Function of Presidential-Administrative Separation* (Washington, D.C.: University Press of America, 1978), pp. 80–81.

22. U.S., *Constitution*, art. I, sec. 8, par. 18.

23. See infra, ch. 2, nn. 42, 43. See also Merry, *Constitutional Function of Presidential-Administrative Separation*, pp. 84–87, 94–96.

24. Louis Loeb and Daniel M. Berman, *American Politics: Crisis and Challenge* (New York: Macmillan Co., 1975), p. 363. See infra, app., 39.

25. J. Roland Pennock, *Administration and the Rule of Law* (New York: Rinehart, 1941), p. 216.

26. Nelson W. Polsby, *Congress and the Presidency*, 3d ed. (Englewood Cliffs, N.J.: Prentice-Hall, 1976), p. 4.

CHAPTER TWO: *The General Character of Constitutional Distribution*

1. "The doctrine of the separation of powers was adopted by the Convention of 1787, not to promote efficiency but to preclude

the exercise of arbitrary power. The purpose was, not to avoid friction, but, by means of inevitable friction incident to the distribution of governmental powers among three departments, to save the people from autocracy." Justice Brandeis quoted by Justice Frankfurter, Youngstown v. Sawyer, 343 U.S. 579, 613–14 (1952).

2. The Supreme Court used the legislative-executive-judicial departmentalization to support self-limitation in refusing to enjoin President Andrew Johnson from enforcing the Reconstruction Acts. Mississippi v. Johnson, 4 Wall. 475 (1867).

3. Wayman v. Southard, 10 Wheat 1, 46 (1825).

4. U.S. v. Hudson & Goodwin, 7 Cranch 32, 33 (1812); U.S. v. Eaton, 144 U.S. 677, 687 (1892); U.S. v. Grimaud, 220 U.S. 506 (1911); U.S. v. Resnick, 299 U.S. 207, 209 (1936); Winters v. New York, 333 U.S. 507 (1948).

5. U.S. v. Hark, 320 U.S. 531, 536 (1944); see also Lockerty v. Phillips, 319 U.S. 182 (1943); Yakus v. U.S., 321 U.S. 414 (1944); M. Kraus and Bros. v. U.S., 327 U.S. 614 (1946).

6. Interstate Commerce Commission v. Brimson, 154 U.S. 447 (1894).

7. Francis D. Wormuth, *The Origins of Modern Constitutionalism* (New York: Harper & Bros., 1949), pp. 59–70; William Gwyn, *The Meaning of Separation of Powers* (New Orleans: Tulane University Press, 1967), pp. 28–65; M. J. C. Vile, *Constitutionalism and the Separation of Powers* (Oxford: Clarendon Press, 1967), pp. 39–51.

8. Wormuth, *Origins of Modern Constitutionalism*, pp. 59, 174; Gwyn, *Meaning of Separation of Powers*, pp. 3, 26, 47–55; Vile, *Constitutionalism and the Separation of Powers*, p. 3.

9. Wormuth, *Origins of Modern Constitutionalism*, pp. 62, 67, 191–93, 205; Gwyn, *Meaning of Separation of Powers*, pp. 5, 13; Vile, *Constitutionalism and the Separation of Powers*, pp. 136, 138.

10. Vile, *Constitutionalism and the Separation of Powers*, pp. 13–18.

11. ". . . no person who has an office or place or profit under the king or receives a pension from the crown shall be capable of serving as a member of the house of commons. . . ." Act of Settlement (1701), in Carl Stephenson and Frederick G. Marcham, *Sources of English Constitutional History* (New York: Harper & Bros., 1937), p. 612. Colin R. Lovell, *English Constitutional and Legal History* (New York: Oxford University Press, 1962), pp. 418–21, 445.

12. Articles of Confederation, art. V.

13. Wayman v. Southard, 10 Wheat. 1, 42, 43 (1825).

14. See G. Burdeau, "Delegation of Powers," *International Encyclopedia of the Social Sciences* (New York: Macmillan Co., 1968), passim.

15. McGrain v. Daugherty, 273 U.S. 135, 174 (1927); Barenblatt v. United States, 360 U.S. 109, 111 (1959).

16. For instance, Madison and Wilson tried repeatedly for adoption of a joint executive-judicial Council of Revision, but no more than three states approved. James Madison, *Notes of Debates in the Federal Convention Reported by James Madison* (New York: W. W. Norton, 1966), June 4, 6, July 21, August 15, 1787.

17. Ibid., June 1, 1787.

18. Lovell, *English Constitutional and Legal History*, pp. 85–91.

19. U.S., *Constitution*, art. III, sec. 1. O'Donoghue v. United States, 289 U.S. 516 (1933). Williams v. United States, 289 U.S. 553 (1933).

20. James Madison, in *Federalist Papers*, no. 47.

21. Ex parte Grossman, 267 U.S. 87, 119, 120 (1925).

22. The two doctrines are "mutually contradictory" despite similar ends; one makes for "division and independence, the other interaction and dependence." Louis W. Koenig, *The Chief Executive*, 3d ed. (New York: Harcourt Brace Jovanovich, 1975), p. 27. ". . . if the separation of powers doctrine tends to make clear and precise distinctions, . . . the concept of checks and balances tends to blur that distinction." Louis C. Gawthrop, *Administrative Politics and Social Change* (New York: St. Martin's Press, 1971), p. 21.

23. App.: 5, 6, 10, 16, 25, 28, 30, 34, 37, 38, 46, 58, 59, 62, 63, 69.

24. Ibid.: 5, 7, 12, 17, 20, 26, 31, 36, 38, 40, 45, 47, 49, 51, 53, 55, 59, 67, 69, 70. Others indicate a blending, fusion, or overlap of powers: 9, 19, 22, 28, 29, 34, 39, 43, 46, 52, 60, 63.

25. Richard E. Neustadt, *Presidential Power: The Politics of Leadership* (New York: John Wiley & Sons, 1960), p. 33; (1976 ed.), p. 101.

26. Dan Nimmo and Thomas D. Ungs, *Political Patterns in America: Conflict, Representation, and Resolution* (San Francisco: Freeman, 1979), pp. 60, 326; Paul Conn, *Conflict and Decision Making: An Introduction to Political Science* (New York: Harper & Row, 1971), p. 218.

27. "The great task of American government is to get these separate institutions to work together with some measure of effectiveness." William Ebenstein, C. Herman Pritchett, Henry A. Turner, and Dean Mann, *American Democracy in World Perspective*, 4th ed. (New York: Harper & Row, 1976), p. 66. Two other leading political scientists assert that the prescribed checks and balances mean "various units of government must cooperate with one another to reach common goals." Kenneth Prewitt and Sidney Verba, *An Introduction to American Government*, 3d ed.

(New York: Harper & Row, 1979), p. 38. See app.: 10, 30, 43.
28. United States v. Nixon, 418 U.S. 683, 707 (1974).
29. "The 'organic power,' which is the power to create and abolish agencies, is entirely contained in Congress. There is no way in which this authority can be inferred from Article II. When the Constitution is viewed in this light, the bureaucracy is always an agent of Congress, unless the legislature chooses to set up different arrangements." Peter Woll, *Public Policy* (Cambridge, Mass.: Winthrop, 1974), p. 29.
30. Louis W. Koenig, *Congress and the President* (Chicago: Scott, Foresman, 1965), p. 120.
31. "It is the *general* power of Congress to act as watch dog and hound dog." Stephen K. Bailey, *Congress in the Seventies* (New York: St. Martin's Press, 1970), p. 84.
32. Even some general explanations of the national government recognize the place of specialized forces in constitutional distribution. ". . . separation of powers depends upon the multiplicity of interests which lessen the likelihood of majority factions. . . . At the same time, the very existence of the independent branches tends to foster the necessary multiplicity." Martin Diamond, Winston Mills Fisk, and Herbert Garfinkel, *The Democratic Republic: An Introduction to American National Government*, 2d ed. (Chicago: Rand McNally, 1970), p. 111. "The bureaucracy . . . reflects the diversity of the dominant elites. The bureaucracy's internal conflicts are the elite's conflicts." David J. Olson and Philip Meyer, *Governing the United States*, 2d ed. (New York: McGraw-Hill, 1978), p. 392. The final statement makes reference to Peter Woll, *American Bureaucracy* (New York: W. W. Norton, 1963). See app.: 13, 15, 17, 25, 30, 35, 41, 49, 51, 54, 57, 59, 64, 66, 70.
33. The development of a legitimizing ideology for special-interest-group process included the articulation of such concepts as "polyarchal democracy." Robert A. Dahl: *A Preface to Democratic Theory* (Chicago: University of Chicago Press, 1956) and *Pluralist Democracy in the United States: Conflict and Consensus* (Chicago: Rand McNally, 1967). "The group model of policy formation suggests that interest groups are the focal point of the policy process, subsuming all of the legitimate political interests of the community." Peter Woll, *Public Policy*, p. 53.
34. Lovell, *English Constitutional and Legal History*, pp. 73, 85–91, 144–47, 168; Bryce Lyon, *A Constitutional and Legal History of Medieval England* (New York: Harper & Bros., 1960), pp. 135, 138.
35. Lovell, *English Constitutional and Legal History*, pp. 156–58;

Lyon, *Constitutional and Legal History of Medieval England*, p. 430.

36. Brian Chapman, *The Profession of Government: The Public Service in Europe* (London: Allen & Unwin, 1959), p. 48.

37. Woodrow Wilson, "The Study of Administration," *Political Science Quarterly* 2 (1887):218. See also Gabriel A. Almond and G. Bingham Powell, Jr., *Comparative Politics: A Developmental Approach* (Boston: Little, Brown, 1966).

38. Edmund S. Morgan, *The Birth of the Republic, 1763–1789* (Chicago: University of Chicago Press, 1956), p. 124.

39. Ibid., p. 125. Merrill Jensen, *The New Nation: A History of the United States during the Confederation, 1781–1789* (New York: Knopf, 1950), p. 360; Leonard D. White, *The Federalists: A Study in Administrative History* (New York: Macmillan Co., 1948), p. 309.

40. Harold Seidman, *Politics, Position, and Power: The Dynamics of Federal Organization*, 2d ed. (New York: Oxford University Press, 1975), pp. 123–24; Thomas E. Cronin, *The State of the Presidency* (Boston: Little, Brown, 1975), pp. 188–92, 199–201.

41. See, for instance, Seidman, *Politics, Position, and Power*, pp. 150–60; Cronin, *State of the Presidency*, pp. 69–70.

42. Some texts stress the elitist approach. See Thomas R. Dye and L. Harmon Ziegler, *The Irony of Democracy: An Uncommon Introduction to American Politics*, 4th ed. (North Scituate, Mass.: Duxbury, 1978); Michael Parenti, *Democracy for the Few*, 2d ed. (New York: St. Martin's, 1977); and Kenneth M. Dolbeare and Murray J. Edelman, *American Politics: Policies, Power, and Change*, 3d ed. (Lexington, Mass.: D. C. Heath, 1977).

43. See, for instance, Thomas R. Dye, Lee S. Greene, and George A. Parthemos, *American Government: Theory, Structure, and Process*, 2d ed. (Belmont, Calif.: Duxbury, 1972), p. 179.

44. "In the past decade Washington has seen a great proliferation in the number and activity of so-called 'public interest' lobbying organizations. . . ." Martin Levin, "Ask Not What Our Presidents Are 'Really Like'; Ask What We and Our Political Institutions Are Like: A Call for a Politics of Institutions, Not Men," in *American Politics and Public Policy*, ed. Walter Dean Burnham and Martha Wagner Weinberg (Cambridge, Mass.: M.I.T. Press, 1978), p. 131.

45. Anthony King, ed., *The New American Political System* (Washington, D.C.: American Enterprise Institute for Public Policy Research, 1978). The contributions of Fred I. Greenstein, Hugh Heclo, Samuel C. Patterson, Jeane J. Kirkpatrick, and Austin Ranney are particularly relevant.

46. Anthony King, "The American Polity in the Late 1970s: Build-

ing Coalitions in the Sand," ibid, pp. 389–91. On coalition politics with respect to presidential elections, see Stephen J. Brams, *The Presidential Election Game* (New Haven, Conn.: Yale University Press, 1978), pp. 134–72.

47. King, ed., *New American Political System*, p. 393.

48. See ch. 8 infra, pp. 171, 173–74.

49. See Henry J. Merry, *Constitutional Function of Presidential-Administrative Separation* (Washington, D.C.: University Press of America, 1978), pp. 24–27, 31–33, 46–48, 103–5.

50. "It took a year and a half for the Administration to discover, in Mr. Kraft's words, that 'the whole Executive Branch is a sieve.'" Martin Tolchin, "New Pro in the White House," *New York Times Magazine*, December 17, 1978, pp. 29, 56.

51. "At the end of his first four years, President Nixon found that his attempts to get a handle on the bureaucracy had not proved successful. Following his re-election, therefore, he decided to deal with the problem in a more vigorous and systematic fashion. . . . In addition to reshuffling his Cabinet, Nixon also asked for the resignation of some two thousand other political appointees. . . . The more important vacancies created by these firings were to be filled with people from the President's already bloated White House staff and also by individuals from the Committee to Re-elect the President (CREEP). It was felt that these Nixon loyalists could more effectively monitor the activities of the bureaucracy from positions within that bureaucracy rather than from the White House. In all, some eighty-four White House staffers and CREEP workers were strategically located in various departments and agencies throughout the bureaucracy. Even with these replacements, however, the firings had been so sweeping that many positions were still vacant several months later." Robert DiClerico, *The American President* (Englewood Cliffs, N.J.: Prentice-Hall, 1979), pp. 132–33.

CHAPTER THREE: *The General Character of the Executive Branch*

1. See supra, ch. 1 and ch. 2.

2. Stephen Hess, *Organizing the Presidency* (Washington, D.C.: Brookings Institution, 1976), p. 143. The cases mentioned are Kendall v. United States, 12 Peters 524 (1838), and Humphrey's Executor v. United States, 295 U.S. 602 (1935).

3. On the special legal meaning of *ministerial*, see Louis Fisher, *The Constitution between Friends: Congress, the President, and the Law* (New York: St. Martin's Press, 1978), pp. 39–46.

4. Kendall v. United States, 12 Pet. 524 (1838).
5. United States v. Eliason, 16 Pet. 291 (1842); Williams v. United States, 1 How. 290 (1843). Cf. Butterworth v. Hoe, 112 U.S. 51 (1884).
6. Mississippi v. Johnson, 4 Wall. 475, 500 (1867).
7. United States v. Curtiss-Wright Export Corp., 299 U.S. 304 (1936); Youngstown Co. v. Sawyer, 343 U.S. 579 (1952).
8. The concurring opinion of Justice Jackson in the Youngstown steel seizure case included this classification:

"Presidential powers are not fixed but fluctuate, depending upon their disjunction or conjunction with those of Congress. We may well begin by a somewhat over-simplified grouping of practical situations in which a President may doubt, or others may challenge, his powers, and by distinguishing roughly the legal consequences of this factor of relativity.

1. "When the President acts pursuant to an express or implied authorization of Congress, his authority is at its maximum, for it includes all that he possesses in his own right plus all that Congress can delegate. In these circumstances, and in these only, may he be said (for what it may be worth) to personify the federal sovereignty. . . .

"2. When the President acts in absence of either a congressional grant or denial of authority, he can only rely upon his own independent powers, but there is a zone of twilight in which he and Congress may have concurrent authority, or in which its distribution is uncertain. Therefore, congressional inertia, indifference or quiescence may sometimes, at least as a practical matter, enable, if not invite, measures on independent presidential responsibility. In this area, any actual test of power is likely to depend on the imperatives of events and contemporary imponderables rather than on abstract theories of law.

"3. When the President takes measures incompatible with the expressed or implied will of Congress, his power is at its lowest ebb, for then he can rely only upon his own constitutional powers minus any constitutional powers of Congress over the matter. Courts can sustain exclusive presidential control in such a case only by disabling the Congress from acting upon the subject." Youngstown Co. v. Sawyer, 343 U.S. 579, 635–38 (1952).

See Philip B. Kurland, *Watergate and the Constitution* (Chicago: University of Chicago Press, 1978), pp. 205–10.
9. In re Neagle, 135 U.S. 1 (1890).
10. James W. Davis, Jr., *The National Executive Branch* (New York: Free Press, 1970), p. 1.
11. U.S., *Constitution,* art. II, sec. 2, par. 1.
12. 1 Stat. 28–29, 49–50, 65.
13. Ibid, 65–67.

14. Leonard D. White, *The Federalists: A Study in Administrative History* (New York: Macmillan Co., 1956), pp. 18–19.
15. Williams v. U.S., 1 How. 290 (1843).
16. Peter Woll, *Public Policy* (Cambridge, Mass.: Winthrop, 1974), p. 29.
17. Ibid., p. 30.
18. Louis W. Koenig, *The Chief Executive*, 3d ed. (New York: Harcourt Brace Jovanovich, 1975), p. 183.
19. Grant McConnell, *The Modern Presidency*, 2d ed. (New York: St. Martin's Press, 1976), pp. 8, 9.
20. James Madison, *Notes of Debates in the Federal Convention Reported by James Madison* (New York: W. W. Norton, 1966), June 4, 6, July 21, August 15, 1787.
21. Erwin C. Hargrove, *The Power of the Modern Presidency* (Philadelphia: Temple University Press, 1974), p. 237; Richard E. Neustadt, "Politicians and Bureaucrats," in *The Congress and America's Future*, 2d ed., ed. David B. Truman (Englewood Cliffs, N.J.: Prentice-Hall, 1973), p. 119; Stephen K. Bailey, *Congress in the Seventies* (New York: St. Martin's Press, 1970), p. 83; William L. Morrow, *Public Administration: Politics and the Political System* (New York: Random House, 1975), p. 113; Hugh Heclo, *A Government of Strangers: Executive Politics in Washington* (Washington: Brookings Institution, 1977), pp. 17–18; Richard M. Pious, *The American Presidency* (New York: Basic Books, 1979), pp. 213, 214.
22. Panama Canal Co. v. Grace Line, 356 U.S. 309, 319 (1958).
23. Herbert Kaufman, "The Administrative Function," *International Encyclopedia of the Social Sciences* (New York: Macmillan Co., 1968), 1:61–67.
24. Ibid., pp. 62, 63, 65.
25. Peter Woll, *American Bureaucracy*, 2d ed. (New York: W. W. Norton, 1977), pp. 195.
26. Ibid., pp. 248–49.
27. Robert Presthus, *Public Administration*, 6th ed. (New York: Ronald, 1975), p. 3.
28. Kenneth M. Dolbeare and Murray J. Edelman, *American Politics: Policies, Power and Change*, 3d ed. (Lexington, Mass.: D. C. Heath, 1977), p. 14.
29. Louis Loeb and Daniel M. Berman, *American Politics: Crisis and Challenge* (New York: Macmillan Co., 1975), p. 363.
30. 5 U.S.C. § 551–59.
31. Robert C. Fried, *Performance in American Bureaucracy* (Boston: Little, Brown, 1976), p. 274.
32. Fred A. Kramer, *Dynamics of Public Bureaucracy* (Lexington, Mass.: Winthrop, 1977), p. 13.
33. Paul H. Appleby, *Policy and Administration* (University, Ala.:

University of Alabama Press, 1949), pp. 29–30. The eight political processes are: (1) presidential and (2) general nominating
processes; (3) electoral, (4) legislative, and (5) judicial processes; (6) the process of party maintenance and operation;
(7) the agitational process (including the organization of
groups; petitioning; public comment, debate, and demands);
and (8) the administrative process.

34. Davis, *National Executive Branch*, p. 1.

35. Ibid., p. 122.

36. Ibid., p. 126.

37. Richard E. Neustadt, *Presidential Power: The Politics of Leadership* (New York: John Wiley & Sons, 1960), pp. 33–57; (1976
ed.), pp. 101–25.

38. Louis C. Gawthorp, *Administrative Politics and Social Change*
(New York: St. Martin's Press, 1971), p. 29.

39. See infra, "Departmental Disunity."

40. Theodore J. Lowi, *American Government: Incomplete Conquest*
(Hinsdale, Ill.: Dryden, 1976), p. 451.

41. See David H. Rosenbloom, *Federal Service and the Constitution*
(Ithaca, N.Y.: Cornell University Press, 1971), passim.

42. McConnell, *Modern Presidency*, pp. 8, 9.

43. Dorothy B. James, *The Contemporary Presidency*, 2d ed. (Indianapolis: Bobbs-Merrill, 1974), pp. 6–7.

44. Hess, *Organizing the Presidency*, p. 153.

45. Lowi, *American Government*, pp. 507, 508.

46. Philippa Strum, *Presidential Power and American Democracy*
(Pacific Palisades, Calif.: Goodyear, 1972), p. 43.

47. Thomas E. Cronin, *The State of the Presidency* (Boston: Little,
Brown, 1975), pp. 92–93.

48. William E. Mullen, *Presidential Power and Politics* (New York:
St. Martin's Press, 1976), p. 188.

49. David C. Saffell, *The Politics of American National Government*, 2d ed. (Cambridge, Mass.: Winthrop, 1975), p. 294.

50. "A Scorecard on Carter's Cabinet," *Business Week*, May 1,
1978, p. 54.

51. James, *Contemporary Presidency*, pp. 147–48.

52. Lowi, *American Government*, pp. 433–34.

53. Ibid., p. 435.

54. Aaron Wildavsky, "The Past and Future Presidency," *The Public Interest* 41 (Fall 1975):67–68.

55. Heclo, *Government of Strangers*, p. 111.

56. Ibid.

57. See infra, ch. 4, "Conditions of Tenure."

58. Mullen, *Presidential Power and Politics*, p. 188; Louis W. Koenig, *Congress and the President* (Chicago: Scott, Foresman,

1965), p. 93; Strum, *Presidential Power and American Democracy*, p. 42; Gawthrop, *Administrative Politics and Social Change*, p. 24; Rowland Egger, *The President of the United States*, 2d ed. (New York: McGraw-Hill, 1972), p. 47; Stephen K. Bailey, "The President and His Political Executives," in *The Dynamics of the American Presidency*, ed. Donald B. Johnson and Jack L. Walker (New York: John Wiley & Sons, 1964), pp. 238–39; Robert E. DiClerico, *The American President* (Englewood Cliffs, N.J.: Prentice-Hall, 1979), p. 213.

59. Milton C. Cummings, Jr., and David Wise, *Democracy under Pressure*, 3d ed. (New York: Harcourt Brace Jovanovich, 1977), p. 422.

60. Gawthrop, *Administrative Politics and Social Change*, p. 25.

61. Heclo, *Government of Strangers*, p. 12; Louis W. Koenig, *Chief Executive*, p. 184; Harold Seidman, *Politics, Position, and Power: The Dynamics of Federal Organization*, 2d ed. (New York: Oxford University Press, 1975), p. 81; McConnell, *Modern Presidency*, p. 75.

62. Neustadt, *Presidential Power*, p. 39 (1960 ed.); p. 107 (1976 ed.).

63. James MacGregor Burns, *Presidential Government: The Crucible of Leadership* (Boston: Houghton Mifflin, 1973), p. 141; James, *Contemporary Presidency*, p. 212.

64. Bailey, "The President and His Political Executives," p. 237.

65. Kramer, *Dynamics of Public Bureaucracy*, p. 90.

66. There was a "transitional period of about two years" after the change of presidential party in 1801. "Jefferson did not adopt a theory of rotation in office, but he did find ways and means in these years to satisfy the clamor of his followers." Leonard D. White, *The Jeffersonians: A Study in Administrative History, 1801–1829* (New York: Macmillan Co., 1951), p. 348. Newspaper reports published in 1830 and 1832 indicate that during the first eighteen months of the Jackson presidency there was "a total of 919 removals out of 10,093 officeholders or somewhat less than 10 per cent." Id., *The Jacksonians: A Study in Administrative History, 1829–1861* (New York: Macmillan Co., 1954), pp. 307–8.

67. "During the first year or two of Washington's administration the question of loyalty to the new government was important, and, while never specifically stated as a *sine qua non*, was nevertheless a matter of concern. . . . None of the leading Federalists, however, sought to make room for party adherents by removing officials and employees whose political reliability had become uncertain. But they were not averse to finding places for their family connections." Id., *The Federalists*, pp. 271, 278.

68. Gawthrop, *Administrative Politics and Social Change*, p. 24.
69. See infra, ch. 4, "Continuity of Specialized Relationships."
70. Egger, *President of the United States*, p. 45.
71. Arthur M. Schlesinger, Jr., "The Limits and Excesses of Presidential Power," *Saturday Review*, May 3, 1969; reprinted as "Strengthening and Restraining the President" in *The Power of the Presidency: Concepts and Controversy*, 2d ed., ed. Robert S. Hirschfield (Chicago: Aldine, 1973), p. 368.
72. Hargrove, *Power of the Modern Presidency*, p. 238.
73. Cronin, *State of the Presidency*, pp. 188–201; Seidman, *Politics, Position, and Power*, pp. 100–101; Hargrove, *Power of the Modern Presidency*, pp. 257–65.
74. A 1976 poll on "Who Runs America" rated the chairman of the Federal Reserve Board above the secretary of the treasury and any other cabinet member except the secretary of state (then Henry Kissinger). *U.S. News and World Report*, April 1976.
75. Bertram M. Gross, *The Legislative Struggle: A Study in Social Combat* (New York: McGraw-Hill, 1953), p. 105.
76. Peter Woll, *American Bureaucracy*, p. 248.
77. McConnell, *Modern Presidency*, p. 65.
78. Davis, *National Executive Branch*, p. 126.
79. James, *Contemporary Presidency*, p. 212.
80. Seidman, *Politics, Position, and Power*, p. 74.
81. Dolbeare and Edelman, *American Politics*, pp. 228, 237.
82. See app., 10.
83. "A president attempting noble innovations thus stands in great need of public support and, especially, of strong partisan backing. A partyless government is almost invariably an arbitrary and reactionary regime. This country has an extraordinary need for revitalized parties: first, to serve as instruments of support for, and to discipline the whims of, elected leaders; and, second, to serve as vehicles for the two-way communication of voter preferences on policy." Cronin, *State of the Presidency*, p. 318. Another scholarly analysis of the presidency has similar views on the reforms needed for the system: "Perhaps the single most desirable improvement would be a regeneration of the political parties and the restoration of them to meaningful participation in the selection of candidates and the operation of government." Mullen, *Presidential Power and Politics*, p. 264.
84. Stanley Bach, "The Presidency and Democratic Stability," in *Perspective on the Presidency*, ed. Stanley Bach and George T. Sulzner (Lexington, Mass.: D. C. Heath, 1974), pp. 9–10.
85. Hess, *Organizing the Presidency*, p. 163.
86. Woll, *Public Policy*, p. 255; Norton Long, "Bureaucracy and Constitutionalism," *American Political Science Review* 46 (Sept.

1952):818; Ernest S. Griffith, *Congress: Its Contemporary Role* (New York: New York University Press, 1951), p. 39; Dale Vinyard, *The Presidency* (New York: Charles Scribner's, 1971), p. 116; Charles E. Jacob, "The Presidential Institution," in *The Performance of American Government: Checks and Minuses,* ed. Gerald W. Pomper (New York: Free Press, 1972), pp. 252–53; Emmet John Hughes, *The Living Presidency* (New York: Coward, McCann and Geoghegan, 1973), p. 184; Morrow, *Public Administration,* p. 102.

87. Hargrove, *Power of the Modern Presidency,* p. 79. See also Philip B. Kurland, *Wall Street Journal,* December 12, 1973.

88. Kenneth J. Meier, *Politics and the Bureaucracy: Policymaking in the Fourth Branch of Government* (North Scituate, Mass.: Duxbury, 1979).

89. Blanche D. Blank, *American Government and Politics: A Critical Introduction* (Chicago: Aldine, 1976), p. 126; David A. Caputo, *Politics and Public Policy in America: An Introduction* (Philadelphia: J. B. Lippincott, 1974), p. 105; Leonard Freedman, *Power and Politics in America,* 3d ed. (North Scituate, Mass.: Duxbury, 1978), p. 278; Thomas G. Ingersoll and Robert E. O'Connor, *Politics and Structure: Essentials of American National Government,* 2d ed. (North Scituate, Mass.: Duxbury, 1979), p. 224; Harvey M. Karlen, *The Pattern of American Government,* 2d ed. (Beverly Hills: Glencoe Press, 1975), p. 275; Fred R. Mabbutt and Gerald J. Ghelfi, *The Troubled Republic: American Government, Its Principles and Problems* (New York: John Wiley, 1974), p. 170; Dennis J. Palumbo, *American Politics* (New York: Appleton-Century-Crofts, 1973), p. 271; Kenneth Prewitt and Sidney Verba, *An Introduction to American Government,* 3d ed. (New York: Harper & Row, 1979), p. 435; Sam C. Sarkesian and Krish Nanda, *Politics and Power: An Introduction to American Government* (New York: Alfred, 1976), p. 367; Raymond E. Wolfinger, Martin Shapiro, and Fred I. Greenstein, *Dynamics of American Politics* (Englewood Cliffs, N.J.: Prentice-Hall, 1976), p. 474; Peter Woll and Robert Binstock, *America's Political System,* 3d ed. (New York: Random House, 1979), p. 72.

CHAPTER FOUR: *The Dimensions of the Continuing Government*

1. See supra: ch. 1, nn. 17, 19; ch. 2, nn. 84–88.
2. U.S., *Constitution,* art. II, sec. 2, par. 2.
3. U.S., *Statutes at Large,* vol. 1: ch. 4, pp. 28–29; ch. 7, pp. 49–50; ch. 12, pp. 65–67.

4. Ibid., pp. 29, 50, 65, 67.
5. Leonard D. White, *The Jacksonians: A Study in Administrative History, 1829–1861* (New York: Macmillan Co., 1954), p. 357.
6. See, in general: David H. Rosenbloom, *Federal Service and the Constitution: The Development of the Public Employment Relationship* (Ithaca, N.Y.: Cornell University Press, 1971); James W. Davis, Jr., *The National Executive Branch* (New York: Free Press, 1970); and Robert Presthus, *Public Administration*, 6th ed. (New York: Ronald, 1975).
7. 5 U.S.C. § 5308, 5311–17, 5332.
8. Administrative Personnel, 5 C.F.R. § 3, 6, 9, 332.
9. 5. U.S.C. § 5331–38, 5341–49.
10. U.S., Civil Service Commission, *1975 Annual Report* (Washington, D.C.: Government Printing Office, 1976), p. 34; id., *1976 Annual Report* (ibid., 1977), p. 39; *1977 Annual Report* (ibid., 1978), p. 33.
11. Hugh Heclo, *A Government of Strangers: Executive Politics in Washington* (Washington, D.C.: Brookings Institution, 1977), p. 37.
12. A leading analyst, while acknowledging that *civil service* and *merit system* are generally used interchangeably, undertakes to articulate a difference between the terms. This does not seem to distinguish the civil service system proper from other systems for limited classes of officials, such as, e.g., the Foreign Service or doctors of the Veterans Administration. Rather, it is a difference in attitudes, between the negative protectionism of the civil service reform that began in the mid-nineteenth century and more recent efforts to develop positive improvements in the technical aspects of selection and in the motivation of employees and officials. Presthus, *Public Administration*, pp. 161–72. The Civil Service Reform Act of 1978 does not utilize that distinction; rather, it uses the term *merit system* to stand for all procedures that recruit on the basis of occupational standards and capacities. See infra, ch. 8, p. 176. This work uses the term in a similar manner.
13. Administrative Personnel, 5 C.F.R. § 332.402.
14. Ibid., § 6.2.
15. Kenneth J. Meier, *Politics and the Bureaucracy: Policymaking in the Fourth Branch of Government* (North Scituate, Mass.: Duxbury, 1979), pp. 37–38.
16. Ibid., p. 38.
17. Administrative Personnel, 5 C.F.R. § 9.
18. "Agencies such as the State Department rely heavily on career personnel in policy-making." Louis W. Koenig, *Toward a Democracy: A Brief Introduction to American Government* (New

York: Harcourt Brace Jovanovich, 1973), p. 248. "Frequently administrative personnel are drawn from the very industry they are charged with regulating, their business background being taken as proof of their 'expertise'. They often return to higher positions in the same industry after serving their terms in office. Likewise, many career administrators eventually leave government service to accept higher paying jobs in companies whose interests they favored while in office." Michael Parenti, *Democracy for the Few*, 2d ed. (New York: St. Martin's Press, 1977), p. 282. See also infra, nn. 51, 52.

19. Meier, *Politics and the Bureaucracy*, p. 24. Moreover, the political executives nominally heading the departments often become captive spokesmen for the constituent bureaus. Robert C. Fried, *Performance in American Bureaucracy* (Boston: Little, Brown, 1976), p. 207.
20. Presthus, *Public Administration*, pp. 181–82.
21. U.S., Civil Service Commission, *Federal Civilian Workforce Statistics* (September 1977), p. 36.
22. Table, U.S., Commission on Organization of Executive Branch of the Government, Personnel and Civil Service (Washington, D.C.: Government Printing Office, 1955). Reprinted in John M. Pfiffner and Robert V. Presthus, *Public Administration*, 4th ed. (New York: Ronald Press, 1960), p. 157.
23. Heclo, *Government of Strangers*, p. 38.
24. Ibid., pp. 84, 113.
25. Ibid., p. 38.
26. Presthus, *Public Administration*, p. 179, gives these figures on executives of supergrade level in the several merit systems:

General Schedule (GS 16–18)	5,804
Foreign Service	1,924
Public Law (P.L. 313)	1,244
AEC, VA (med.), TVA	682
Other	794
Total	10,448

27. Heclo, *Government of Strangers*, p. 38.
28. Ibid., p. 40.
29. Ibid., pp. 39–40.
30. On the Senior Executive Service established by the Civil Service Reform Act of 1978, see infra, ch. 8, pp. 173, 187–89.
31. James Madison, *Notes of Debates in the Federal Convention of 1787 Reported by James Madison* (New York: W. W. Norton, 1969), pp. 596–97, 600–602, 606.
32. Madison and James Wilson proposed a Council of Revision,

composed of the executive and members of the judiciary, to review legislation. Ibid., June 4, 6, July 21, and August 15, 1787. No more than three states gave approval.

33. Myers v. United States, 272 U.S. 52 (1926).

34. William Howard Taft, *The President and His Powers* (New York: Columbia University Press, 1967), p. 71. This was published originally in 1916 under the title *Our Chief Magistrate and His Powers* based upon lectures delivered in 1915.

35. Humphrey's Executor v. United States, 295 U.S. 602 (1935).

36. Weiner v. United States, 357 U.S. 349 (1958).

37. The opinion in the Humphrey case gave some weight to the fact that the office had a fixed term. 295 U.S. 624.

38. Thomas E. Cronin, *The State of the Presidency* (Boston: Little, Brown, 1975), pp. 198–201.

39. James M. Naughton, "The Ford Upheaval and Some Explanations," *New York Times*, November 6, 1975, p. A14.

40. Richard F. Fenno, Jr., *The President's Cabinet* (Cambridge, Mass.: Harvard University Press, 1959); Grant McConnell, *The Modern Presidency*, 2d ed. (New York: St. Martin's Press, 1976), p. 69; Louis C. Gawthrop, *Administrative Politics and Social Change* (New York: St. Martin's Press, 1971) p. 24.

41. See David T. Stanley, Dean E. Mann, and Jameson W. Doig, *Men Who Govern: A Biographical Profile of Federal Political Executive* (Washington, D.C.: Brookings Institution, 1967), pp. 55–68.

42. J. Edgar Hoover was appointed director of the FBI in 1924; he died while still in office, May 2, 1972, at the age of 77. He was in legal status a noncareer political executive. His appointment by eight successive Presidents is exceptional. During the forty-seven years he was director, there were fifteen commissioners of Internal Revenue. Guy C. Helvering, who held his office from June 6, 1933, to October 8, 1943, had the longest tenure. *Standard Federal Tax Reporter*, vol. 9 (Chicago: Commerce Clearing House, 1979), pp. 68, 508–9.

43. Fried, *Performance in American Bureaucracy*, pp. 206–7.

44. Stephen Hess, *Organizing the Presidency* (Washington, D.C.: Brookings Institution, 1976), p. 153.

45. Gawthrop, *Administrative Politics and Social Change*, p. 25.

46. Ibid.

47. Marian D. Irish, James W. Prothro, and Richard J. Richardson, *The Politics of American Democracy*, 6th ed. (Englewood Cliffs, N.J.: Prentice-Hall, 1977), p. 350.

48. "Literature in public administration has stressed the role of agencies as implementors of consensus, as accommodators of heterogeneous interests, and as arenas wherein political tension

is controlled. . . . Delay, obstruction, and incrementalism may be preferable to the adoption of irrevocable, arbitrary programs that would cultivate an omnipotent bureaucracy." William L. Morrow, *Public Administration: Politics and the Political System* (New York: Random House, 1975), p. 244.

49. Heclo, *Government of Strangers*, pp. 172–75, 178.

50. Robert E. DiClerico, *The American President* (Englewood Cliffs, N.J.: Prentice-Hall, 1979), p. 115.

51. Louis W. Koenig, Glendon Schubert, Lloyd S. Musolf, Lawrence I. Radway, and John H. Fenton, *American National Government: Policy and Politics* (Glenview, Ill.: Scott, Foresman, 1971), p. 300; David J. Olson and Philip Meyer, *Governing the United States*, 2d ed. (New York: McGraw-Hill, 1978), p. 403. See also supra, nn. 18, 19.

52. Meier, *Politics and the Bureaucracy*, p. 24.

53. Kenneth Prewitt and Sidney Verba, *An Introduction to American Government*, 3d ed. (New York: Harper & Row, 1979), pp. 439–41.

54. Rowland Egger, *The President of the United States*, 2d ed. (New York: McGraw-Hill, 1972), p. 46. On congressional investigation of executive officials, see Morris S. Ogul, *Congress Oversees the Bureaucracy: Studies in Legislative Supervision* (Pittsburgh: University of Pittsburgh Press, 1976).

55. Joel D. Aberbach and Bert A. Rockman, "Clashing Beliefs within the Executive Branch: The Nixon Administration Bureaucracy," *American Political Science Review* 70 (June 1976): 456–68. The interviews also disclosed that on a continuum with five choices of more or less government provision for social services, the left to right categories of the political appointees were 22, 12, 35, 20, and 11 percent, while those of the career supergrades were 31, 22, 25, 12, and 10 percent. That, of course, is evidence that differences are relative and perhaps substantial rather than absolute.

56. Lewis C. Mainzer, *Political Bureaucracy* (Glenview, Ill.: Scott, Foresman, 1973), p. 112.

57. Ibid., p. 18. On the politics/administration controversy, see ibid., pp. 69–72. One extensive analysis of the national administration explains that the system involves both a pluralistic politics and a coalition politics. James W. Davis, Jr., *The National Executive Branch* (New York: Free Press, 1970), pp. 121–23.

58. "Early scholars of administration, such as Woodrow Wilson and Frank Goodnow, treated the president and bureaucracy as one, a situation that today is inconsistent with reality." Meier, *Politics and the Bureaucracy*, p. 145.

59. See supra, n. 41.

60. "Political executives are often poorly equipped to organize a reliable political recruitment process for their own agency. . . . A cabinet secretary without control of key political appointments will be able to exert little influence on the semiautonomous fiefdoms that make up most departments." Heclo, *Government of Strangers*, pp. 96, 97.

61. The decline of the centralizing power of the major political parties has increased the relative position of groups and constituencies: fragmentation aids the image of independence and individualism.

62. Egger, *President of the United States*, p. 45.

63. Dorothy B. James, *The Contemporary Presidency*, 2d ed. (Indianapolis: Bobbs-Merrill, 1975), p. 212.

64. McGeorge Bundy, *The Strength of Government* (Cambridge, Mass.: Harvard University Press, 1968), p. 37.

65. Philippa Strum, *Presidential Power and American Democracy* (Pacific Palisades, Calif.: Goodyear, 1972), p. 46; 2d ed. (1979), p. 88.

66. Morrow, *Public Administration*, p. 97.

67. Eugene Lewis, *American Politics in a Bureaucratic Age: Citizens, Constituents, Clients, and Victims* (Cambridge, Mass.: Winthrop, 1977), p. 72; Charles W. Dunn, *American Democracy Debated: An Introduction to American Government* (Morristown, N.J.: General Learning Press, 1978), pp. 216–17. "Bureaucracy can perform quite efficiently, contrary to common belief, but its efficiency and effectiveness are related to the groups it serves." Dunn, ibid., p. 358. See also J. Leiper Freeman, *The Political Process*, rev. ed. (New York: Doubleday, 1955), pp. 14–16. See also infra, app.: 1, 13, 14, 17, 25, 30, 35, 37, 41, 48, 49, 57, 66, and 70.

68. Fred A. Kramer, *Dynamics of Public Bureaucracy: An Introduction to Public Administration* (Cambridge, Mass.: Winthrop, 1977), p. 7.

69. Heclo, *Government of Strangers*, pp. 12, 13; see also p. 224. Erwin C. Hargrove, *The Power of the Modern Presidency* (Philadelphia: Temple University Press, 1974), p. 237.

70. Quoted in Cronin, *State of the Presidency*, p. 69.

71. Ibid.

72. Stephen K. Bailey, *Congress in the Seventies* (New York: St. Martin's Press, 1970), p. 28; and Gawthrop, *Administrative Politics and Social Change*, pp. 28–29.

73. Donald T. Allensworth, *The U.S. Government in Action: Policy and Structure* (Pacific Palisades, Calif.: Goodyear, 1972), p. 57; James MacGregor Burns, J. W. Peltason, and Thomas E. Cronin, *Government by the People*, 10th ed. (Englewood Cliffs, N.J.:

Prentice-Hall, 1978), p. 372; CRM Books, *American Govern-ment Today* (Del Mar, Calif.: Ziff-Davis, 1974), p. 274; William Ebenstein, C. Herman Pritchett, Henry A. Turner, and Dean Mann, *American Democracy in World Perspective*, 4th ed. (New York: Harper & Row, 1976), p. 371; Koenig, *Toward a Democracy*, p. 254; Louis Loeb and Daniel M. Berman, *American Politics: Crisis and Challenge* (New York: Macmillan Co., 1975), p. 271; and Sam C. Sarkesian and Krish Nanda, *Politics and Power: An Introduction to American Government* (New York: Alfred, 1976), pp. 377–79.

74. Milton C. Cummings, Jr., and David Wise, *Democracy under Pressure: An Introduction to the American Political System*, 3d ed. (New York: Harcourt Brace Jovanovich, 1977), p. 425 (bureaucracy and client groups); Martin Diamond, Winston Mills Fisk, and Herbert Garfinkel, *The Democratic Republic: An Introduction to American National Government*, 2d ed. (Chicago: Rand McNally, 1970), pp. 249–50; Thomas R. Dye, Lee S. Greene, and George S. Parthemos, *American Government: Theory, Structure, and Process*, 2d ed. (North Scituate, Mass.: Duxbury, 1972), p. 352; John C. Livingston and Robert G. Thompson, *The Consent of the Governed*, 3d ed. (New York: Macmillan, 1971), p. 408; and Ruth C. Silva, Edward Keynes, Hugh A. Bone, and David W. Adamany, *American Government: Democracy and Liberty in Balance* (New York: Alfred A. Knopf, 1976), p. 313.

75. Leonard Freedman, *Power and Politics in America*, 3d ed. (North Scituate, Mass.: Duxbury, 1978), p. 282; Robert L. Keighton and Martin P. Sutton, *One Nation* (Lexington, Mass.: D. C. Heath, 1972), p. 239; Robert L. Morlan, *American Government: Policy Process*, 3d ed. (Boston: Houghton Mifflin, 1979), p. 219; Olson and Meyer, *Governing the United States*, p. 392; Robert H. Salisbury, *Governing America: Public Choice and Political Action* (New York: Appleton-Century-Crofts, 1973), pp. 303–4; Peter Woll and Robert Binstock, *America's Political System*, 3d ed. (New York: Random House, 1979), p. 372.

76. "The notion of iron triangles and subgovernments presumes small circles of participants who have succeeded in becoming largely autonomous. Issue networks, on the other hand, comprise a large number of participants with quite variable degrees of mutual commitment or of dependence on others in their environment; in fact it is almost impossible to say where a network leaves off and its environment begins. Iron triangles and subgovernments suggest a stable set of participants coalesced to control fairly narrow public programs which are in the

direct economic interest of each party to the alliance. Issue networks are almost the reverse image in each respect. Participants
move in and out of the networks constantly. Rather than groups
united in dominance over a program, no one, as far as one can
tell, is in control of the policies and issues. Any direct material
interest is often secondary to intellectual or emotional commitment. Network members reinforce each other's sense of issues
as their interests, rather than (as standard political or economic
models would have it) interests defining positions on issues."
Hugh Heclo, "Issue Networks and the Executive Establishment,"
in *The New American Political System,* ed. Anthony King
(Washington, D.C.: American Enterprise Institute for Public
Policy Research, 1978), p. 102.

CHAPTER FIVE: *The Dimensions of the Presidential Government*

1. "Beginning with Kennedy the president became progressively
   less a man who presided over the processes of government in
   Washington and became progressively more a one man genera-
   ator and executor of national policy." Joseph C. Harsch, "The
   Ford Presidency," *Christian Science Monitor,* March 6, 1975,
   p. 12. A former White House adviser made this statement to a
   political-science interviewer: "It is more important to symbolize
   solutions than it is to achieve them in operations. Getting legislation passed or getting a department to do things is never
   going to be as important as talking to people through the media
   and providing symbolic leadership about new directions."
   Thomas E. Cronin, *The State of the Presidency* (Boston: Little,
   Brown, 1975), p. 10.
2. Louis Harris, Survey, *Detroit Free Press,* April 4, 1977, p. 8E.
3. "According to Carter, the comprehensive approach offers a final
   decisive solution to problems." Aaron Wildavsky and Jack Knott,
   "Jimmy Carter's Theory of Governing," in *American Politics and
   Public Policy,* ed. Walter Dean Burnham and Martha Wagner
   Weinberg (Cambridge, Mass.: M.I.T. Press, 1978), p. 61. The
   package label of a comprehensive proposal tends to override
   particular conflicts and limitations and to give a virtuous impression. The Carter administration first proposed broad reforms in several areas, but proposals became more specific as
   time passed. Yet the campaigns for congressional acceptance
   placed more stress upon the label than upon the contents. The
   absence of a governing philosophy is asserted by James Fallows,
   a former Carter speechwriter (1976–78). "Carter believes fifty
   things but no one thing. . . . He thinks he 'leads' by choosing the

correct policy; but he fails to project a vision larger than the problem he is tackling at the moment." James Fallows, "The Passionless Presidency," *Atlantic Monthly* 243 (May 1979): 42–43.

4. Richard E. Neustadt, *Presidential Power: The Politics of Leadership* (New York: John Wiley & Sons, 1976), p. 224.

5. Henry C. Lockwood, *The Abolition of the Presidency* (New York: R. Worthington, 1884), p. 191. Robert S. Hirschfield, ed., *The Power of the Presidency: Concepts and Controversy*, 2d ed. (Chicago: Aldine, 1973), p. 251.

6. Lockwood, *Abolition of the Presidency*, p. 192. "It isn't stretching words too much to say that John F. Kennedy became a king and both Lyndon Johnson and Richard Nixon were emperors." Harsch, *Christian Science Monitor*, March 6, 1975, p. 12.

7. Henry James Ford, *Rise and Growth of American Politics* (New York: Macmillan, 1898), pp. 284, 293. See Hirschfield, *Power of the Presidency*, p. 268; Aaron Wildavsky, ed., *The Presidency* (Boston: Little, Brown, 1969), p. 435.

8. Clinton Rossiter, *The American Presidency*, 2d ed. (New York: New American Library, 1960, rev. 1962), 16, 17.

9. Alfred de Grazia, "The Myth of the President," in Wildavsky, ed., *The Presidency*, p. 50.

10. Louis W. Koenig, *The Chief Executive*, rev. ed. (New York: Harcourt Brace Jovanovich, 1968), p. 5; similarly, ibid., 3d ed., 1975), p. 11.

11. James D. Barber, *The Presidential Character: Predicting Performance in the White House*, 2d ed. (Englewood Cliffs, N.J.: Prentice-Hall, 1977), p. 4. Unchanged from 1972 edition.

12. Richard M. Pious, *The American Presidency* (New York: Basic Books, 1979), p. 8.

13. Walter Bagehot, *The English Constitution* (1867; reprint ed., London: Oxford University Press, 1928), p. 30. "For millions of citizens, the president becomes the unifying symbol of the nation. He performs for American society many of the functions of the British monarch." Robert H. Salisbury, *Governing America: Public Choice and Political Action* (New York: Appleton-Century-Crofts, 1973), p. 290. See also Rowland Egger, *The President of the United States*, 2d ed. (New York: McGraw-Hill, 1972), p. 3.

14. George E. Reedy, *The Twilight of the Presidency* (New York: New American Library, 1970), p. 21.

15. Barber, *Presidential Character*, p. 5.

16. John F. Murphy, *The Pinnacle: The Contemporary American Presidency* (Philadelphia: J. B. Lippincott, 1974), p. 27.

17. Koenig, *Chief Executive*, p. 6.

18. Joseph Kallenbach, *The American Chief Executive* (New York: Harper & Row, 1966), p. 3. See also Dale Vinyard, *The Presidency* (New York: Charles Scribner's Sons, 1971), p. 4.

19. Grant McConnell, *The Modern Presidency* (New York: St. Martin's Press, 1967), p. 3; 2d ed. 1976), p. 6. Egger, *President of the United States*, p. 5.

20. Barber, *Presidential Character*, p. 5.

21. American conceptions of democracy seem to range from animalistic anarchism to angelic authoritarianism.

22. Rossiter, *American Presidency*, pp. 252, 251.

23. Baron de Montesquieu, *L'Esprit des Lois* (1748), bk. 8, secs. 16–20. His primary solution was confederation, ibid., bk. 9, secs. 1–3; but his final interest was in a limited monarchy, ibid., bk. 9, secs. 4–6. Baron de Montesquieu, *The Spirit of the Laws* (New York: Hafner, 1949), 2 vols. in 1, vol. 1, pp. 120–22, 126–28, 129–30.

24. "If the President were not a king, the system could not survive. If he were not elected, he could not be trusted with the powers he must exercise if the system is to survive." Egger, *President of the United States*, p. 4.

25. Woodrow Wilson, *Constitutional Government in the United States* (New York: Columbia University Press, 1908, 1964), p. 70. Hirschfield, *Power of the Presidency*, p. 92.

26. Clinton Rossiter, "The Presidency: Focus of Leadership," *New York Times Magazine*, November 11, 1956, p. 26. Hirschfield, *Power of the Presidency*, pp. 263, 264.

27. Thomas E. Cronin, *State of the Presidency*, uses the label *textbook presidency* for exaggerated versions; but he has a broad meaning for *textbook*, which includes the press and the broadcast media (p. 24) and even campaign rhetoric (p. 31). He considers Theodore White's books on the making of the President as textbooks for millions of adults. Cronin seems most disturbed by those who give the presidency a religious dimension (p. 34). Yet he does not include political scientists in that group. "Political scientists have usually not read in such meaning, or at least have not infused their view of the presidency with connotations of a civil religion." Ibid., p. 35. The author made a considerable survey of political-science textbooks for the basic university course in American national government. He concluded that those texts presented a balanced, sober picture of the presidency even in the 1960s. Clinton Rossiter, in his special analysis of the presidency, uses the expression "the American people's one authentic trumpet" (*American Presidency*, p. 31), but no instance of such remarks has been found in pre–Watergate texts for the basic course.

28. Robert S. Hirschfield, "The Power of the Presidency," in Hirschfield, ed., *Power of the Presidency,* pp. 290, 285–89, 291.
29. John F. Kennedy, "Foreword," in Theodore C. Sorensen, *Decision-Making in the White House* (New York: Columbia University Press, 1963), p. xi.
30. Neustadt, *Presidential Power,* pp. 110, 77.
31. William F. Mullen, *Presidential Power and Politics* (New York: St. Martin's Press, 1976), p. 265.
32. Reedy, *Twilight of the Presidency,* pp. 32–35.
33. "The President represents in the Executive department the whole people of the United States as each representative of the legislative department represents portions of them." President Polk, quoted in Wilfred E. Binkley, *President and Congress,* 3d rev. ed. (New York: Random House, 1962), p. 124.
34. James MacGregor Burns, *Presidential Government: The Crucible of Leadership* (Boston: Houghton Mifflin, 1965, 1973), p. 318. The 1973 edition shows no change in the quoted statements. On the myth of the President as representative of the entire people, see Mullen, *Presidential Power and Politics,* p. 253.
35. Louis W. Koenig, "More Power to the President (Not Less)," *New York Times Magazine,* January 3, 1975, p. 7; Hirschfield, ed., *Power of the Presidency,* pp. 362–63.
36. Woodrow Wilson, *Constitutional Government in the United States,* p. 70. John F. Kennedy made this statement by Woodrow Wilson the theme of his prenomination speech before the National Press Club, January 14, 1960. See Hirschfield, *Power of the Presidency,* p. 130.
37. Dorothy B. James, *The Contemporary Presidency,* 2d ed. (Indianapolis: Bobbs-Merrill, 1974), p. 168.
38. A President nowadays "cannot be as small as he might like." Richard E. Neustadt, *Presidential Power,* p. 73.
39. Philippa Strum, *Presidential Power and American Democracy* (Pacific Palisades, Calif.: Goodyear, 1972), pp. 83, 78.
40. "It should be noted that in our political system the President is not always motivated to control the bureaucracy. . . . The American Presidency is a great institution, but the President is not in fact 'Chief Administrator.' He cannot, nor does he really wish to, control all the complex activities engaged in by the administrative branch. In many key areas of presidential responsibility he demands, and generally receives, loyalty from administrative agencies. But in other fields the agencies function with partial autonomy in the policy spheres that have been assigned to them by Congress." Peter Woll, *American Bureaucracy,* 2d ed. (New York: Norton, 1977), pp. 246, 247.
41. John H. Kessel, *The Domestic Presidency: Decision-Making in*

the White House (North Scituate, Mass.: Duxbury Press, 1975), pp. 4–7.

42. Ibid., p. 6.

43. Ibid., p. 5.

44. Koenig, *Chief Executive*, pp. 369–80.

45. Compare Aaron Wildavsky, "The Two Presidencies," and Donald A. Peppers, "The Two Presidencies: Eight Years Later," in *Perspectives on the Presidency*, ed. Aaron Wildavsky (Boston: Little, Brown, 1975), pp. 448–61 and 462–71 respectively. Wildavsky's 1966 article did not contend absolute separation or complete dissimilarity. For instance, his statistics on passage of presidential proposals during 1948–64 were: domestic, 40%; defense, 73%; foreign, 58%; and immigration, 13%. Ibid., pp. 449–60.

46. James, *Contemporary Presidency*, pp. 176, 227.

47. For a scholarly analysis of the legal and operational aspects of the war powers of Congress and the President, including the War Powers Resolution of 1973, see Louis Fisher, *The Constitution between Friends: Congress, the President, and the Law* (New York: St. Martin's Press, 1978), pp. 214–46.

48. The Duke University School of Law devoted an issue of *Law and Contemporary Problems* (35 [Summer 1970]) to "The Institutionalized Presidency."

49. Lester G. Seligman, "Leadership: Political Aspects," *International Encyclopedia of the Social Sciences* (New York: Macmillan, 1968), vol. 9, p. 109. Randall B. Ripley, *American National Government and Public Policy* (New York: Free Press, 1974), p. 128

50. The Budget and Accounting Act, approved June 10, 1921, 42 Stat. 20; 31 U.S.C. § 11–16. Louis Fisher, *President and Congress: Power and Policy* (New York: Free Press, 1972), pp. 101–5.

51. On the structure of the Executive Office of the President, see James W. Davis, Jr., *The National Executive Branch* (New York: Free Press, 1970), pp. 126–28; Harold Seidman, *Politics, Position, and Power: The Dynamics of Federal Organization*, 2d ed. (New York: Oxford University Press, 1975), pp. 74–86; Cronin, *State of the Presidency*, pp. 117–75.

52. See William Ebenstein, C. Herman Pritchett, Henry A. Turner, and Dean Mann, *American Democracy in World Perspective*, 4th ed. (New York: Harper & Row, 1976), p. 351.

53. For a list of the agencies that have been included in the Executive Office of the President since 1939, see Cronin, *State of the Presidency*, pp. 326–27.

54. Lester G. Seligman and Cary Covington, "The Process of Presi-

dential Institutionalization" (Paper delivered at the Midwest Political Science Convention, Chicago, April 19, 1979), pp. 22–23.

55. Seidman, *Politics, Position and Power*, pp. 191–93; Cronin, *State of the Presidency*, p. 132.

56. See Cronin, *State of the Presidency*, pp. 326–27.

57. *New York Times*, July 16, 1977, p. 22.

58. "A full generation's experience with bigger and better presidencies has left the situation substantially unchanged." Robert C. Wood, "When Government Works," in *Perspectives on the Presidency*, ed. Wildavsky, p. 396. Another political scientist states that the "persistent drive for overhead consolidation may be marching us to the rear." Frederick G. Thayer, "Presidential Policy Processes and 'New Administration': A Search for Revised Paradigms," in *Perspectives on the Presidency: A Collection*, ed. Stanley Bach and George T. Sulzner (Lexington, Mass.: D. C. Heath, 1974), p. 268. See also Robert S. Gilmour, "The Institutionalized Presidency: A Conceptual Clarification," in *The Presidency in Contemporary Context*, ed. Norman C. Thomas (New York: Dodd, Mead, 1975), pp. 158–59. "The 'inner Presidency' of the White House staff and the Executive Office has not jelled." Ernest S. Griffith, *The American Presidency: The Dilemmas of Shared Power and Divided Government* (New York: New York University Press, 1976), p. 33.

59. On domestic policymaking in the White House, see Kessel, *Domestic Presidency*, pp. 108–9; Cronin, *State of the Presidency*, pp. 124–27; Kenneth J. Meier, *Politics and the Bureaucracy: Policymaking in the Fourth Branch of Government* (North Scituate, Mass.: Duxbury Press, 1979), p. 147.

60. President Carter eliminated the more or less formal council of eight or nine cabinet members and stressed a policy staff headed by Stuart E. Eizenstat. Hedrick Smith, "A Man the President Listens to," *New York Times*, November 6, 1977, sec. 4, p. 2.

61. See Davis, *National Executive Branch*, pp. 183–92; Seidman, *Politics, Position, and Power*, pp. 189–91; and Fisher, *President and Congress*, pp. 85–110.

62. Louis Fisher, *Presidential Spending Power* (Princeton: Princeton University Press, 1975), p. 258.

63. Ibid., pp. 46–58. Richard P. Nathan, *The Plot that Failed: Nixon and the Administrative Presidency* (New York: John Wiley & Sons, 1975).

64. Louis C. Gawthrop, *Administrative Politics and Social Change* (New York: St. Martin's Press, 1971), p. 34.

65. Nathan, *Plot That Failed*, pp. 59–76.

66. See supra, n. 58.

67. Godfrey Sperling, Jr., "Who Has Jimmy Carter's Ear?" *Christian Science Monitor,* December 29, 1978, p. 3.
68. Wilson, *Constitutional Government in the United States,* p. 70.
69. James, *Contemporary Presidency,* p. 174; Strum, *Presidential Power and American Democracy,* p. 85; 2d ed. (1979), p. 152.
70. Cronin, *State of the Presidency,* pp. 16, 255–56.
71. "It is with his staff that a president most frequently interacts." Mullen, *Presidential Power and Politics,* p. 181. See also Patrick Anderson, *The Presidents' Men* (New York: Doubleday, 1969), p. 235.
72. Reedy, *Twilight of the Presidency,* pp. 17, 22. See also nn. 10–20.
73. Richard E. Neustadt, "Approaches to Staffing the Presidency: Notes on FDR and JFK," *American Political Science Review* 57 (December 1963):856.
74. Certain policy expectations may have become routine. James, *Contemporary Presidency,* pp. 90, 168, 171.
75. Hugh Heclo, *A Government of Strangers: Executive Politics in Washington* (Washington, D.C.: Brookings Institution, 1977), p. 12; Eugene Lewis, *American Politics in a Bureaucratic Age: Citizens, Constituents, Clients, and Victims* (Cambridge, Mass.: Winthrop, 1977), p. 163; Dale Vinyard, *The Presidency,* p. 116; James, *Contemporary Presidency,* p. 148; Seidman, *Politics, Position, and Power,* p. 91; Peter Woll, *American Bureaucracy,* 2d ed. (New York: Norton, 1977), p. 246.
76. Richard L. Strout, *Christian Science Monitor,* March 7, 1978, pp. 1, 18.
77. Mullen, *Presidential Power and Politics,* pp. 1, 265.
78. Erwin C. Hargrove, *Presidential Leadership: Personality and Political Style* (New York: Macmillan Co., 1966), p. 147.
79. James Fallows, "The Passionless Presidency: The Trouble with Jimmy Carter's Administration," *Atlantic Monthly* 243 (May 1979): 42, 43.
80. Koenig, *Chief Executive,* pp. 349–50; Patrick Anderson, *The President's Men* (Garden City, N.Y.: Doubleday, 1969), pp. 191–92.
81. Anderson, *President's Men,* p. 319.
82. Reedy, *Twilight of the Presidency,* p. 96.
83. Dan Rather and Gary Paul Gates, *The Palace Guard* (New York: Harper & Row, 1974), p. 33. *New York Times,* March 31, 1977, p. A20; ibid., February 21, 1978, p. 24.
84. James MacGregor Burns, J. W. Peltason, and Thomas E. Cronin, *Government by the People,* 10th ed. (Englewood Cliffs, N.J.: Prentice-Hall, 1978), p. 294. See also *Time,* May 15, 1978, p. 22. This last quotes a White House aide: "One of the biggest mistakes we made during the transition was letting the Cabinet

secretaries play such an independent role in naming their assistants."
85. A plan submitted to Congress would permit the President to increase the number of top salary positions on the White House staff from fourteen to twenty-five. *New York Times*, April 5, 1978, p. A23.
86. Samuel I. Rosenman, "The Presidency As I Have Seen It," in Emmet John Hughes, *The Living Presidency* (New York: Coward McCann and Geoghegan, 1972), pp. 361, 362.
87. Cronin, *State of the Presidency*, p. 158. "In this sense the executive branch operates much like a trading arena in which different participants hope that their preferences will prevail. Few on either side of the White House–departmental exchange are easily pleased." Ibid., p. 160.
88. "Presidents cannot control the bureaus because the department secretaries cannot control them. The presidential chain of command breaks down because department secretaries lack incentives and resources—administrative and political—to control the bureaus. Secretaries have four functions: they must manage their departments and set priorities; represent constituencies to the president and the president to constituencies; help make administration policy and propose new policy initiatives; offer advice to the president. Most secretaries are least effective as managers." Richard M. Pious, *American Presidency*, p. 236. " . . . a Cabinet appointee and his assistant secretaries frequently have very little expertise in the substantive concerns of their department." Consequently they "are forced to rely heavily upon the career bureaucrats." Robert E. DiClerico, *The American President* (Englewood Cliffs, N.J.: Prentice-Hall, 1979), p. 115.
89. Fallows, "Passionless President," *Atlantic Monthly* 243 (May 1979):42.
90. Richard E. Neustadt, *President Power*, (1960 ed.) p. 162, (1976 ed.) p. 230.

Chapter Six: *The Character of the Emerging Fifth Branch*

1. The five branches in this study have no relation to the five branches in John Rawls's *A Theory of Justice* (Cambridge, Mass.: Harvard University Press, 1971), pp. 275–83. Rawls's five are types of functions: allocation, stabilization, transfer, distribution, and exchange. Herein the branches are institutions or, more accurately, groups of officials.
2. Harold Seidman, *Politics, Position, and Power: The Dynamics of Federal Organization* (New York: Oxford University Press,

1970), pp. 100, 101. A 1970 article makes a definite split, with State, Defense, Treasury, and Justice in the inner cabinet. Thomas E. Cronin, " 'Everybody Believes in Democracy until He Gets to the White House': An Examination of White House–Departmental Relations," *Law and Contemporary Problems* 35 (Summer 1970):609. Erwin C. Hargrove, *The Power of the Modern Presidency* (Philadelphia: Temple University Press, 1974), pp. 238–39, adopts Cronin's distinction. Cronin's recent work, *The State of the Presidency* (Boston: Little, Brown, 1975), p. 190, repeats the division.

3. Hargrove, *Power of the Modern Presidency*, pp. 238–39.
4. Cronin, *State of the Presidency*, pp. 191, 197–98. Cronin explains the general White House–departmental tensions and the special case of the outer-cabinet: "As tension builds around whether or to what extent domestic policy leadership rests with the departments or with the Office of Management and Budget or the White House, and as staff and line distinctions become blurred, the estrangement between the domestic department heads and the White House staff deepens. . . . Outer-cabinet members have complained bitterly about the unmanageability of their departments and the many pressures on them." Ibid., pp. 199–200.
5. Stephen K. Bailey, "The President and His Political Executives," *Annals of the American Academy of Political and Social Science* 307 (Sept. 1956):25.
6. Grant McConnell, *The Modern Presidency* (New York: St. Martin's Press, 1967), p. 58. Essentially similar, ibid., 2d ed. (1976), p. 67.
7. Bailey, *President and Political Executives*, p. 30.
8. Louis W. Koenig, *The Chief Executive*, 3d ed. (New York: Harcourt Brace Jovanovich, 1975), p. 185.
9. William E. Mullen, *Presidential Power and Politics* (New York: St. Martin's Press, 1976), pp. 190–91.
10. Robert Presthus, *Public Administration*, 6th ed. (New York: Ronald, 1975), p. 364.
11. Robert E. DiClerico, *The American President* (Englewood Cliffs, N.J.: Prentice-Hall, 1979), p. 114; Richard M. Pious, *The American Presidency* (New York: Basic Books, 1979), p. 238. See ch. 5 supra, "White House Government."
12. Richard F. Fenno, Jr., *The President's Cabinet* (Cambridge, Mass.: Harvard University Press, 1959), p. 231.
13. Cronin, *State of the Presidency*, pp. 160, 168, 158, 200, 199–200.
14. Robert C. Fried, *Performance in American Bureaucracy* (Boston: Little, Brown, 1976), p. 201.
15. Ibid., pp. 197–98.

16. Richard E. Neustadt, "Politicians and Bureaucrats," in David B. Truman, ed., *The American Assembly: The Congress and America's Future*, 2d ed. (Englewood Cliffs, N.J.: Prentice-Hall, 1973), pp. 125–26.

17. Ibid., pp. 138–39.

18. Pious, *American Presidency*, p. 238.

19. Kenneth M. Dolbeare and Murray J. Edelman, *American Politics: Policies, Power, and Change*, 3d ed. (Lexington, Mass.: D. C. Heath, 1977), p. 236.

20. Ibid., p. 210.

21. Cronin, *State of the Presidency*, p. 169.

22. Ibid., pp. 97, 158, 169.

23. Hugh Heclo, *A Government of Strangers: Executive Politics in Washington* (Washington: Brookings Institution, 1977), p. 95.

24. Ibid., p. 109.

25. Ibid., p. 103.

26. Ibid., p. 249.

27. Ibid., p. 250.

28. See infra, ch. 8, pp. 173, 181–83, 187–89.

29. "Given the formidable administrative task Cabinet secretaries face, it is not altogether surprising that they and their assistant secretaries come to rely heavily upon the career bureaucracy within their departments." DiClerico, *American President*, p. 114. "Political executives are hardly settled into office when they resign, get fired, or win promotions. They rarely gain the expertise to control their bureaus. With high turnover the normal pattern, the incentive for careerists is to 'educate from below,' to delay making ordered changes, and to manipulate their superiors. Bureau chiefs rely on 'end runs' to Congress and their constituencies to evade the presidential chain of command. Each side blames the other for conflict and delay." Pious, *American Presidency*, p. 238. "Cabinet members and bureaucrats have such different responsibilities and views from presidential advisers that the relationship between these bodies can easily become tense and conflictual." Steven A. Shull, *Presidential Policy Making: An Analysis* (Brunswick, O.: King's Court, 1979), p. 171. See also supra: ch. 3, "Departmental Disunity"; ch. 4, "Specialized Knowledge and Information."

30. Roger Hilsman, *To Govern America* (New York: Harper & Row, 1979), p. 223.

31. "Top White House officials, reportedly dissatisfied with the way energy policy has been handled and concerned about potential political damage to President Carter, are moving to take control of the situation from the Department of Energy.

"As part of this effort, they are reported to be seeking to ease out John F. O'Leary, Deputy Secretary of Energy, who was Energy Secretary James R. Schlesinger's choice for the post. . . .

"The White House wants 'someone who is a Carter person and who is under political control,' one Energy Department official said. . . .

"The involvement of the White House staff ·in the energy situation first became substantial in April, when Stuart E. Eizenstat, the President's assistant for domestic affairs, took over the chairmanship of the Energy Task Force and began using the group's daily meetings as a way of reviewing virtually all coming energy decisions. . . .

"The decision to take energy policymaking into the White House is based principally on a view that the Department of Energy is incapable of coping with the problem on its own. . . .

"Another reason for the shift in control is said to be a conviction of top White House officials that the energy problem has become the principal issue threatening the President's political health. Solving immediate energy problems is essential to a second term for the President, they are said to believe.

"Finally, some White House officials offer a more conventional explanation: that the energy situation has broadened into a problem that affects virtually every Government department and agency and therefore merits close White House attention." Steven Rattner, "White House Is Moving to Reduce Policy Role of Energy Department," *New York Times*, July 3, 1979, p. A1. There is another key point in the final explanation. When the problem became multidepartmental, it was shifted to the White House and not to the cabinet.

32. See ch. 4 supra, "Method of Appointment as a Basis of Classification."

33. A leading analyst suggests three types of federal personnel: "full career, in-and-outers, and high-level entrants." The first "constitute fully three-fifths of the sample" and are the "true bureaucrats"; the "in-and-outers" comprise one-fifth of the sample. Presthus, *Public Administration*, pp. 181–82.

34. Fried, *Performance in American Bureaucracy*, pp. 34, 378; James W. Davis, Jr., *The National Executive Branch* (New York: Free Press, 1970), pp. 33–41.

35. However, Richard Nixon named Republicans to head five of the "Big Six" regulatory commissions within a year of taking office. Milton C. Cummings and David Wise, *Democracy Under Pressure: An Introduction to the American Political System*, 3d ed. (New York: Harcourt Brace Jovanovich, 1977), p. 417.

36. Leonard Freedman, *Power and Politics in America*, 3d ed. (North Scituate, Mass.: Duxbury Press, 1978), pp. 3–5.

37. The House Education and Labor Committee "found itself writing an obituary for OEO, 10-year-old symbol of the late President Johnson's 'war on poverty,' in an attempt to meet the objections of Republican committee members." *Congressional Quarterly Weekly Report* 32, May 18, 1974, p. 1313. The Community Services Act of 1974 was enacted January 4, 1975, 88 Stat. 2292, 42 U.S.C. § 2790, 2791.

38. Myers v. United States, 272 U.S. 52. See ch. 4 supra.

39. William H. Taft, *The President and His Powers* (New York: Columbia University Press, 1967), p. 71.

40. Seymour S. Berlin, "The Federal Executive Service," *Civil Service Journal* 11 (April-June 1971):9–13.

41. Cronin, *State of the Presidency*, pp. 96, 97.

42. 5 U.S.C. § 5308.

43. *Congressional Quarterly Weekly Report* 32, October 12, 1974, p. 2873; 33, March 22, 1975, p. 627; 34, October 9, 1976, p. 2890.

44. William E. Mullen, *Presidential Power and Politics* (New York: St. Martin's Press, 1976), p. 253.

45. Koenig, *Chief Executive*, pp. 221, 237; Cronin, *State of the Presidency*, pp. 121, 138–39, 306-11.

46. Erwin C. Hargrove and Roy Hoopes, *The Presidency: A Question of Power* (Boston: Little, Brown, 1975), p. 51.

47. See in particular Robert J. Sickels, *The Presidency: An Introduction* (Englewood Cliffs, N.J.: Prentice-Hall, 1980), pp. 123–51.

48. Francis Lieber, *On Civil Liberty and Self-Government* (London: Bentley, 1853), 3d ed. (Philadelphia: J. B. Lippincott, 1883), p. 125.

49. "In social background, the national bureaucracy is more broadly representative of society than are Congress and the president." Louis W. Koenig, *Toward a Democracy: An Introduction to American National Government* (New York: Harcourt Brace Jovanovich, 1973), pp. 241–43. See also Seidman, *Politics, Position, and Power*, p. 109; Presthus, *Public Administration*, pp. 56–59; Lewis C. Mainzer, *Political Bureaucracy* (Glenview, Ill.: Scott, Foresman, 1973), p. 127.

50. Peter Woll, *Public Policy* (Cambridge, Mass.: Winthrop, 1974), p. 255. Another political-science analyst of the national administration considers the role of the bureaucracy during the Watergate affair and finds constitutional support for the restraining force of the civil servants. His analysis includes these statements: "Ironically, liberalism seems to have been better served by bureaucratic agencies that displayed the usually condemned resistance to White House suggestions. Bureaucratic resistance to change, or fear of controversy, which we may condemn as unresponsiveness, now seems the very bulwark of constitutionalism

and legality in the American administrative process." Fried, *Performance in American Bureaucracy,* p. 214.

51. Eugene Lewis, *American Politics in a Bureaucratic Age: Citizens, Constituents, Clients, and Victims* (Cambridge, Mass.: Winthrop, 1977), p. 162.

52. William L. Morrow, *Public Administration: Politics and the Political System* (New York: Random House, 1975), pp. 189–90, 191–92.

CHAPTER SEVEN: *The Essential Interactions of Five-Branch Government*

1. For instance, a leading analysis of the American bureaucracy includes this statement in its conclusion: "It is difficult to grasp the concept that the bureaucracy is not subordinate to one or more of the three initial branches of American government. But the fact is the three primary branches have necessarily supported the creation of a semiautonomous bureaucracy as an instrument to enable our government to meet the challenges it has faced." Peter Woll, *American Bureaucracy,* 2d ed. (New York: W. W. Norton, 1977), p. 248. See also ch. 3 supra, nn. 2, 21, 23, 27, 33, 38, 58, 71, 84, 86, and 88. See infra n. 12.

2. For a fuller examination of the principles of constitutional distribution, see Henry J. Merry, *Constitutional Function of Presidential-Administrative Separation* (Washington, D.C.: University Press of America, 1978).

3. U.S., *Constitution,* art. II, sec. 2, par. 2.

4. See ch. 3 supra, nn. 75–88.

5. "The top officials in each agency and those on whom the President relies for general policy advice are not regarded as part of the civil service. They are ordinarily chosen because the President likes their political beliefs or because their appointment to high posts is politically advantageous for the administration—not necessarily because of skill or expertise and certainly not because they score high on a competitive examination. Cabinet secretaries and assistant secretaries, commissioners in the regulatory agencies, top White House aides, ambassadors, and some other leading figures in the executive branch fall into this group." Kenneth M. Dolbeare and Murray J. Edelman, *American Politics: Policies, Power and Change,* 3d ed. (Lexington, Mass.: D. C. Heath, 1977), p. 324. For distinctions made by other political scientists between political and career executives, see supra, ch. 1, n. 17.

6. See ch. 3 supra, nn. 86–89.

7. Ibid., nn. 71–72.
8. Peter Woll asserts a parallel specialization of the administration and the society. "Perhaps the most important implication of bureaucratic power and organization today is that in relation to constitutional theory and methods pertaining to the control of faction. . . . The separation of powers was to prevent any unified group from gaining control of the national governmental apparatus. . . . It should be realized that there are both governmental and private interest groups. . . . One of the most complex and important implications of the rise of the administrative branch is the proliferation of such governmental interest groups." Peter Woll, *American Democracy*, 2d ed. (New York: Norton, 1977), pp. 30, 31. See also ch. 6 supra, nn. 51–52.
9. The press is sometimes called a fourth branch. Douglass Cater, *The Fourth Branch of Government* (Boston: Houghton Mifflin, 1959); Charles Peters and James Fallows, eds., *The System: The Five Branches of American Government* (New York: Praeger, 1976). This last adds interest groups as well as the press to the three official branches.
10. "The president will continue to be our ceremonial leader, and the media will continue to lavish attention on every move of his family and himself, treating them as if they were a kind of royal family. This was true even of the unpretentious Jerry Ford. And when Jimmy Carter and his family chose to walk the inaugural parade rather than ride in the presidential limousine, the media went into paroxysms of delight, as though he were a king who was deigning to walk." Leonard Freedman, *Power and Politics in America*, 3d ed. (North Scituate, Mass.: Duxbury, 1978), p. 227.
11. See in general: "Centripetal Forces: Party Leadership and Organization," in Stephen K. Bailey, *Congress in the Seventies* (New York: St. Martin's Press, 1970), pp. 39–49. See also: John S. Saloma III, *Congress and the New Politics* (Boston: Little, Brown, 1969); Morris P. Fiorina, *Congress: Keystone of the Washington Establishment* (New Haven, Conn.: Yale University Press, 1977).
12. "The proliferation of staff has inevitably turned many congressmen and senators into managers as well as legislators, and has consequently skewed their attention to problems of internal conflict resolution within their several fiefdoms. Whether this represents a net gain for congressional efficiency and deliberation is doubtful." Bailey, *Congress in the Seventies*, p. 61. "Congress Frets about Its Own Bureaucracy," *U.S. News and World Report*, May 15, 1978, pp. 21–22.
13. See ch. 5 supra, "Lower Limits of the Presidential Government."

14. See supra: ch. 1, n. 5; ch. 2, "Narrow Realm of Unshared Functions."

15. See ch. 5 supra, "Elevation of the Presidency" and "External Roles of the Presidency."

16. See, in general, Lewis Mayers, *The American Legal System*, rev. ed. (New York: Harper & Row, 1964); Herbert Jacob, *Justice in America: Courts, Lawyers, and the Judicial Process*, 2d ed. (Boston: Little, Brown, 1972).

17. See, in general, Sheldon Goldman and Thomas P. Jahnige, *The Federal Courts as a Political System*, 2d ed. (New York: Harper & Row, 1976).

18. See ch. 2 supra, n. 39. See also Merry, *Constitutional Functions of Presidential-Administrative Separation*, pp. 80–81.

19. See ch. 3 supra, n. 66.

20. Louis C. Gawthrop, *Administrative Politics and Social Change* (New York: St. Martin's Press, 1971), p. 24; David H. Rosenbloom, *Federal Service and the Constitution: The Development of the Public Employment Relationship* (Ithaca, N.Y.: Cornell University Press, 1971).

21. U.S., Civil Service Commission, *1975 Annual Report* (Washington, D.C.: Government Printing Office, 1976), p. 34; id., *1976 Annual Report* (ibid., 1977), p. 39.

22. Rowland Egger, *The President of the United States*, 2d ed. (New York: McGraw-Hill, 1972), p. 45.

23. Ibid.

24. See ch. 4 supra, nn. 25–30.

25. See ch. 6 supra, "Dimensions of the Emerging Fifth Branch."

26. Hugh Heclo, *A Government of Strangers: Executive Politics in Washington* (Washington, D.C.: Brookings Institution, 1977), pp. 110, 111, 112.

27. Ibid., p. 111.

28. See ch. 4 supra, n. 41.

29. *Congressional Quarterly Weekly Report* 36 (January 28, 1978), p. 175.

30. See ch. 4 supra, n. 30.

31. Dolbeare and Edelman, *American Politics*, p. 317. "It is policemen, income tax auditors, welfare department caseworkers, . . . and thousands of other public employees, often in relatively lowly positions, who decide whether individuals and groups of individuals will be helped or hurt by the statutes, court decisions, and executive orders they apply and interpret." Ibid., pp. 317–18.

32. "Americans overrate the President's political power as often as they underrate the professional bureaucracy as a powerful element of American national government." Robert S. Ross, *Amer-

ican National Government: An Introduction to Political Institutions, 2d ed. (Chicago: Rand McNally, 1976), p. 133.

33. See ch. 3 supra, "Departmental Disunity."
34. Robert C. Fried, *Performance in American Bureaucracy* (Boston: Little, Brown, 1976), p. 232.
35. Louis W. Koenig, *The Chief Executive,* 3d ed. (New York: Harcourt Brace Jovanovich, 1975), p. 183.
36. Charles M. Hardin, *Presidential Power and Accountability: Toward a New Constitution* (Chicago: University of Chicago Press, 1974), p. 15.
37. Dorothy B. James, *The Contemporary Presidency,* 2d ed. (Indianapolis: Bobbs-Merrill, 1974), p. 212.
38. Koenig, *Chief Executive,* pp. 183–84.
39. Peter Woll and Rochelle Jones, "The Bureaucracy as a Check upon the President," *The Bureaucrat* 3 (April 1974):19.
40. See ch. 4 supra, "Continuity of Specialized Relationships."
41. Heclo, *Government of Strangers,* pp. 84–112; see supra, n. 5.
42. "At most, the President can be only a quasi-party leader. A variety of forces and pressures compel him to temper and contain his partisanship. . . . although the party system has enabled a national popular majority to choose a President, when he attempts to translate his electoral promises into policy he finds himself in a government that permits only limited majority rule because of separation of powers and checks and balances, among other things. . . . Within the past two decades, disparate forces have been effecting alterations of the parties to the point that, compared with their historic appearance, they have become scarcely recognizable. Television, primaries, campaigning by jet aircraft, the increasingly augmented ranks of the independent voter, ticket-splitting, and such potent social forces as affluence, more widespread education, and enhanced population mobility have swiftly outmoded the traditional parties." Koenig, *Chief Executive,* pp. 146, 147. "Political appointees in Washington are substantially on their own and vulnerable to bureaucratic power." Heclo, *Government of Strangers,* p. 112. See also James, *Contemporary Presidency,* pp. 292–94.
43. Heclo, *Government of Strangers,* pp. 103–112; see ch. 4 supra, n. 41.
44. See ch. 4 supra, "Continuity of Specialized Relationships."
45. See ch. 6 supra, nn. 19–24.
46. See ch. 5 supra, "Elevation of the Presidency" and "External Roles of the Presidency."
47. See supra, nn. 34–37.
48. "It is a maxim of the law, admitting few if any exceptions, that every duty laid upon a public officer, for the benefit of a private

person, is enforceable by judicial process." Butterworth v. Hoe, 112 U.S. 51, 57 (1884). See also Fried, *Performance in American Bureaucracy*, p. 261.

49. A 1937 report recognized that "well over two-thirds of all legislation emanating from Congress originates in and is often drafted by the bureaucracy." Peter Woll, *Public Policy* (Cambridge, Mass.: Winthrop, 1974), p. 187.

50. See ch. 6 supra, "Potentials of Specialized Activism" and "Prospects for More Neutral Administration."

51. "The doctrine of monocratic administrative responsibility holds that the superior is responsible (blamable) for all activities of the subordinates—although it is not possible for the superior to know about them or to prevent them. The superior has the right to command and veto without appeal. Subordinates act to carry out his orders (or the orders of someone else he has ordered them to obey). Their actions are determined by him; therefore, the superior is responsible. . . . There is considerable confusion about the doctrine of administrative responsibility, especially in the United States. It was consistently applied to General Yamashita, commander of the Japanese forces in the Philippines late in World War II. . . . In the trials of Nazi war criminals, on the other hand, the Allies agreed that the command of a superior officer would not be a defense. They adopted a pluralist doctrine. The German soldier was not only responsible to his boss, but to higher laws as well—the laws of humanity. If he violated them, even while carrying out the commands of a superior, he could be convicted and punished.

"This pluralist doctrine of administrative responsibility is illustrated by Ralph Nader [1972] when he urges that all government employees 'blow the whistle' when they disagree with their superiors. Many spokesmen for the news media have taken this view to justify the publication of secret government information, although much of the media was very critical of the doctrine at the time of the Nazi war trials.

"The media . . . claims the right to interview all employees (and even inmates), attend all meetings, and see all documents, thereby disregarding the elaborate system of rights and duties that constitutes modern bureaucracy.

"Former special Watergate prosecutor Leon Jaworski had a serious problem with the doctrine. He felt that he must be independent of his boss's wishes and orders (for example, in order to subpoena him); and he needed to be able to prosecute the president's subordinates whether they were carrying out orders or not. . . .

"The House Judiciary Committee, considering impeachment

of President Nixon, looked long and hard at the monocratic doctrine of the president's responsibility for all the acts of his subordinates, the classic Madisonian doctrine of the presidency. However, since the subordinates individually had been held responsible for their actions, were indicted, and many convicted to prison terms, it would hardly be logical to claim that the president was the one responsible for their actions. To have both superior and subordinates responsible, one must interpret the organization as a conspiracy. This is the direction in which the Judiciary Committee and the special Prosecutor went, disregarding the presidential branch as an institution." Victor A. Thompson, *Bureaucracy and the Modern World* (Morristown, N.J.: General Learning Press, 1976), pp. 91–92. The conviction of individual members of President Nixon's staff indicates that not even the White House office is an administrative monolith with a unified legal structure of responsibility and obedience. Much less can we expect the whole executive branch to have hierarchical integrity. Administrative decisionmaking is so far from an exact science that there are likely to be many policy dissenters; and even on doubtful issues, a dissenter may feel obliged to "blow the whistle." Whistle blowing is not apt to be confined to costly overruns.

52. See app. infra. See also ch. 3 supra, "Political Competition within the Executive Branch."

53. See ch. 4 supra, n. 30.

54. See ch. 6 supra, "Potentials of Specialized Activism."

55. See ch. 2 supra, nn. 26–28; see also Merry, *Constitutional Function of Presidential-Administrative Separation*, pp. 68–70. "While the Constitution diffuses power the better to secure liberty, it also contemplates that practice will integrate the dispersed powers into a workable government. It enjoins upon its branches separateness but interdependence, autonomy but reciprocity." United States v. Nixon, 418 U.S. 683, 707 (1974).

56. See ch. 4 supra, "Continuity of Specialized Relationship."

57. "Anne Wexler moved from the Democratic National Committee to harness the lobbying strength of special-interest groups behind administration measures in Congress." "New Faces in the White House Pecking Order," *U.S. News and World Report,* January 22, 1979, p. 34.

58. *New York Times,* June 6, 1979, p. 1; ibid., June 7, p. 1.

59. "The most frequently proposed method of controlling bureaucracy is making bureaucracy subordinate to the will of elected public officials. . . . Overhead democracy as a control mechanism is divisible into two distinct stages. The first stage requires popular control over elected officials through the sanc-

tion of elections. . . . The second stage, . . . requires that elected officials control bureaucrats through one of the many means they have at their disposal. Some people feel the most effective means of control is hierarchical control by the president; others favor congressional control over bureaucracy via budgets, oversight, and casework. Many people believe that supremacy of law and the right of disaffected persons to appeal administrative wrongs to the courts for redress is the major check on bureaucracy. Still others place little faith in current institutions and advocate the independent office of the ombudsman to prevent administrative abuse of power." Kenneth J. Meier, *Politics and the Bureaucracy: Policymaking in the Fourth Branch of Government* (North Scituate, Mass.: Duxbury Press, 1979), pp. 130–32.

60. On the size of the administrative force in 1790 and 1800, see *supra*, ch. 1, n. 8. Two political science analyses present views on the future of the bureaucracy:

"Public attention is chiefly focused on the branches of government that have traditionally wielded power and made the key policy choices: the President, Congress and the Supreme Court. But day-to-day decisions by administrative organizations seem to have an increasing impact on the quality of every citizen's life, and also to predetermine a great deal of what the President, Congress and the courts can do. Concern is widespread about the bureaucratization of society, and even more insistent calls are heard for administrative accountability and for means by which individuals can insulate themselves from bureaucratic influence and controls.

"Nonetheless, there is little reason to expect any lessening of bureaucratic power or slowing of its growth, short of holocaust. Administrative agencies have to respond to interests that can hurt them, and so sometimes become instruments of groups that wield social and economic power. Though they combat such groups in token fashion, they also strengthen them. To survey American bureaucratic organizations is to identify the centers of power and the interests of Americans with influence; it is also to identify both the cutting edge and the cement of the contemporary governmental process." Dolbeare and Edelman, *American Politics*, p. 344.

"It is easy to criticize the errors of omission and commission of professional public bureaucracies, but it is even easier to see the problems raised in a government administered by decentralized groups of amateurs. Although there are problems, public bureaucracy seems able to maintain an acceptable level of support from the citizenry. Barring a political revolution, observers in the year 2000 will see public personnel systems that are not too far different from what we have today. The forces that will shape public personnel administration in the future are already happening today. Affirmative action will force a sharpening of the tools to measure merit; jobs will be restructured to accommodate upward mobility from within; specialization and professionalization will continue. The most active force in changing public personnel administration in the future, however, will be the rise in power of public employee unions." Fred A. Kramer, *Dynamics of Public Bureaucracy: An Introduction to Public Administration* (Cambridge, Mass.: Winthrop, 1977), p. 121.

61. See n. 59 supra.
62. A leading analyst of bureaucratic policymaking and its control examined several types of individual control mechanisms (see, for instance, n. 60 supra) and found each inadequate in some manner or degree. He concluded that there is a need for multiple efforts. "To adequately control bureaucracy, a control system must be designed that is better than the sum of the individual checks on bureaucracy." Meier, *Politics and the Bureaucracy*, p. 189.

CHAPTER EIGHT: *The Fifth Branch in Civil Service Reform*

1. Civil Service Reform Act of 1978, Pub. L. No. 95–494, 92 Stat. 1111–1227 (1978). President Carter's transmittal message stressed two objectives: (1) increasing "the government's efficiency by placing new emphasis on the quality of performance of Federal workers" and (2) ensuring "that employees and the public are protected against political abuse of the system." U.S., Congress, House, *Civil Service Reform: Message from the President of the United States Transmitting a Draft of Proposed Legislation to Reform the Civil Service Laws*, 95th Cong., 2d sess., 1978, H. Doc. 95–299 (Washington, D.C.: Government Printing Office, 1978), p. 1.
2. A strong critic of the bureaucracy says the Carter reform program "was only the tiniest, most incremental step toward the massive changes that are required to restore accountability to the federal service." Charles Peters, "A Letter to Jimmy Carter," *Washington Monthly* 11 (July/August 1979):15. See also Hugh Heclo, "The Overselling of Civil-Service Reform," *Washington Post*, August 12, 1978.
3. One newspaper editorial stated that for "the first time in recent history, we now should be able to see what an administration

262 FIVE-BRANCH GOVERNMENT

committed to good management in the public sector can do."
Detroit Free Press, September 15, 1978.
4. Editorial, *U.S. News and World Report*, August 28, 1978.
5. Judith H. Parris, *Civil Service Reform: The President's Bill*, Issue Brief No. IB 78066 updated September 15, 1978 (Washington, D.C.: Library of Congress, 1978), p. 1.
6. 5 U.S.C. § 1101 et seq. See, in general, David H. Rosenbloom, *Federal Service and the Constitution: The Development of the Public Employment Relationships* (Ithaca, N.Y.: Cornell University Press, 1971); Robert Presthus, *Public Administration*, 6th ed. (New York: Ronald, 1975), pp. 157–267.
7. Cf. Administrative Personnel, 5 C.F.R., 1978 and 1979.
8. Civil Service Reform Act of 1978, Pub. L. No. 95–494, 92 Stat. 1111–1227 (1978). For summary explanations of principal provisions, see *Congressional Quarterly Weekly Report* 36: July 15, 1978, pp. 1777–84; August 12, 1978, pp. 2125–29; August 26, 1978, p. 2239; September 16, 1978, pp. 2458–62; October 7, 1978, pp. 2735–36; October 14, 1978, pp. 2945–51.
9. Jimmy Carter may be more a merchandiser than a politician. He was willing and quite able to engage in nomination and election politics, but he at first shunned operational politics and was not always skillful at legislative and executive politics. His efforts to obtain congressional approval for selected proposals have been more package-selling than governmental politics. On the promotion of the civil-service-reform bill, see *Christian Science Monitor*, July 31, 1978, p. 4; and David S. Broder, *Washington Post*, July 10–11, 1978.
10. House, *Civil Service Reform*, p. 10.
11. U.S., Civil Service Commission, *Civil Service News*, April 20, 1978.
12. Id., *Federal Civilian Workforce Statistics*, September 1977, pp. 34–36.
13. Id., *Civil Service News*, April 20, 1978.
14. Ibid., p. 1. "Approximately 2 million Federal employees had completed their probationary year and had thus acquired appeal rights. The overall discharge rate for these employees was about 0.3 percent and the discharge rate for unsatisfactory performance was less than 0.02 percent." Ibid. These statements show not only that some 6,000 employees with appeal rights were discharged within the year but also that discharge for unsatisfactory performance does not give a sound picture of the disciplinary actions.
15. Firing an official may be more than having legal authority and being disappointed. President Carter kept two cabinet members

for a year or two after they had disturbed inner-circle harmony. The replacements in July 1979 had a newly relevant political orientation. From a slightly different angle, an official may be valuable even though lacking managerial excellence. "A political appointee to the Department of Agriculture, say, recommended by a large farm organization that has supported the president, cannot readily be removed. . . . He is a political officer in his own right, rather as if he had won office by election." Grant McConnell, *The Modern Presidency*, 2d ed. (New York: St. Martin's Press, 1976), p. 67.

16. In the present climate of less government for less taxes, public anxiety about the bureaucracy might be eased more by tighter hiring methods than by more flexible firing processes.

17. See Editorial, *Detroit Free Press*, September 15, 1978. Even such newspapers as the *New York Times* and *Washington Post* seem to give the public surprisingly little explanation of the rate of turnover among political and career executives. In fact, they rarely differentiate the two types of policymakers.

18. The terms are often used interchangeably. See Jack C. Plano and Milton Greenberg, *The American Political System*, 3d ed. (Hinsdale, Ill.: Dryden, 1972), p. 222.

19. On a recent differentiation between *civil service* and *merit system* as general terms, see ch. 4 supra, n. 12.

20. See discussion infra, "Political Aspects of the New Personnel Management" and "Protection of Employee Rights."

21. The President's transmittal message said that the Civil Service Commission administers a merit system. House, *Civil Service Reform*, p. 3.

22. House, *Civil Service Reform*, p. 13.

23. The term is used as a chapter heading by Hugh Heclo in *A Government of Strangers: Executive Politics in Washington* (Washington, D.C.: Brookings Institution, 1977), pp. 34–83.

24. See, in general, ch. 2 supra.

25. See ch. 3 supra, "Congressional Basis of the Executive Branch."

26. See ibid., fig. 1.

27. See ibid., "Spread of Specialized Functions."

28. See ibid., "Checks and Balances within the Executive Branch."

29. See ch. 4 supra, "Specialized Knowledge and Information" and "Continuity of Specialized Relationships."

30. See ibid., "Method of Appointment as a Basis of Classification" and "Conditions of Tenure." The 10,000 figure is in Presthus, *Public Administration*, p. 179 (5,804 general schedule, 1,244 public law, and 3,400 other). Heclo, *Government of Strangers*, pp. 38, 39, indicates 7,000 in this category; but his figure in-

264 FIVE-BRANCH GOVERNMENT

cludes only general schedule and public law positions. The 72,000 figure for the lower group is in President Carter's transmittal message. House, *Civil Service Reform*, p. 3.

31. On types of status and employment, see Administrative Personnel, 5 C.F.R., ch. 2, pts. 210–13, 301, 302, 315, 316.

32. See ch. 4 supra, n. 41.

33. See ch. 3 supra, "Political Competition within the Executive Branch" and "Departmental Disunity."

34. There are levels of officials also in the independent agencies, even though their titles and functions may differ to some degree.

35. 5 U.S.C. § 3131(13).

36. Fred A. Kramer, *Dynamics of Public Bureaucracy: An Introduction to Public Administration* (Cambridge, Mass.: Winthrop, 1977), p. 3. Another broad definition of *politics* is "the process by which power is employed to affect whether and how government will act on any given matter." Kenneth M. Dolbeare and Murray J. Edelman, *American Politics: Policies, Power, and Change*, 3d ed. (Lexington, Mass.: D. C. Heath, 1977), p. 14.

37. See ch. 3 supra, n. 33.

38. See ibid., n. 36.

39. Heclo, *Government of Strangers*, p. 38.

40. "The executive branch of the federal government has been described as two-and-one-half million people of whom one (two if you count the vice president separately) has been elected. The rest consists of the bureaucracy and the political appointees, who, except for those on the White House staff, soon find themselves absorbed into it. To assume, as the textbooks tell us, that the executive branch is an arm of the President is to face away from reality.

"In anticipation of power struggles with each new administration, the bureaucracy's first order of business is the taming and gradual absorption of political appointees." Leonard Reed, "The Bureaucracy: The Cleverest Lobby of Them All," *Washington Monthly* 10 (April 1978):50. See ch. 3 supra, n. 58.

41. Heclo, *Government of Strangers*, p. 38.

42. Noncareer appointments to the Senior Executive Service are limited to 10 percent of the total appointments. 5 U.S.C. § 3134b.

43. House, *Civil Service Reform*, p. 8.

44. Timothy B. Clark, "Senior Executive Service—Reform from the Top," *National Journal* 10 (September 1978):1542.

45. James MacGregor Burns, in *Presidential Government: The Crucible of Leadership* (Boston: Houghton Mifflin, 1973), at p. 175, gives some recognition to "four national parties" arising from the conflict between the president and congressional forces. See

also id., *The Deadlock of Democracy: Four-Party Politics in
America* (Englewood Cliffs, N.J.: Prentice-Hall, 1963).

46. Positive presidential legislative success has been limited to the
years 1933–36 and 1964–65.

47. See ch. 2 supra, "Wide Realm of Shared Functions," and ch. 3
supra, "Congressional Basis of the Executive Branch."

48. 5 U.S.C. § 1101–5, 1201–5; 92 Stat. 1119–31.

49. See Burns, *Presidential Government*, pp. 124–42. See also Arthur M. Schlesinger, Jr., *The Imperial Presidency* (Boston:
Houghton Mifflin, 1973).

50. Herman Finer, *The Presidency: Crisis and Regeneration* (Chicago: University of Chicago Press, 1960); Charles M. Hardin.
*Presidential Power and Accountability: Toward a New Consti-
tution* (Chicago: University of Chicago Press, 1974); Stephen
Hess, *Organizing the Presidency* (Washington, D.C.: Brookings
Institution, 1976). This last is post–Watergate and probably the
least reformist. Hess points out the advantages of "a more collegial presidency" with a stronger role for the cabinet. See
analysis of a collegial or plural presidency, Thomas E. Cronin,
The State of the Presidency, (Boston: Little, Brown, 1975), pp.
263–68.

51. After the Nixon resignation, two former advisers to President
John F. Kennedy urged that presidential authority not be reduced. Schlesinger, *Imperial Presidency*, and Theodore C. Sorensen, *Watchmen in the Night: Presidential Accountability after
Watergate* (Cambridge, Mass.: M.I.T. Press, 1975).

52. The principal congressional limitation on the presidency as a
consequence of the Johnson-Nixon "imperialism" is the War
Powers Act of 1973. Its efficacy is yet to be tested.

53. Clark, "Senior Executive Service," p. 1545.

54. *Congressional Quarterly Weekly Report* 36, September 16, 1978,
pp. 2460–61.

55. 5 U.S.C. § 3318a.

56. Heclo, "The Overselling of Civil Service Reform."

57. The independent regulatory commissions have been criticized
increasingly since they began nearly a century ago. One analysis
includes a curiously pertinent remark: "The same general conditions that have tended to estrange political executives from
line agencies have also estranged regulatory boards from their
intended role." William L. Morrow, *Public Administration: Politics and the Political System* (New York: Random House, 1975),
p. 76.

58. Incentive systems for political executives were proposed in
1975 by one political-science specialist in the presidency as a

means of "making the President an effective executive." Cronin, *State of the Presidency*, pp. 284–87.

59. 5 U.S.C. § 3131–36.

60. Heclo, *Government of Strangers*, p. 38.

61. Senior Executive Service position is one in which the GS-15 plus incumbent "(a) directs the work of an organizational unit, (b) is held accountable for the success of specific line or staff programs or projects, (c) monitors the progress of the organization toward goals and periodically evaluates and makes appropriate adjustments to such goals, or (d) supervises the work of employees other than personal assistants." This reflects the broad meaning of *executive* which has been used by the Civil Service Commission for several years.

62. *Congressional Quarterly Weekly Report* 36, October 14, 1978, p. 2945. *National Journal* 10 (September 1978):1542.

63. 5 U.S.C. § 3132, 3134.

64. *National Journal* 10 (September 1978):1544. The final law also provided that the number of career SES employees never could be less than the number of SES-level positions reserved for career employees prior to enactment of the bill, that not more than 30 percent of all SES positions could be filled by persons who have less than five years continuous experience in the civil service just prior to their appointment to SES, and that career appointees could not be involuntarily reassigned within 120 days after appointment of a new agency head or a new immediate superior. *Congressional Quarterly Weekly Report* 36, October 14, 1978, p. 2949.

65. ". . . in our special sort of bureaucratic system the bureaucrat is not only permanent in tenure but permanent in place, that is, that careers are not in the civil service, but in the Internal Revenue Service or the Bureau of Mines." Rowland Egger, *The President of the United States*, 2d ed. (New York: McGraw-Hill, 1972), p. 45.

66. There seems to be a decline in the extent to which civil servants are permanent in place and a growth in the number of generalists in the broad sense of the term. One survey shows that of 596 supergrade employees, 270 were generalists, having been employed in two or more departments, whereas 326 were specialists in that they had been employed in one department throughout their careers. Presthus, *Public Administration*, p. 212. For recent analysis of public bureaucratic administration by political scientists, see Victor A. Thompson, *Bureaucracy and the Modern World* (Morristown, N.J.: General Learning Press, 1976) and Ralph P. Hummel, *The Bureaucratic Experience* (New York: St. Martin's Press, 1977).

67. Graeme C. Moodie, *The Government of Great Britain*, 3d ed. (New York: Crowell, 1971), pp. 154–56.

68. Ibid, pp. 64–70, 88–89, 121–22, 128–32.

69. Richard Rose, *Politics in England* (Boston: Little, Brown, 1964), p. 153. A ministry generally has six "administrative grades," ranging from many assistant principals to the permanent secretary (usually one). Moodie, *Government of Great Britain*, p. 159. Thus, the career executives in an English ministerial department come to a pyramidal point and are three or four levels higher than the American career service. Another analysis indicates that the top civil servant may be the real head of the department or ministry. "(All political appointees shuffle from department to department every few years; very few spend their whole ministerial career dealing with one subject). The Permanent Secretary is the chief civil service advisor to the minister, and receives a salary 40 per cent higher than his. By virtue of his ability and detailed knowledge of the department, the Permanent Secretary often influences the administration and formulation of policy. The Ministry of Pensions is divided into a number of functional units, dealing with legal, medical, and other problems, it is also divided into regional units covering the country. Each unit is normally headed by a senior civil servant." Rose, *Politics in England*, pp. 196–97.

70. Moodie, *Government of Great Britain*, p. 150.

71. 5 U.S.C. § 5401–4.

72. See supra, n. 30.

73. 5 U.S.C. § 5335.

74. House, *Civil Service Reform*, pp. 1, 3, 4.

75. 5 U.S.C. § 2301c-8; 92 Stat. 1114.

76. 5 U.S.C. § 1204–7; 92 Stat. 1121–34.

77. Ibid., 92 Stat. 1125. *Congressional Quarterly Weekly Report* 36: July 15, 1978, pp. 1770, 1783, 1784; August 12, 1978, p. 2127; October 14, 1978, p. 2947.

78. 5 U.S.C., ch. 71. *Congressional Quarterly Weekly Report* 36: July 15, 1978, pp. 1782–84; August 12, 1978, pp. 2126, 2129; August 26, 1978, p. 2239; September 16, 1978, pp. 2458, 2460–62; October 14, 1978, pp. 2945, 2950.

79. U.S., Civil Service Commission, *1976 Annual Report*, p. 39.

80. House, *Civil Service Reform*, p. 1.

81. See ch. 3 supra, "Political Competition within the Executive Branch."

82. "It is with his staff that a president most frequently interacts." William F. Mullen, *Presidential Power and Politics* (New York: St. Martin's Press, 1976), p. 181. It "is tempting for a president

to rely on a small brigade of hand-picked and personally loyal White House aides." Cronin, *State of the Presidency,* p. 172.

83. See ch. 3, supra, "Departmental Disunity."

84. "Presidential reputations are made in policy and political leadership rather than in managing the executive branch." Robert C. Fried, *Performance in American Bureaucracy* (Boston: Little, Brown, 1976), p. 197. It is "questionable whether the presidency has kept up with the centrifugal tendency of the government." McConnell, *Modern Presidency,* p. 75.

85. "A Carter aide told one of your authors in the summer of 1977 that giving so much power to the cabinet members 'was probably President Carter's biggest mistake in 1977.'" James MacGregor Burns, J. W. Peltason, and Thomas E. Cronin, *Government by the People,* 12th ed. (Englewood Cliffs, N.J.: Prentice-Hall, 1978), p. 294. See also *Time,* May 15, 1978, p. 22. This last quotes a White House aide: "One of the biggest mistakes we made during the transition was letting the Cabinet secretaries play such an independent role in naming their assistants."

86. "Quite often the political executives nominally heading the departments, instead of asserting control on behalf of the president, become instead 'captive' spokesmen, advocates, and instruments for the constituent bureaus in the White House and Congress." Fried, *Performance in American Bureaucracy,* p. 207.

87. "For every organized economic interest there is an agency at some level of government." Eugene Lewis, *American Politics in a Bureaucratic Age: Citizens, Constituents, Clients and Victims* (Cambridge, Mass.: Winthrop, 1977), p. 72; "The behavior of an administration results from the interaction of some seven factors: the character and work habits of the president, the power situation outside the White House, the attitudes of persons appointed to responsible positions, the attitudes of the voters as expressed in the most recent election, the policy areas with which the administration must deal, the complexity of the political environment, and the constraints set by the political calendar." John H. Kessel, *The Domestic Presidency: Decision-Making in the White House* (North Scituate, Mass.: Duxbury, 1975), pp. 21–22.

88. Hugh Heclo, "Issue Networks and the Executive Establishment," in *The New American Political System,* ed. Anthony King (Washington: American Enterprise Institute for Public Policy Research, 1978), p. 102.

89. See articles by John Herbers in the *New York Times,* November 12, 13, and 14, 1978.

90. See ch. 5 supra, "White House Government."

91. "It has been suggested more than once that the crushing load upon the president should be divided among a number of people—assistant presidents or a cabinet of vice-presidents. While undoubtedly some presidential chores could be well done by assistants, most of the work of the presidency cannot be divided or given over to others, whatever their titles, without a radical and probably dangerous change in the system of responsibility. . . . The president's burden may be heavy, but he must carry it." McConnell, *Modern Presidency*, p. 111.